Warrior Women with Angel Wings

Stories of Love, Faith, Hope, Courage and Angels

Compiled by Sundi Sturgeon

Published by:

Cover Design by Claudia Ibarra

Cover Artwork by Katarina Moon-Zaphire
www.katzaphire.deviantart.com

Editors Christina Mercer and Sharon Gulley

Dedication

This Book is Dedicated to Una Jasmin White. She was an amazing visionary healing artist.

She touched many lives and will be remembered with love. Her beautiful gifts of Soul Portraits will live on forever.

She is forever in our thoughts and our hearts. Her life and work here touched so many and was truly a gift.

She was truly an angel among us. We have included on her beautiful stories in the book to honor her.

Table of Contents

Foreword

Inspirational. Heartfelt. Triumphant. These are descriptions I use to describe this collection of stories written straight from the hearts of women. Upon these pages, the authors have courageously opened themselves up to you, the readers, to offer a glimpse into their pasts so that you might share in their pains, triumphs, and profoundly inspiring experiences. These offerings are given to the world as a reminder of the power of Divine Love in a world sometimes shrouded by darkness.

Women finding freedom after years of abuse, surviving those with chemical dependency, witnessing divine beings, overcoming the stigma of being different, the power of prayer, the helping hands of guardian angels, the existence of spirit guides, finding your life's purpose, and pushing through grief are some examples of the triumphant and inspirational themes found within this book. Real women, real stories. Some of them write professionally, some for the pure joy of opening their hearts to others. And all of their voices shine with authenticity and valor.

I've known Sundi Sturgeon, the complier and co-author of this anthology, since we were tweens in the throes of adolescence. We've watched one another progress over the decades, struggle through times of despair and soar in times of joy. We share a vision of love and peace, yet understand that life can often appear grim even though we are always surrounded by angels. With this understanding, Sundi lovingly provided a platform for a group of "warrior women" with stories to tell. I'm honored to be one of the co-authors and co-editors sharing in this beautiful collection, and I invite you to join us in reading its thoughtful prose.

For me personally, this anthology offered an opportunity to tell my story *The Grim and the Fairy* while also stretching my writing in a unique way. As a published author, primarily of fiction, I took the raw truth of my experiences and wove it within the setting of a fairy tale. Though this style differed from the format of the other pieces, I found it every bit as telling and cathartic. Writing my story pushed and pulled and drew from me feelings too intense to put into words, yet the guise of fiction allowed them to pour onto the pages. I am thankful for the opportunity and experience to be a part of this book.

Our greatest gifts are our stories, and our listening hearts lead us to unity.

Christina Mercer, B.S., CPA
Award-Winning Author
www.christinamercer.com

Una Jasmin White
Eternally Entangled Through the Light of the Soul

How a journey of tragic loss elevated
the expansion of art, love, and life
through the light of my soul.

Soon after my burning desire to meet the love of my life the predictions became reality. Before meeting my husband John, I traveled between Europe and California introducing my healing methods as a transpersonal art therapist and soul portrait artist. Planning to go back to France to teach art therapy the direction of my destiny changed in an instant. After checking with my inner guidance for confirmation, I followed the advice of an astrologer urging me to stay in Santa Barbara where I was, not knowing I would soon meet my future husband John. Always optimistic, I followed her advice with total faith, committed to continuing my healing work.

John and I met at a spiritual gathering. We instantly recognized each other's light of the soul and common soul purpose and became aware of our divinely created union. From that first moment on we were inseparable. Feeling an intimate sense of belonging to each other, knowing each other's thoughts and feelings, we were uplifted and inspired. Our deep love and Divine commitment unified our purpose and mission. Unconditional faith, support, and guidance from our angels, guides, and God, empowered us to transform any obstacles and challenges into opportunities guiding us safely on our love's journey.

In the midst of a transitional period in our lives, I met a woman in a Costa Mesa print shop who was standing next to me. Through her we were introduced to a gentleman who was intimately connected to a property formerly owned by Prince Mozumdar, a spiritual teacher and healer from India, already on the other side. As a result of painting his soul portrait conveying messages from Prince Mozumdar, we were invited to live on this property on the top of a mountain in Southern California. It was a former sanctuary for world peace and healing. It was through the inspirational books of Prince Mozumdar and the high energy and vibrations of our mountaintop home, that our perception of invisible realities, angels, fairies, and dimensions of light expanded inspiring our work in healing and global peace.

We arrived on February 1,1998, to our new mountaintop sanctuary. Little did I know I would lose my John on this snowy mountain two years later on the same day.

It was fifteen years ago I lost my John to a tragic incident. It was snowing heavily that bitterly cold winter night of January 31st, 2001. I was absorbed in the writing of a channeled description of my Reiki III teachings at the time. I was so involved in my work that I did not realize that time had passed. Suddenly I felt the urgency go upstairs to check on John. I could not find him in the house. At that moment, Mother Mary appeared to me communicating to me that I could never ever reach him again physically, that he was in another realm. Feeling that her message was true, I started to cry hysterically. Suddenly our visions and dreams were shattered by a tragic incident: John's sudden death of a massive heart attack.

My dear neighbor and I found John at midnight lying in the snow by the side of his car. At first, we thought he was unconscious and tried to lift him up, we did not believe he was dead. I then covered him with a red scarf and with loving caresses and tender words. We immediately called 911 and the emergency medical team that arrived confirmed his death after a brief attempt to revive him. The emergency medical team took John away so suddenly, with no compassion for my grief. Leaving me in a state of shock, I was not given the precious time and opportunity to say goodbye to my sweetheart, to feel him physically for the last time, and to give him a last kiss and embrace for the last time.

The sudden realization of his death intensified my horrible pain. It was as if my body and soul shattered into pieces, and my whole world crumbled. According to the coroner, he died of a sudden massive heart attack. I had learned later that John's heart had always had a weakness. I do believe that the stress he had endured on the mountain for various reasons contributed to the cause of his heart attack. I decided to stay on the mountain by myself for some months until my future path became clear to me. I am forever grateful to all my angels, archangels, and God, Mother Mary and close friends for the loving support and healing during my transformational and challenging journey.

It took me a long time to accept the reality that John was never coming back physically. Slowly I learned to surrender to God's will and to accept his passing without resentment. It was important for me to be patient and caring with myself and to move through my grieving process respecting my own rhythm. Surrendering to Divine guidance with peace in my heart empowered me to take a quantum leap into the unknown with the confidence that I could master my life. Soon after his passing I organized a memorial with my friends in the amphitheater located in the deep snow. During this ceremony, I decided to continue our mission for peace and healing in the future and to create a healing center when the time was right. The day after John's passing he came to me expressing his sadness, asking forgiveness for having left me behind so suddenly and he told me it was beyond his control. Forgiveness and gratitude with us and our life partners as expressions of true love and compassion is essential for overcoming struggles, misunderstandings, and shortcomings.

Guided by my angels, my healing services, my creative capacities and determination to master my life, I received inspiration about my new direction and what actions to take. I was given all the support necessary from known and unknown sources and friends for my survival, healing, and for continuing my soul's purpose and journey.

Taking long walks in the snow in the solitude of the mountain, away from people and distractions, was very important for experiencing moments of deep peace, joy and bliss. Listening to my inner voice soothed my pain and any fear disappeared. My soul's path and my life's mission expanded and evolved as I asked to be aligned with my new higher calling. I was guided by life transforming messages and gifts from this and the Other Side, beneficial for my healing work as an artist of the soul.

A whole new world was revealed to me as I discovered new ways of communication with John beyond the veil. United in a vibratory energy field of Divine love and light, I experienced the energy and aliveness of our boundless love. The reality of the afterlife, nurtured by our daily communications channeled directly from his soul and spirit, flowed into my heart. These loving communications from John turned into channeled writings and art that I called, Love Letters from Heaven. These cherished communications offered me hope, courage, strength, confidence, trust, and a new direction and love of life with renewed purpose, new perspectives, and miracles.

His never-ending communication through inspired writings, and drawings, still continue to this day. Some examples of these inspirations are illustrated through John's sharing of his walking over the rainbow bridge to the Other Side, and being received by his parents. At this time, I did not know when we die our family meets us on the Other Side.

Also, illustrated to me, an angel showing the way to happiness; an eternal love beyond the veil; portal to cosmic love, and another drawing showed the light-filled essence of flowers, (a vision of their subtle and dense reality) .... and much more. John revealed his new "heavenly Self" through a soul portrait I painted of him expressing his love, and everlasting presence shining on me revealing the triumph of our divine spark that prevails forever. In another drawing I was shown the light of my soul, and much more....

One day a professional intuitive came to see me to offer a psychic reading with messages from John. This meeting offered clear insights and directions, paving my way to new places, people, guiding my love's journey safely into the future. John assured me of his collaboration, guidance and inspiration from the Other Side, available to me at all times by offering creative, spiritual, artistic healing gifts for my healing artwork, becoming an essential part of my life's mission. Ignited in me, the revelation of the rainbow bridge connected me to invisible dimensions of light, angels, guides, and departed loved ones. Thus, my passion to "unite heaven and earth" by connecting people with their departed loved ones. Loving messages revealed in these soul portraits carry expressions of luminous beauty and wholeness.

Love was all around me, I felt I was not alone and I knew I could trust my guidance to follow my Divine destiny with total trust, as long as I honored my commitment to continue the legacy of our healing work. As I connected with the realms of light integrating the heavenly gifts transmitted from John, multidimensional images of angels, guides, and Ascended Masters appeared in my soul portraits. Soon after this experience it was time to move from the solitude of the San Bernardino Mountains to New York City.

I was called to share my work as soul portrait artist/healer in Columbus Ohio on various TV shows. Then I was invited to offer a lecture/workshop at the New Living Expo in New York that prompted me to move to New York. John was "working through people" in practical ways assisting me to enhance my soul portrait clientele. John's presence in a photo called "United in the Light, was the inspiration for the creation of my website. After my move to California, a close friend offered the gift of the Holistic Regenesis technology, a quantum energy tool for holistic healing. This is a pioneering healing tool with light and sound encoded information promoting alignment with the Divine blueprint restoring wholeness on all levels.

I have always been guided towards the right people, places, events, working together with John from the other side. I continue the legacy of our work: co-creating world peace, healing, raising consciousness, inspiring people to integrate their Divine nature through Divinely inspired soul portraits via quantum energy healing through art.

In closing, the loss of my beloved husband was a tragedy. Our souls and lives were so entangled that I could not imagine at that time living by myself. But the expansion of my artistic healing methods (tools) gifted to me by John are an essential part of my love's journey from tragedy to triumph, matured me as the healing soul portrait artist I am today. I am forever grateful for my sacred relationship with John who keeps inspiring me to co-create our work from the world of light and to continue our legacy. His continuous support, protection, and guidance have convinced me of the reality of the afterlife. Knowing that life and love are boundless, I am committed to uniting heaven and earth by painting celestial soul portraits offering closure, hope, peace and guidance on their journey from grief to peace.

It is my purpose to inspire people to discover themselves as Divine beings, to experience and express the loving light, beauty, wisdom, power of their soul, to actualize their highest potential for true fulfillment, peace, harmonious relationships and the joy of wholeness. I am currently offering quantum-healing sessions through art and guided healing journeys to assist people in their personal and spiritual evolution. During transition, depression, and challenging times my work assists others to adapt to life's changes with grace and ease. According to today's research we are interconnected through a quantum energy field. Past, present and future co-exist. We can tap into this quantum energy field offering us infinite possibilities at any time. More and more people and conferences are exploring the afterlife. Dannion Brinkley was one of the first persons presenting this reality to mainstream through his books.

Now living in the San Francisco Bay Area, I am traveling worldwide offering my innovative healing work, seminars and healing soul portraits for individuals, couples, departed loved ones, and pets, in person and through the internet. For several years, I have been working together with Sundi and Joe Sturgeon, the founders of the Holistic Light Rejuvenation Center. Located in Kihei, Maui, Hawaii, we continue developing new pioneering programs and services. Along with other teachers and practitioners, Sundi and Joe have founded a tax-exempt educational and charitable organization to provide expanded services in the quantum energy arts.

Sundi Sturgeon
Earth Angel

Angels have surrounded me and loved me since I was involved in the first story I ever shared. When I learned to be embraced by their love, I let go of being a warrior. My angels guide and direct me with many angel signs such as the repetition of numbers such as 444, 222 and 555. Doreen Virtue and "Signs from your Angels" gives you an amazing insight into Angels and how they come to you in the time of your need, comfort you in your time of fear and transition, and are always there.

I often experience feathers, coins, breezes and other little tingly feelings that let me know they are always there protecting me, for you see, they are the warriors, I am the wings.

You are an earth angel my dear. You were drawn to read this book today because you have an inner need for healing. Over the years' angels have communicated with me in subtle ways. As an earth angel, I would direct you to the book "Assertiveness for Earth Angels". You will see many ways to protect yourself and to heal yourself from wounds caused by trauma.

Part of this journey included this book and the many to come. I was called upon to help others to share their experiences and stories. As you read each of the stories, you will be inspired, encouraged, guided and blessed. Each of those who shared their stories were so brave and courageous.

Personally, I have been called an Earth Angel and I am honored with that title. As I tap into my own guides and my gifts, I am able to help others. The most amazing journey and love comes from using our gifts and walking on our intended path. I believe that all you have to do is ask for guidance and your Angels will provide it.

They are there waiting to guide you, to help you and protect you. But you must ask. You must be open to receive. You must tap into the energy and guidance. You are surrounded by love and light every day. But you must to open to receive it. You must learn to tap in to it and use it to change your life and the lives of others around.

My mission in life is to help others heal. It's what I was born for in this world. It's my life work and journey. It's the reason I started the Holistic Center and why I do everything I do. It is why I chose to create this opportunity for others to share their stories and this journey.

I wish and hope for you is that you will find your life's purpose and passion. And that you will follow your guides and live up to your purpose.

About the Author

Sundi Sturgeon's unique approach and gifts empower her clients to reach their highest potential in a loving and safe environment. She provides her clients with the tools necessary to obtain a coherent fulfilled state of being. Her loving accepting and presence is felt in her nurturing embrace. Sundi's clients describe her as a truly gifted "Earth Angel."

Her passion stems from her life lessons and travails, including traumatic health challenges, overcoming cancer, fibromyalgia, and a variety of addictions and abuses, marked with two near-death experiences. Through her personal dark night of the soul experience, Sundi birthed a new belief system inspiring her discovery of unrealized potential, self-worth, and personal empowerment.

Sundi Sturgeon is a Certified Reiki Master, Intuitive Empath/Healer, CHT, NHC, a certified Doreen Virtue Angel Practitioner, and is currently enrolled in a doctorate program in integrative medicine with a focus in holistic/quantum medicine which will be completed in 2016.

Sundi is also a wife, mother, and grandmother who is devoted to caring for all of Earth's living beings. She is a resident of Kihei, Maui, where she lives with her husband, Joseph as Quantum Energy Healing practitioners. They co-founded the Holistic Light Rejuvenation Center, an educational and charitable organization promoting holistic and cellular rejuvenation services.

Sundi's story has been included in *Pink Think, Grow Richer, Activating the DNA of Wealth, In the Presence of Angels*, Karen Tants, and Doreen Virtue's latest book, *How to Get Your Life Back - 40 Women Luminaries Share Intimate Stories of Spiritual Awakening: Illuminate Your Joy, and now* the books,

Women on a Mission, I am Beautiful, Echoes in the Darkness, and is publishing her own upcoming book series: *Warrior Woman to Angel Wings,* in 2018.

Reach out to her at: http://www.holisticrejuvenate.com. You can learn more about Sundi at her website.

Carole Booth
The Angel Man Who Saved Our Lives

It was the summer of 1976. Forty-one years ago, I had just taken my three children to the dentist for a checkup. After the visit, we got back in the car and headed home. My eleven-year-old son, Vincent, sat in the front seat with me. The other two children—eight-year-old Sundi and three-year-old Steffan—were sitting in the back seat. About fifteen minutes into driving, I passed out onto my oldest son's lap.

When I had passed out, my foot pushed on the gas pedal and accelerated the car to an estimated thirty-five miles per hour. Vincent and his sister saw a man running along the driver's side of the car. He hung on the door, reached into the car, and turned off the key. He steered the car off the road near a row of trees where it slightly bumped into a tree.

Then the man disappeared as quickly as he had appeared.
 A car with doctors stopped to help on their way to the hospital. The paramedics and police came, and I was taken by ambulance.

I will never forget the paramedic in the ambulance. He said, "You're going to be okay, dear."

I looked up at him and thought he was so handsome. He looked like Elvis, and I thought to myself, *I've died and gone to heaven!*

My children were also taken to the hospital, and my husband was notified. He came and picked us all up from the hospital, and after getting home, our two oldest children told us the whole story of what had happened with the man running alongside the car saving us while I was passed out.

It was determined that my medical situation was caused by a seizure disorder. When I was nine years old, I fell out of my bed onto a cement floor, hitting my left temple and suffering from a concussion. Twenty years after that, I starting having grand mal seizures that had to be controlled by medication. But I've always had the protection of my angels.

Over the years, there have been many, many times when my angels watched over me: When we had our fourth child, Sarah, six years after the accident; after the passing of my oldest son, Vincent, at forty-four years of age in 2010; and so on.

This is my first writing of these experiences. I used to write all the time, and paint and draw. My story comes forth now because of the beautiful, kind spirit of my daughter, Sundi Sturgeon, who compiled this anthology. I think of her and remember that little girl forty-one years ago in the backseat of my car with her three-year-old brother watching the angel man save us. It is because she asked, "Mom, would you like to write something for this book that you experienced in your life?" that I was able to break a cycle. Now I can write, paint, draw, do pottery. I can move forward again!

My Wings to Grow Again

Angels walk with me; they ride with me too;
Each day of my life, all the day through.

I cannot see them, but I know that they are there;
Their beautiful wings of faith, that envelop us with such care;
Sending grace and beauty upon us everywhere.

In the quiet moments and in the troubled times;
Their wings are here to guide us, cover us, and shield us;
Sending us the peace and protection
the split second it is needed.

Angels are a gift from God and a light to show us
He is not very far away;

They follow our very footsteps, day after day.

About the Author

My name is Carole Booth. I was born in San Diego, California. I have been married for 52 Yrs. to my wonderful husband Roger, (The love of my life). We have Four children two boys, & 2 girls. I'm a Grandmother of four, and a Great grandmother of four beautiful Grandchildren. My interests are drawing, painting, and writing poetry. I also love interior designing. I retired 2 years ago from my own domestic engineering business of 30 years. After retirement, I still love to help anyone with questions they would have about the interior, or exterior of their homes. Designing pathways, Arbors, plants, etc. Helping people with questions about what they can do to make their surroundings a peaceful, relaxing, and fun place to live.

Christina Mercer
The Grim and the Fairy

Once upon a life in a faraway mountain region, a fairy named Bee lived in a cozy tree with her family. Seasons came and went, blue skies and gray, and Bee grew into her wings, though she didn't yet know how to fly. It was a special, yet fragile time for her and her family, so when the earth began to quake with warnings of danger, fear seeded within them all.

Bee's parents grew distant; her brother developed a case of daggers, impelling him to strike out or hide away from others; and Bee fell under the dominance of a wild goblin pack. As if the earth hadn't shaken their lives enough, a rough fairy with a booming voice and leather skin crashed into their tree like a runaway dragon. Consumed by an infestation of Grims—sticky needlers and icy vamphetas and all sorts of drownies—the plagued fairy had an endless hunger for poison. And for Bee's mother.

His rough ways somehow hypnotized her mother, and she allowed him to steal her away from their home and family. After all efforts to call her back failed, Bee's father ran from the mountain and tucked himself deep in a cave. There he found refuge in the dark and quiet, and he slept for a very long time.

Bee and her brother struggled on their own. Their broken tree provided no more comfort, no more protection from the world. Bee sought refuge from the goblin pack, but their attentions proved dark, only paralyzing her more. As if caught in a spider's web, she found it hard to move, hard to think, and believed she might remain trapped forever under their control. But as all hope began to wither, she heard the birdsong, and light spun around her once again.

The bluebird had called to her throughout her childhood, and this time its song penetrated the sticky cocoon and freed her from the goblins' web. Bee and her brother fled the mountains to the bluebird's nest and an ocean of dreams where they could start anew. However, several Grims chased Bee's brother, and he soon left the nest and sandy shores to the valley lands in a desperate attempt to rejoin with their mother.

The bluebird's song encouraged Bee to remain seaside, and she found solace with other fairies also struggling to find their ways. They all, including Bee, tangled with Grims— mostly smokles and starlucies—but the fairies were much freer and happier than the goblins back in the mountains, and they all sought to one day fly.

One fairy in particular filled Bee's heart with hope. His name was Dew, and he had golden horns and sky bright eyes. He exuded rays of warmth and rainbows of ambition, despite the lingering clouds that hung around him from his battles. He'd arrived at the western seashore only months before Bee had, wretchedly thin and riddled with the nightmares of his past. Despite his suffering, he spoke of creating a better life where the trees had roots and the rocks never sought to crush bones.

Dew's story described his journey across thousands of miles, much of it on foot, some of it in carriages driven by others. Before his travels, a creature made of iron fists and stone had held him captive for years. Barely old enough to grow wings, he escaped from his tormentor and ran hundreds of miles away. He scavenged for food, found shelter in abandoned carriages, and even fought through the scarlet sickness on his own.

He found odd jobs harvesting elephantine leaves or frying toads for the dwarves, but the coinage he earned was small. Then one day, despite his youth, a kind dwarf gave him a job helping the sun-spindlers who brought warmth to the caves where the dwarves lived. Dew learned how to spin sunshine into heat, and when the summer months arrived, he learned how to syphon cold air from the sky. And at the end of one summer, he decided to pack his small bag and chase the sun west to start life anew.

Bee and Dew talked for hours about their memories and also about their dreams for a life of soaring high above all the Grims and those made of iron and stone. They promised eternal love to one another, and though they were still very young and clumsy with flying, they knew they were destined to be together. Their love for the sea would remain for a lifetime, but they decided to make their home where their coins could stretch further.

So, they moved inland to the valley lands between the ocean and mountains, a place with plenty of sunshine and the same region where Bee's mother dwelled, where her brother had fled to, and where her father slept quietly in his cave. Bee carried the bluebird's blessing in her heart and heard its soft encouragement often. Her greatest wish was for their lives to flourish in the valley and for her family to find peace once again.

While Dew worked hard at his job, Bee learned the art of counting coins. They shed pesky Grims and tried hard to avoid more, but the long-held drownies clung to Dew like swamp vines. However, despite their hold and through persistent efforts, Bee and Dew built a life with branches and roots, tucked away coins, and began to stretch their wings and fly a little higher.

Bee continued to worry for her family. The lives of her and her brother touched like the fluttering of a butterfly's wings, delicate and fleeting, yet rooted in the depths of time. They each wove in different ways into their mother's realm, sometimes finding light and mirth and other times a black and blue darkness. They also tried to coax their father from his smokle-filled cave, but he never ventured beyond its borders. Their one consolation was a fairy with ivory horns and a unique song who discovered their father and brought him bowls of porridge that warmed the edges of his cave.

Bee's life with Dew offered both highs and lows, but their flying grew stronger with each passing year. The bluebird offered them both a constant reminder to stay on their paths and aim for the stars, and they flew higher and higher, made babies from their love, and out of sweat and tears and laughter, the air filled their wings. But just when Bee thought they'd flown high enough above the world's gloom, she discovered one of the most mysterious Grims of all living deep within her mind.

A codeep was the sort of Grim that hid inside, that could fester and grow for years without its host knowing it existed, and then one day when it became too big for its hideaway, its red rawness showed through and inflicted great pain. Like a giant mirror, a codeep absorbed the suffering from those with Grims and then reflected it back out in a blinding image that intensified the pain of Grim victims. Bee struggled with her horrid discovery, feared that the Grim inside her would never go away, and knew that as long as she suffered with a codeep, she endangered everyone she loved who battled with Grims.

Because Dew was her other half, her codeep and his drownies clashed and mirrored and pulled at the strength of their tree until its branches began to crack. Desperate for help, Bee sought out wizards, finally finding a wizardess who showed her the way. She taught her how to stop fighting, fixing, and needlessly suffering from the enslavement of Grims. The key was simple, yet terrifying, and it meant surrendering to the beating of her heart alone. Letting go of all she held most dear nearly broke her into pieces, and yet it also broke the codeep's hold. And as she lifted from its shards to the skies as a lone fairy, Dew's eyes opened wide and he stretched his wings bigger than he'd ever done before, and raised himself from the swamp-heavy drownies and joined her in the bright clear blue.

Life was theirs again. Renewed joy fed their dreams, healed their life's tree, and allowed them to find the sort of flying only experienced by some. They reaped the treasures of undying love and teamwork, and the scars of their past Grims turned into badges of courage. Bee thanked the moon and stars, and basked in the glitter of the higher skies, though still, deep inside, she felt the pull of her family.

She visited her father from time to time, enjoying moments of warmth and laughter, but always within the confines of his sleepy cave. Then a day came when the smokles there grew so strong they turned into sticky globes all over his body. They changed his feet into blocks, distorted his bones, and stole all but a thin wisp of his breath away. He pled for relief, yet his fear to leave the cave terrified him more than the horrid Grim. Bee, her brother, and the ivory-horned fairy buzzed around him, doing everything to ease his suffering, but only the alchemists with powerful potions could take the edge off his pain.

The smokles grew larger with each passing day, bringing him closer to his end, but he refused to let either body or soul leave his dark, quiet cave. So, Bee and Dew moved her father, his cave, and the ivory fairy to the base of their tree where he could be closer. There, Bee helped tend to his suffering until his days turned to months turned to years, and though Bee's wings grew heavy and the rainbows of her life dimmed in the heaviness of his plight, she sought out the glitter lining of daily hugs and "I love you's that edged the gray.

All the while Grims plagued Bee's mother. Her mother and the leather fairy had lived for years in a house of twisters and feathered webs and walls covered in astrowheels. Bee always wished the light would return to shine on her mother's wings, and she tried many times to show her what it felt like to fly again, but her efforts had fed the codeep and later scratched at its scar, so Bee learned to walk ever gently, trying never to trip off the thin rope between love and Grim sickness.

Then one day, the leather fairy crashed into a wall of black stone, breaking his head into a thousand pieces. Wizards glued the pieces back together, though the fairy would never again roar like a dragon, and though his crash had taken away all of his Grims, he withered away like an autumn leaf. Bee's mother whirled around his fragile body day and night for many years, but when he rolled out the door and hit black stone again, another wizard scraped up the tiny fragments and moved him to a place of sleeping.

The Grims grew stronger within Bee's mother. Icy vamphetas and oily smokles riddled her body and clawed into her mind. She sought out others like her infested with Grims to fill the void the leather fairy left behind. Her splintered body flitted to and fro in a fiery hunger, seeking to fill a craving that promised nothing but more misery, more loss of reason, more darkness for herself and her family. Time clicked backwards and forward without logic. And the cricket's chirping carried on without end until the foam sputtered and teeth and bones clattered to the ground.

Bee fretted and frayed over her mother's plight, and when the inky blue started scrawling mindlessly across the blank surfaces in her mother's home, Bee's mind spun in panic. She sought out Grim-wizards to help, one after another who took her mother in only to spit her back, pushing Bee to seek out different wizards. Nobody could help. Nobody could save her. And when the feeler-wizards finally sealed her mother in a hollow of safekeeping, Bee scrubbed and cleaned and sorted the chaos of her mother's home, counted her small bag of coins and stacks of owe-ings, and tucked away her belongings. Bee became bombarded with all the constant needs and wants and have to's of others until her wings no longer lifted and her eyes swam with the oceans of her past.

Despair over both of her parents swarmed around Bee, and her heart grew so heavy, her wings began to fail. As hard as she tried to flap them, the ground came closer and closer, her body grew stiff and cold, and she felt as if her mind would crack. She closed her eyes as the tears spilled forth and waited for the crash, but then the great tree of life that she and Dew built reached out a branch and caught her. It pulled her close into its strong arms filled with the love of Dew and their offspring and stilled her quaking. And when the quiet returned, the bluebird's song filled her head with peace. It sung from the heavens, reminding her to, again, surrender. And so, she did.

She surrendered to her father's fate, knowing that no matter how long he remained in his cave or when he soared to the heavens, his love for her and her love for him was eternal, and all the rest was in the hands of the angels.

And she surrendered to her mother's fate, knowing that the darkness left in the wake of Grims was not for Bee to heal, and though she loved her mother and kept her safe and wished for all the light in the skies to return to her precious wings, fixing her, or anyone else, was never in her power. For we are all in the divine hands of the angels.

About the Author

Christina Mercer is an award-winning author of fiction for children and teens, in addition to writing for adults. Titles include young adult fantasy *Arrow of the Mist* and its sequel *Arms of Anu*, young adult paranormal romance *Honey Queen*, and an upcoming young adult paranormal series called the *Wood Witch Series*. Christina is also a once-upon-a-time CPA and the author of *Bean Counting for Authors-Helping Writers & Creative Business Owners Grasp Accounting & Taxes*. Her works have been honored by *Publisher's Weekly*, *Writer's Digest*, and multiple writing competitions. She's been a guest speaker, instructor, and panelist at several writing conferences and continues to offer support to her fellow authors. For Christina, writing is a passionate endeavor that provides the perfect outlet for creative expression.

It also provides a continuing platform for growth and connecting with others, which she considers to be the most precious reward of all. In other areas of her life, Christina is a lover of nature, a Certified Herbalist, and hobbyist beekeeper. In years, past, she became certified in various healing modalities, including Massage Therapy, Reflexology, and Reiki. Christina is blessed to do what she loves, and she enjoys life in the foothills of Northern California with her husband, sons, pack of large dogs, and about 100,000 honey bees. For more about her and her writing, visit: www.christinamercer.com or connect with her on Facebook | Twitter | Instagram | Pinterest | Goodreads

Monica Pleinis
Adriana's Story

It's March of 1987, I'm young, single and pregnant with my first child and only daughter. I knew her name was going to be Adriana Nicole. Adriana was born on March 15th at a petite 6lbs. 6oz. at 11:49 am. She was everything to me, my whole world. It was going to be her and me living a beautiful life of just us girls. After two hours went by, the nurses cleaned her up and they printed her foot prints on a card for me, and even cut a piece of her hair and taped it to a card for my memory book.

I hear her cries of being cold, poked, prodded and in good time she will soon be in my arms; as I'm holding her and staring at her in awe, I'm noticing she was starting to turn blue around her mouth. I brought it up to my nurse and showed her, she didn't seem too worried. A little more time went by and now the color was becoming more prominent.

I'm now in panic mode and insist that the nurse take my baby to be checked out. My nurse agrees and wraps her up tightly, she has me give her a kiss and tell her that will see her later. Adriana was layer in her rolling bassinet and off they went. Not realizing this will be the last time I'll ever get to hold my baby alive.

The Pediatric Cardiologist walked into my room a little later that evening to talk to me about Adriana's condition. Her main heart valve wasn't functioning properly due to it being partially developed. Doc says it would be an easy fix by going in during surgery and placing an artificial piece of valve to mimic the real one.

The nurses and Doctor have me sign all the consent forms for the surgery, I was so overwhelmed I signed away as long it would help my baby to get better. Surgery was scheduled that next morning; it was a long waiting period before they let me know it was a success.

It's been three days since Adriana was born, since she's had her surgery and it is Saint Patrick's Day and the hospital is decorating and celebrating. That morning the nurse came in my room, woke me up and said, your daughter needs you right now, the nurse was acting a little nervous than usual; as I put my two gowns on and my slippers, I sit on wheelchair and the nurse pushes me up to the INCU on the third floor.

I see my baby Adriana hooked up to wires, a breathing tube and they had to paralyze her body with a paralytic because they had said she was trying to pull her wires out. Saddened at the site of her looking like this, I was allowed to touch her, speak to her and sing to her but not able to pick her up.

As I sat back down on the wheelchair but still touching her, all the machines that were keeping her alive went alarming! The staff rushed to her side, giving her CPR with three fingers; there was so much controlled chaos I was so scared and I didn't realize what just happened.

The INCU staff turned off all the machines, told me they were so sorry they had tried all they can do to keep her alive, I was in shock! Adriana my baby girl died on March 17th three days after she was born on Saint Patrick's Day, she was unhooked from all wires, wrapped in her blanket and given to me. The nurse had said I can take her into a private room and spend the last moments with her before she becomes cold and stiff. A nurse came in with a Polaroid camera and had taken a few pictures, at the time I wasn't even paying attention to what these pictures would mean to me thirty years later.

I was also privileged with more time with Adriana's limped body in my hospital room.; as the nurse was wheeling me back to my room, I was stopped in the hallway by a patient as she looked at my daughter the lady says, oh look how beautiful your baby is, she's sleeping so well. I didn't have the heart to tell her, I just grinned and bared it.

I finally made it to my room, I rolled into bed with her, I saw there was a gift at the end of my bed, I opened it and it was a little dress from her grandma on her dad's side. I dressed her little body with this beautiful pink dress and booties. This was such a bitter sweet moment, confused, saddened. I wanted to dote on her as any new mother would but the circumstances weren't right.

I remember my High school friend Carlos coming to visit me at this time; he was informed of what had happened as he was the one who basically took care of me while being pregnant, as well as his girlfriend being only a month behind me in pregnancy. Carlos was my first friend to hold Adriana's little limp body, as he kissed her and prayed over her, I deemed him her Godfather thereafter.

The next thing I realize I had a room full of family and friends that were praying over her and passing her around. As Adriana came back to me the nurse came in to take her, I rebelled, cried, yelled wrapped my body around Adriana so she wouldn't be taken from me. I heard loud cries coming from my family and friends, as the nurse and I were in a little tug of war with Adriana's body.

I was finally pried open and my baby was taken from me once again. I'm home now back at my parent's house, we have a house full of people paying their respects; of course, I don't want anything to do with anyone at this time. I'm sitting on my bed looking around at all the baby furniture, clothes, diapers and memories of the past few days.

As I'm crying and numb all at the same time, I feel my blouse getting wet, I look down and my breast are leaking and I have no baby to nurse, this was the tipping point that set my depression to spiral. My Mom and I walk into the funeral home, I asked my mom where was Adriana's casket? My mom said it's under all the flowers, the flowers were overflowing over the tiny casket; it was a closed casket due to mortuaries does not embalm new born babies.

The next moment I remember is being at the cemetery, as they lowered her casket into the ground all I could think of was to throw myself in the deep hole with her. I was eighteen years old at this time; it would be seventeen years of grief, turmoil, agony, depression, addiction and contemplated suicide. I remember throwing myself on my knees, raising my arms to Heaven asking God, if your real please show me why I am going through this! Will there ever be an end? There soon came a Healing in the forms of physical healing, emotional healing, Spiritual healing and growing to understand the death and dying process.

I am now a Mother of two handsome young men, working with a Non-profit organization as a Touch Therapist for the terminally

Ill. I've worked for other Hospice care providers and Doctors. I currently am a massage therapist for the Sacramento Naturopathic Medical Center and supporting Natural medicine. I've been studying under my Medium Ship Teacher, Tana Hoskinson. I'm now in the advance classes, which have healed me on a much deeper level than I can ever imagine.

Through all the meditations and lessons, I was taught by Tana; I am now able to see, speak and communicate with Adriana on a profound level. March 15th 2017 I with 16 of my favorite family and friends who have gone through this healing journey with me had celebrated Adriana's Thirtieth Birthday with four doves which represented the Trinity, thirty rose color balloons, not pink because in channeling, Adriana had said she wasn't a baby anymore, I even asked her what kind of cake she wanted and I clearly heard fruit basket! So, a fruit basket cake it was.

Candace our Dove lady had brought her four beautiful doves and her husband was attending a funeral with their four other doves miles away from the cemetery we were at. Adriana's doves once released flew and circled around us three times and supposedly supposed to fly home, well they decided to hook up with the other four released doves from the husband's flock of doves, came back to where we were, now there is a total of eight doves flying around us many times and putting on quite the show.

Our dove lady Candace was almost out of her mind saying aloud, this has never happened! Your daughter is Some Big Spirit!

The next morning, I went into Meditation to speak to Adriana and I had said, Adriana, you know you put quite a show on for us and her response was, "It was for the other children," as she gave me a visual of all the diseased children sitting on their gravestones watching the Doves above.

This is how much I've Healed in thirty years.

Thank You, Adriana, my only Daughter

With Love your Momma

Healing Hands Healing Hearts
P.O. Box 1865
Bakersfield, CA 93303
www.HealingHandsHealingHearts.org
(916) 968-0091
m.martinez2@hotmail.com

About the Author

I am a State Certified Massage Therapist by the California Massage Therapy Council; I have also obtained a Volunteer Training Certification with the Sacramento Sutter Cancer Consortium; and am a Certified Instructor and Touch Therapist for the Terminally Ill' with Healing Hands Healing Hearts. I attended and received my massage therapist degree from Trinity College-Sacramento-Campus, graduating in 2004 with a 4.0 (high honors), twice on the Dean's List. In 2007, I was certified by the California Massage Council.

My specialties include Healing Massage, Trigger Point Therapy, Touch Therapy for the terminally ill, and Pranic Energy Healing. I also offer Basic Tools, Technique and Meditation Classes along with Teach Touch Therapy for the terminally ill.

I currently reside in West Sacramento and am married to a wonderful man. I have two amazing sons and a lovable Labrador retriever named Jaycee. I also have a huge adoration for horses and believe equine therapy is a positive step for people with various types of special needs. For years, I was in between various jobs trying to find my "center", I discovered along my journey that the joy of therapeutic massage was my passion. I believe nothing is more powerful than human touch in nurturing the body, mind and spirit of human and animal beings.

Ruby Sharon Evans – (Sa Eeda)
My Breast Cancer Survival Experience

It is my intention to tell my breast cancer survival story through the alternative, metaphysical and medical experience of my being. It is my prayer that through sharing these experiences, you the reader or someone close to your heart will be encouraged and lifted to a higher level of understanding. I also realize the people who are meant to read or learn from this story will be led to it, in some form or fashion.

In the last week of Feb. 2007, I noticed a lump under my arm. I've had breast cyst for many years; so, I used to feel lumps, but this was different. I went to the doctor and got a biopsy and the diagnosis was third stage breast cancer. I returned home feeling 'numb.' I went into an immediate prayer and meditation mode. I asked Spirit, was it my time to die? The answer was No! You've been chosen to be a testament to others. That answer put me at peace and thus my journey began.

I went on a (Macrobiotic diet,) sometimes called the (Cancer Prevention Diet,) (eat lots of cooked and some raw greens, grains and fruits, wash all vegetables and fruit well; eat nothing moldy or white food such as rice and pasta. I got wheat and corn, no gluten or sugar and very little meat; I also stopped eating all dairy products and absolutely no processed foods; I stopped going to 'fast food' establishments.)

It wasn't easy. But I lost forty pounds from my five foot two inch 168-pound frame in a six-month period. It's better to lose it slowly because it's more apt to stay off. I also drank pure or filtered water, (no tap,) well water is okay if it has been tested to be safe. I detoxified my body of impurities by taking a couple of herbal concoctions such as **(Essiac and Kambucha – mushroom tea.)** I also drank a lot of decaffeinated green tea; Remember, fat holds the cancer and sugar feeds it!

I was determined to cure myself in that first six months. I did not go back to the medical profession at that time. The lump under my arm stopped hurting and shrunk. I didn't talk about what I had because I didn't want people to feel sorry for me; other than my family and very close friends; I told no one. Two profound things happened next that turned my whole life around.

I received word that a beautiful healer and friend of mine (Carol) had died of brain cancer. We belonged to the same metaphysical church, Honolulu Church of Light, when I was living in Hawaii. We held weekly world healing sessions over the internet; where people could call in for prayer request and we received hundreds of testimonies from people of many countries testifying as to how powerful our prayers were. Carol was one of the officiators of the program and a beautifully voiced spokesperson.

I was devastated!

I questioned God. How could such a wonderful, powerful healer die of cancer? I mourned for three or four days. I finally got myself together and did a special meditation and ceremony for her spirit; I lit a white candle, burned some frankincense and placed a small glass of water and fresh flowers on a table. I then prayed to God to bless her spirit and the members of her family that were left behind, to be in peace.

I am an Ordained Spiritualist Minister with the gifts of sight and hearing. Her spirit came to me as I prayed; I saw her in all her glory, bathed in a gorgeous, golden light and she was so beautiful, physically as well as spiritually. Carol spoke as I quietly sat and listened to her words; she said, she had been doing the same thing I was doing but by the time she turned to the medical profession, it was too late. "Don't make the same mistake, you must do both, the alternative and the medical; Do so and you will be fine." She then disappeared into the others. I sat quietly for some time, crying off and on for joy, and gratitude that she would come to me and give me such a profound message. I then got up, called my doctor and made an appointment to get medical care.

The second thing happened within the same week. I noticed a tiny red patch on my breast; I had read about these spots and rashes and had an ideal of what it might be. When I went to my appointment, the doctor has it biopsied and as I suspected, it was inflammatory; the nastiest kind of breast cancer you can get. It spreads rapidly and means an automatic mastectomy (removal of the breast.)

The doctor started me on chemotherapy immediately. There are different types of chem. Cocktails, depending upon what kind of cancer you have; even breast cancer has different kinds (I had Two.) I was told the cancer was not hormone related, so due to protocol, they knew what mixture to give me. Protocol has to do with your height and weight, what type of cancer and what stage you're in. I protested, how could you give the same amount of chemo to everybody based on that when we are all so individual?

It stands to reason that some people will react differently, regardless of the same weight and height. The doctor responded "This is what we do with good success rates." She was a gentle and caring doctor, so then, and there I knew I needed to trust her. She went on to explain that they're learning more about cancer every day and the process of giving chemo before an operation, gives the patient a better chance of survival.

It is minimal to remove the shrunken tumor, but cutting into live cancer cells may unknowingly cause it to travel to other parts of the body and flare up, later thus, chemo treatment before operation. The hospital I chose was also a medical school that trained doctors. I felt they had the latest equipment and knowledge so, again I felt that I needed to trust more. I received chemo intravenously.

I knew what the side effects were and I prayed I wouldn't have them, No such Luck! The (Andromiacyn) in my cocktail made me deathly sick, even though I envisioned golden light flowing into my veins; I chanted (under my breath,) a (Nichren Dishonen Buddist chant;) Nam, Myoho, Renge, Kyo; which I also practice. I suffered terrible nausea and could not keep anything down on my stomach; my head felt like a balloon, soon to burst at any moment from the pain, not to mention the woozy sensation that made me feel like I would blast off into outer space at any moment. The anti-nausea medicine only made me feel worse.

The sores in my mouth were excruciating and my throat swelled, so it was hard to swallow, needless to say, I didn't eat too well and I lost twenty more pounds. My son brought his clippers, so I could cut my hair close. I wore wigs, most of the time so that when I became bald, no one would notice. I had to have a plasma transfusion because my white blood cells were too low and I had no energy and that helped a lot.

I turned to my non-denominational church at Christ Unity who helped me with different resources such as financial and prayer support. One of my church family members was Gail Derin, an oriental medicine doctor and acupuncturist; she worked with me daily, giving me an acupuncture treatment, dried roots and herb mixtures to make teas out of. I definitely consider her, one of my saving graces. I'd also go to her office immediately after my chemo treatment which was every two weeks for eight weeks; it took two days for the adverse effects to 'kick in.'

My symptoms would straighten up towards the end of the second week and then treatment side effects would start all over again. The herbs and acupuncture quickly took away the regurgitation actions but, it took longer to re-coup from the other adversities in-which I did quite well. The first eight-week cocktail was then changed to a different concoction; kind of a One-Two punch to the cancer cells. The culprit, this time was (Taxol.)

It deadened my taste buds so I either couldn't taste my food or, it tasted horrible. I developed neuropathy; nerve damage to the fingers and toes, causing some pain, tingling, and numbness all at the same time. I suffered terrible joint pain all over my body. It turned my nails black with black patches on my tongue, palms and bottom of my feet. I had no feelings of touch in these areas, yet my feet felt they were as large as footballs even though they looked normal size.

Nuroptin is a medicine to help with the side effects, only brought back the nausea and wooziness, so I refused to take it. Dr. Derin meanwhile stuck with me; giving me weekly treatments and I quickly bounced back, and also received other healing modalities from practitioners of massage, Reiki and Deeksha, both latter two having to do with different types of healing energy transferables. The doctor gave me a three week break from any treatments before the operation.

During that period of time, my sister and I did a special ceremony for my breast; we used the mineral kingdoms aid of two carved, puffed heart, rose quartz. We prayed to Gaia (Mother Earth,) and asked her to receive the two crystals in honor of my breasts, and all it stood for in the past. We asked that she bless me and receive these crystals as a blessing to her.

I then dug a deep hole in her breast, (underground,) placed some sage and the rose quartz in it. We paid homage to her and thanked her for receiving these gifts. My heart and eyes filled with tears as I symbolically said good-bye to my breast. I only needed one breast removed but since I had a benign tumor on the other side, I opted for the other breast also to be taken. The operation is called a bilateral mastectomy. I had talked to different people, some who only got the infected breast removed and they felt lopsided afterwards; some people had cancer return to the other breast at a later time, regretting not having it removed during the initial operation.

My reasoning was to try to avert those things from happening to me. My feelings were that I am more than my flesh and I am certainly more than my breast. Nine lymph nodes were removed from under my arm. These nodes removed fluid from under my arm, and without them swelling, (lymphodemia,) can occur. I now cannot do any heavy lifting with that arm. I cannot have shots or needles put in it or blood pressure cuffs used on it. Even elevation caused by travel in the mountains or airplane flights can also cause the arm to swell, so there's a special spandex sleeve that was recommended for me to wear; it prevents the arm from swelling during these activities. I also have to be careful with bug biting me on that arm or getting any kind of cuts or punctures.

The operation went well, even though it took twelve hours from procedure through recovery. I was in the hospital for four days, due to a locked bowel; the doctors wanted to send me home sooner, but I protested. I needed to feel my bowels were working properly, since I live by myself. They kept me an extra day and I used that time praying to my anatomy to 'straighten up' so I could return home and I did. The pain meds in the hospital made me feel good, but was changed when I went home.

The new meds made me feel nauseous, so I didn't take them. I used herbal pain killers (arnica) and when the pain increased, which wasn't too often, I bought over the counter products such as extra strength Tylenol. I had three tubes or drains from my operation site which were removed; one the first week and the others, two weeks later. I waited a month before my radiation treatments began. I went out into nature during that time as much as possible. I did deep breathing exercises and asked for healing help from the elementals (nature spirits, fairies, etc.) I placed my bare feet upon mother earth's breast (ground or grass) and continued praying and chanting.

Radiation was a 'piece of cake' compared to the chemo therapy. It only took about ten minutes from set-up to the end of the treatment session. It did not hurt but, I could feel the energy going in me, almost but not quite like a slow electrical current. I gave myself Reiki treatments, immediately after each session, before I got dressed. I am a Karuna/Reiki Master healer and Teacher, and Spirit had reminded me to do this during one of my meditations. I was too sick (most of the time,) during chemo to give myself Reiki but, chanting, the use of the sound vibration of my voice helped me.

Dr. Derin meanwhile, was still there giving me treatments. Radiation treatments were five days a week for six weeks. The last week, the treatment was cut to fifty seconds and directed only at the incision site. The reason stated was that when cancer comes back it usually starts from the point, so that's an extra precaution they take. I got quite tanned from the rays, but I did not blister. The couple of days, I felt some stinging; I used Shea butter, Vitamin E and Aloe Vera to help keep my skin in condition. I opted for this instead of the doctor's recommended cream.

I next had to take a special chemo treatment called (Herception,) intravenously. This lasted every three weeks until a year to the date of my operation; I opted to take this treatment more slowly than usually recommended because I noted that I didn't get sick as quickly and rebounded better, before the next one. I tended to get tired easily but did not suffer pain. It is my belief that I am cancer free due to all of the work that's been done. This work included alternative modalities, the medical professions, chemo, a bilateral mastectomy, radiation, chanting, visualization of seeing myself being totally healed, faith and determination; with at all times, a positive attitude. All these are choices you may choose to make.

I feel almost as well as I did before the ordeal started. My family and friends comment on how much energy I have and how good I look; there is radiance around me. The doctors are very pleased with how well I came through the whole process. I lost sixty-five more pounds all together and even though I complained at losing so much weight; I feel so much lighter, like I am walking on air. I don't plan to pick up much more weight.

Talk to people, tell your story. There is someone who will want or need to hear it. Modify your diet, get more rest, relieve the stress from your life, and most of all, have Faith, trust and keep the determination to 'Beat It.' I Thank All the people who prayed for and helped me in some way. I am so grateful to be alive, and I will do my best to help others travel through their cancer journeys. Be Well!

Feb. - 2014, I am now 7 years' out

June - 2016, I am now 9 years out and still cancer free.

Now- 2017, I am now in 2017 10 years out and still cancer free. From here on I only go once a year for check- ups.

Namaste (The God in me, recognizes the God in you.)

Nam Myoho Renge Kyo (Through sound and vibration, chant the mystic Law (God) to be wise, heal and be happy.)

About the Author

Ruby Sharon Evans – Sa Eeda

Sa Eeda's interfaith beliefs enable her to work, embrace and teach people of all walks of life through her Spiritual Tool Creations and Energy Transference Healings, and her ability to love you…. "Just the way you are." She has been active and lively in the Metaphysical field for over 40 years. She is an Ordained Minister, trained Psychic Development Teacher, and Karuna - Reiki Master/Teacher, and has perfected her own style of healing techniques in California for a wide array of audiences.

She strongly believes we are all Kings and Queens who deserves the best life has to offer. 'The Trick,' say Sa Eeda, "Is to first recognize the Divine in each other and then reach out to give a helping hand in love." Sa Eeda is a divinely guided, compassionate Intuitive that in using Egyptian Oracles, Dolphin, Fairy and Angel Readings as well as Energy Transference Healings, is here to help you. You can contact Sa Eeda, at the address listed below.

Ruby Sharon Evans- Sa Eeda
P.O. Box 214885
Sacramento, Ca. 95821

Amitola Sky
Mother Loves Her Child

It was a beautiful Saturday in May, the kind of beautiful spring day you love to turn to the sun and close your eyes and let the sun warm your whole body. I live in New Jersey and we drove to Pennsylvania to the Leigh Valley where there are gorgeous mountains and trails. My daughter was almost 8 years old, when a friend invited us to go rappelling. I had never been and neither had my daughter. He gave us a lesson on how to handle the ropes and said this is a great way to face fears. I sent my daughter down first so I could keep an eye from the top and a friend was at the bottom when she landed. Then I went next, it was fun and I did a pretty good job bouncing off the rocks with my feet. We both were at the bottom and my daughter ran out in front of my down the path to go back up the mountain to do it again. There were 2 levels to this mountain and we were on the top level.

I told her to slow down and walk with me but she ran ahead and in a flash lost her footing and fell of the side of cliff. I ran to the side and looked down and she was lying on her back and not moving. I screamed and looked for a spot where I could sit down, and slide down the cliff. I was doing fine sliding down on my butt when all of sudden the ground gave way and I was in the air, I slammed down on a rock ledge and rolled and tumbled off the rock and fell, and rolled for about another 15 feet.

I landed about ten feet from my daughter and tried to get up, and run to her but I could not, so I crawled over to her. She was talking to me and I was holding her in my arms, and when I saw blood on her face, I wiped it away and it kept coming back. I realized the blood was coming from me. Friends and other people hiking were now getting to where we were and I asked a friend to please find my glasses. In a few minutes, she came back and handed me my glasses, she handed them to me folded up neatly, no scratches and in perfect condition, she told me that is how she found them under a tree.

After about an hour an ambulance arrived and took us to a landing site where we were medevac to a local hospital. After being checked out from head to toe they said my daughter had broken her shoulder and I fractured T12 in my back. They took Megan to surgery and I was put in bed, and told to rest until they could fit me with a brace.

That night in the hospital I kept dreaming about the fall, during the dream I saw the 3 Angels; there was a huge blue Angel and that is the one I asked to take my glasses off my face so they would not cut me, they lovingly helped me and neatly folded them, and placed them under the tree where they were found. The smaller green one held my bottom when I landed on that rock so nothing was broken there.

There was a greenish blue large Angel who just kept talking to me and telling me everything was going to be fine, it was not my time to come home. We both should have died we fell seventy feet, the greenish blue one told me Megan would be fine, they had held her as she fell and they just let her have a little thump on the ground that broke her shoulder but it will heal with no problems. It was like talking with friends who loved me more than I could have imagined.

During the time, all of this was happening there was a large white figure above us and it was as if they had encased the area where Megan and I were with light. It felt like it was a bubble, a very loving and safe bubble, where Divine energy work was happening. Over the year's friends who are gifted have often told me they see an Angel on my right side holding my hand and I feel them holding my hand at times also.

We are never alone and help is there constantly. Since that time, I have more Angels with me, I also have animal's guides. I ask them for assistance all the time and do my best to get out of the way so I can hear them. I am a certified Fairyologist and read cards. Blessing to you as you read this, your Angels love you more than your human mind can ever imagine, relax, and keep your heart open to hear them. Your Journey is a very special one and you are needed here.

I am a certified Fairyologist and live in New Jersey, my email is fairyangels61@gmail.com. I do card readings using the Fairy Tarot cards; the Mermaid Dolphin deck and Unicorn Deck, also the Fairy Healing Deck and Archangel Power Tarot Cards. When I do readings, I am guided to the deck or decks to assist you. A lot of what comes through me for my clients is information on how to assist you on your journey. My website is www.fairiesnatureangels.com and my address is P.O.Box 426, Thorofare, NJ 08086.

About the Author

Ellie Leas was born in Pennsylvania. At age five, she moved to a little place called Coventryville and attended first grade in a two-room schoolhouse. Having grown up around farms, Ellie loves nature and all animals. From a young age, the elementals have connected with her, so becoming a Certified Fairyologist spoke to her on a deep level. She has also studied courses in law and nursing, and worked for companies most of her life, but spending time outdoors and enjoying nature and the elementals make her the happiest.

Greta Lilek
Many Lifetimes One Love

Where do I start my story? This is the question I asked myself when I agreed to contribute to this wonderful empowering book. My first real Spiritual encounter after a lifetime of synchronicities and visions came as I walked the bridle path with my two German Shepherds in my home town in Lancashire England. I had been feeling very low and wandering how my life had become so unhappy when I spotted a large Owl just ahead of me. It was sat in a tree watching us approach it, neither dog noticed it and ran ahead. As I passed and looked in awe at this magnificent bird our eyes locked and at that moment an electric shock ran through my body right into my soul and I instantly felt a peace come over me, and a feeling my life was going to change and it did in a big way.

Not long after the Owl I received a booklet in the post full of local functions and services I put it in my bookrack and forgot about it until one day I found it on the floor open I glanced at the page and put it back in the rack, the next day same thing, I put it back the third day I read the page and in a corner, was a small add inviting people to come along to a Reiki Share group. I decided I will go along as I had heard about this form of healing and was curious. I went and that was the beginning of my journey into healing. I became a Reiki Master and then studied several healing Modalities Sachem Reiki Spiritual Healing, Angelic Light system of healing and my beloved Ra-Sheba an ancient Egyptian Healing.

Then I met Kate a medium who held a Spiritual Circle in her home I was invited to join and learnt a lot directly from Spirit wonderful teachings and guidance, and was learning to sit as a Trance Medium.

One day I was on Facebook and I noticed a friend request from a Spiritualist Minister in the USA, the first thing that struck me about him was his stunning blue eyes. The Minister was Rev John Lilek who later on became my husband but that's jumping ahead of my story.

John had just gone through a divorce and his Spirits were low, so he decided to offer tutoring free of charge over the internet, he told me later helping others he was helping himself. I jumped at the chance to learn from a Physical Medium.

As we chatted one day after a rather long tutoring session I felt the familiar electric charge I felt on my walk. I recalled the Owl and at that instant John said you have a guide called Spotted Owl! I was amazed. I also felt compassion and an overwhelming feeling of Love pass through me for this man with the deep blue eyes that I hardly knew but felt so comfortable with. I have to admit it shook me to the core.

I started to feel a deep connection as if I knew his very soul. I felt lifetimes of Love and intimacy come flooding into my mind in those few seconds. The next lesson I had with John he informed me was about remembering past lives, I thought this man knows my mind, I told him I had had a past life regression and I had the cd somewhere, John just started to tell me about one he remembered every detail of, as he was telling his story I felt the electric energy through my very soul he was describing word for word my story from the regression where I was a young Native American girl.

Our stories were the same, I was a young girl considered an outcast by the tribe, only tolerated because my Father was the Chief. Somewhat of an outcast I wandered the forest with my Wolf cub who I had found abandoned and reared myself.

I had been promised to a Brave from our tribe but I was in Love with a Brave from another Tribe and it was forbidden. I secretly met with him and one day I was followed by my suitor and Brother. They attacked my Love and stabbed him several times then dragged me screaming and crying back to our village. John said all he could hear was me screaming and crying until he slipped from that lifetime into Spirit. In my regression, I was asked to describe where I was and the name of the River I had described I called it The Great White Snake. I later found out it was White Snake River in Idaho.

As we discussed this John told me he felt the connection the day he saw my photograph on Facebook and reached out to me. He felt the same he told me. A deep Soul Level Love.
His guides had told him we would be reunited briefly in this lifetime. We later discovered how briefly they meant.

Several months went by where we grew closer and I decided to join him at a Spiritualist Camp in Florida where he was teaching and lecturing and doing séances for 3 weeks. Before I arrived, I knew I was going to be with this man for the rest of my life.

After 3 weeks sitting in Séances Classes, Lectures and in Private I had to return home to Britain. We were both devastated and very much in Love.

I returned home and felt as if my Heart was no longer mine it was with John. I arranged to spend Thanksgiving and Christmas with him in the UDSA and flew back after only being home 6 weeks I walked out of my home and life with 2 suitcases and didn't look back once.

I flew into Seattle Washington and after Thanksgiving John proposed to me and in a whirlwind of not even thinking about the consequences we got married in a small Spiritualist Church in Tacoma by the minister Rev Sheila Kirkland.

Our Life was as roaming gypsies we travelled over 48 States in 2 years John doing demonstrations teaching and I did my Energy work and workshops along the way. We basically lived in our car staying with trusted friends along the way. Then Spirit kept telling me I had to live in Maine we had visited several times and it felt familiar to me, so we bought a house in Maine John wanted to start a Spiritual Centre there and we started to make it happen when after only 2 years 4 months John took sick all of a sudden.

We were together when the diagnosis came through that he had Stage 4 Terminal Lung Cancer and it had spread throughout his body and were told to go home and make preparations.
John worked doing his Spiritual work right up until 2 days before he passed to Spirit on the 14th August 2014 3 months before our 3rd Wedding Anniversary. He was peaceful that day and was seeing his Beloved Rev James Tingley who was his mentor friend, and like a Father to him waiting to take him home.

 I know there are many Earth Angels who walk amongst us and alongside our Master Teachers and Guides. I was privileged to be a part of a Love Story that has spanned many lifetimes as we both found out during our sittings with Spirit in Séance.

And I want to tell our readers with great confidence that Love does not die, it continues on and our loved ones are never far away watching guiding and waiting to welcome us home.

About the Author

Greta Lilek is a well -respected, qualified Preschool Teacher and licensed special needs coordinator born and raised in England.

Greta's passion is healing and energy work. Greta attended Fort Wayne Spiritual Church Indiana was she earned her certification for Spiritual Healing. Greta attended The Centre for Sachem where she earned her degree for Sachem Master. Greta is a Reiki Master Teacher, Ra-Sheba Master and Angelic Light Initiator.

Greta attended North East School of Psychic study was she earned her Mediumship Certificate. Greta moved to the United States in 2011 and travelled with her husband Rev John Lilek around the country helping people with their gifts of Medium ship and Energy Healings.

Greta's readings offer guidance from a higher power. Each reading consists of past, present, and future.

Greta has a unique mixture of Reiki and Channeled Angelic energy to release old energy patterns while cleansing and balancing chakras. This healing releases stress, anxiety and depression leaving you feeling calm and balanced. This is a new age of transformation and Greta's gifts can help you through the adjustment processes need to life in Peace and Harmony.

Michele Amburgey
The Crooked Road Back Home-Part One

Looking up at the sky, my ten-year-old mind grappled with what I was seeing. Three rainbow-colored angels blowing trumpets moved across the sky. I broke my gaze away just long enough to look around at the playground and find it was empty. I heard a door slam in the distance and knew that everyone was back in class from recess; but I couldn't' move. I continued to stare up at the beautiful angels, my whole-body tingling. My heart felt full, and it beat hard in my chest. As the angels began to fade away, I felt the world coming back into focus.

Suddenly realizing I was late, I began to run toward the blue metal door that took me into the hallway leading to the classrooms. At the third door, down, I saw the plaque on the door that said Mrs. Short. I stopped for a moment. *Is this the right room?* I had just started this new school three days earlier since moving back from New York. My father had received another promotion, and we got to move back home to this quiet little suburb of Los Angeles.

My body had begun to shake, so I pushed open the door and ran to the teacher's desk.

"There are angels! Angels on the playground!" I said much louder than I had intended.

Mrs. Short looked up at me. "Excuse me?" Seeing her staring at me quenched my excitement, and my natural shyness kicked right in. I whispered, "There are angels on the playground. I saw them."

There was a moment of quiet, and then the whole classroom burst into laughter. The kids' remarks behind me, "Oh, the new girl saw angels," "she must be retarded," "what an idiot," rang through my head. I turned to look at the class and all of the faces laughing at me. I felt the rush of heat to my face and wanted to die right there.

Mrs. Short smiled at me and said, "Let's call your parents. You might not be feeling well." The next thing I remembered was sitting in the principal's office as my Mother came walking through the door. She was a beautiful woman, and she turned heads everywhere she went. The principal looked up, and I saw the familiar admiration that most men had on their faces when they saw her. "So, what is going on?" she asked sharply.

The principal took her into the next room and I heard murmuring. Then my Mom came back in and said, "They are telling me that you saw angels. Did you?" I looked up at her, still hearing the kids laughing at me. I swallowed hard and said, "Yes, Mom, I did."

She looked annoyed. The principal was standing in the doorway, and they passed a look back and forth. It did not feel good to me, and I knew I was in trouble. Riding home in the car, my Mom explained to me that the school wouldn't let me come back until I had a psychological examination. I wasn't sure what that meant, but I already regretted saying anything to anyone about the beautiful angels.

The next day, I was sitting in a huge leather chair that was so slippery I could barely stay seated. I kept slipping all over it, and the psychologist didn't even seem to notice. He asked me a lot of questions. I tried to stay still without slipping onto the floor.

Then the psychologist asked my mom to come into his office, and he said, "Well, we have more tests to do, but I think it's safe to say your daughter is showing signs of psychosis and will have to be medicated. We find that lithium is a good choice in these instances." My mom almost shouted, "Absolutely not!" She squared off at the psychologist and said, "I want a full examination, and I want her to have an IQ Test. Can that be done right now?"

The doctor said it could, and I was taken into another room where I was given a bunch of test questions. The room smelled like cigarette smoke, and to this day when I have to take tests, I can smell that smell. Fast forward to dinner that night; my mom hadn't said much to me about the psychologist test results, but at dinner, once my dad got home, she made an announcement at the dinner table.

"Your daughter has a 138 IQ; she is a genius. I read this brochure and it said that children geniuses have very active imaginations. This is why she is so imaginative and why she sees people and angels and she knows when Nona is going to call. She is smart, very smart." Then she looked at me. "And from now on, we don't tell people about what you see. I mean the things that other people don't see. We don't talk about those things any more, okay?"

After that, I struggled to figure out what was okay to share and what wasn't. I continued to see angels and dead people. I knew things that other kids didn't. I knew that Caroline Hill's mom was going to die. I brought her flowers the day before, but didn't say anything about it. I said some things about what I saw or knew to my friends and got very good at gauging their responses as to whether or not something was safe to share. I would laugh things off if I saw that it wasn't received well.

I became known as a silly girl, playful, a joker. It kind of helped my shyness, and people generally liked me. I began to settle in our new home and life went on. But I was incredibly lonely. I read a lot of books. My parents were both avid readers. Jack London, James Michener, and JRR Tolkien were a few of the many authors I was privy to. Books became my friends, and they calmed my ever-active imagination.

Fast-forward two years. I was standing in the foyer of my church. The congregation was assembled in the sanctuary and the music was just starting. I heard a knock on the big glass doors at the front of the hall. There was a man and woman standing there. He was dressed in shorts and sandals, and she had on a blue dress. Both looked a little tattered. The bishop of the church came out of his office and saw the people standing there.

He said through the glass doors, "What can I help you with?"

The man answered, "We would like to worship in your church."

The bishop said, "We have dress codes here. Go change your clothes and we would welcome you." He turned his back to go into the sanctuary, and the man knocked again, this time harder.

"What do you want?" the bishop asked sharply as he turned.

The man said again, "We would like to worship in your church."

The bishop said, "Change your clothes and come back." The bishop went into the sanctuary.

I heard the man knock on the big glass door again. As I turned to look at him, a chill ran through my body. I saw Jesus Christ looking at me through the glass. It was Jesus knocking on the door. And The Church of Jesus Christ of Latter-day Saints just turned Him away. I was stunned. I was heartbroken. I walked into the sanctuary and sat at the back, numb. I remember crying through the whole church service. And let me tell you, Mormon Church services are really long. I cried for myself and for the church and for Jesus. How could the bishop have turned Him away? After that, I refused to go to church.

I tried to shut down my gifts at that point. I ignored the sights and sounds I heard from the other places, and I think my love of learning, puberty, and the days of being a twelve-year-old took hold. My younger brother was an ADD nightmare and haunted my existence. He used to say to me, "No one wants you; you should kill yourself." My parents became consumed with keeping him out of trouble and in school. He would light things on fire, beat kids up, steal beer, and generally cause mayhem 24/7. I became consumed with staying as far away from him as possible. A few glimpses into other worlds and some intuitive hits came through, but for the most part, I kept it all under wraps. I was in a twelve-year-old's survival mode.

When I was thirteen, my father became president of an iconic record company in Los Angeles. My life began to shift as I was required to play the part of the president's daughter. Speaking, dressing, and behaving in certain ways were expected, and training and coaching began to be a part of my life. We entertained the most amazing people at our home. I sat and listened in on conversations of how musicians created their music. I heard stories of how these normal people became famous. My father was a great bard and shared stories of the days at "The Tower." My imagination was fueled in a new way!

I began to play and write music. Along with that came the realization that I had been writing poetry and prose since I was five-years-old. I began to put my childhood writings to music. I felt like I had found my niche in life, my purpose! I spent hours in my room or in the backyard pouring over songs and lyrics. I knew I was going to be a music artist.

Then, I presented a poem for a class project. I was going to put it to music, but something inside me said not to. On the day of the presentation, I was so excited. I had heard my dad talk about the debut of artists, and I felt like I was so grown up and this was my debut.

I read my poem in front of the class. Everyone stayed eerily silent, even the teacher. When I was done, my teacher gave me a severe look and told me to go to my seat. No one said a thing. Thankfully, that was the last class of the day and I went straight home. I was so confused. What had happened? When I got home, the house was silent. Where was everyone? I went into the kitchen and saw my mom sitting on a stool looking at the phone. She looked up and scowled at me. "What am I going to do with you?" she asked.

I just stared. I had no idea how to respond. Me? I was the good kid! I was the smart kid! What was she talking about? When my dad got home, there were conversations behind closed doors. No one spoke all evening.

The next morning my mom took me to school. When we got there, I realized that my dad had followed us. They took me into the principal's office and we all sat down. The principal showed my parents the poem I had written. She seemed very angry. All I could do was look at her lips as she talked. "Shelly read this poem as her project for English class." She handed the poem to my parents. Smiles slowly came over both of their faces. As they looked up, my dad said, "This is really good."

The principle replied in a loud voice, "There is no way she wrote this poem."

She looked at me and said, "Where did you steal this from?"

I was stunned. I answered, "I wrote it." The principle argued, "There is no way you wrote this, this is plagiarism and I will find where you got it."

"Tell me right now or you get a fail on this paper and a fail in the class.

Plagiarism is against the law and is morally wrong."

Then she turned her eyes on my dad, a powerful and intelligent man, and said, "And you, Mr. Zimmermann, should know this above all others." Your daughter has stolen the creative work of someone else and has presented it as her own. You need to have a long talk about plagiarism with this, this, this;" She turned her hate-filled eyes on me and said, "Spoiled brat!" Then she stormed out of the room.

I looked up at my dad, hoping he would explain. He asked me, "Did you steal this?"

I told him no, I wrote it. He nodded. "People in my industry go to jail and pay huge sums of money for stealing other people's music. Do you understand that?" I just looked at him and said, "I wrote that myself. I wrote it; I didn't steal it. I wrote it."

We went home and my dad went to work. The day was very quiet and I spent it in my room afraid, and confused. I was devastated that all of my dreams, hopes and plans were gone. A part of me was embarrassed that my teacher thought I would steal a poem, and a part of me was angry that my parents didn't fully defend me. I was awash with emotions that I didn't know how to deal with.

Just before sunset, I decided I needed to go sit by the pool. Water always calmed me down, so I grabbed a towel and went outside. While I was sitting there, I began to notice flickering in the sky. There was a little tree on the hill behind our house and I saw the flickering as if it was coming from behind the tree. I started to feel tingly. My whole body began to buzz. Then I saw them.

In the sky, above me, three rainbow angels blowing trumpets sailed across the sky. I began to cry. I heard a soothing male voice say, "Someday this will all make sense. The road back home is a crooked one. Keep your faith and soon the world will come to know you as Malachim, a Messenger." My voice was trembling as I whispered, "Who are you?" "I am Archangel Metatron."

To Be Continued in *Warrior Women with Angel Wings for the Soul*

About the Author

Michele Amburgey has been creatively writing since she was five years old. Her poetry and prose were famous amongst her family and friends. Michele grew up in a creative family; her father was in the music industry, and music has greatly influenced her writing. Michele now works as an Intuitive Coach, Master Healer, Hypnotherapist, Spiritual Teacher, Radio Show Host, Public Speaker, and Author. Michele was a regular Speaker at the World Healer Conference in San Diego, Ca. for many years. Michele has published articles in *Holistically Savvy*, *Radiance,* and *Awareness* **magazines**. Her first published book was as a co-author in *Toolboxes for Women.*

Michele believes that humanity is ready to be embraced as whole beings that are capable of healing mind, body, and spirit in miraculous ways. Michele's soul purpose is to facilitate healing and spiritual awakening, and to inspire joyous, abundant, healthy, soulful living. Michele's uplifting messages, positive and playful attitude, and healing presence empower people to reach their greatest potential.

Michele currently resides in Orange County, California.

Website: www.MicheleAmburgey.com

Email: Michele.Amburgey@gmail.com

Phone: 1-949-202-7493

Facebook Author Page: Michele Amburgey-Author

Facebook Business Page: Intuitive Coach Michele Amburgey

Facebook Group: Soulful Living Tribe

Linda Farrelly
The Misery of a Child with an Adult's Mind

Wishing life was over! Until I seen the light:

My childhood was a sad and lonely place growing up, all I ever wanted as a child was to end my life. I had to grow up very quickly to survive my nightmare in a sad child's body. I was only 2 years old when my mother left me and only remember bad stuff, I could not remember anything good in my life growing up, I remember my mother walking out on my father with 3 of her children out of 7 and that was my self which my name is Linda and my two brothers aged 3 aged 5. I don't know why this happened but only Knew that I came from a very mixed up family life, as you will discover further on in this chapter. My mother left with the 3 of us and took us to her sister's flat. I can't remember how long we stayed there for but what I can remember and still to this day was the smell of urine. My Aunt would dry her mattress and sheets in front of the fire whenever her kids wet the bed. Another thing I remember was a knock at the door and that the 3 of us was rushed into the kitchen and my mother putting her hands over our mouths as not to say a word.

My father and my older brother pushed their way in once my Aunt opened the door; my father gave my mother an ultimatum to come back with us all now or to never return. The sad thing was she decided to stay with her sister and just let her kids walk away. My father had different women in his life that didn't treat me to good, I was never loved and never got affection, I had no one to talk to or turn too so I had to hold everything inside me, I was very shy and felt I was never good enough for anything, I began to hate myself.

All I remember was wishing I was not here anymore, that life would be so much better of that way; only thing was I was too scared to do anything about it. Let me go into a little detail about my life then you will understand. First of all, my father met this woman, she was a lady that wanted everyone to know she was around and she would make up stories about all of us but to her it was so real, my father would always believe her.

I had 4 older family members 3 brothers and one sister, but they were so much older than us so was able to look after themselves. Things I remember about my childhood would be all bad, some of the things would be I went to school one day and when I got back home I told her my head was very itchy. She checked my hair and noticed I had nits. I got the hardest slap around the face which stung for ages. She felt I passed it on the rest of the family and hit me because I should have told her sooner.

Another thing was I used to wet the bed too, I would be so afraid to tell her as I always was beaten for it. Myself and my cousin would go and visit the old people in the elderly home, one day I said to my cousin I had to go to the loo, when I came back I noticed this old man in a wheel chair with his hand down her knickers.

I didn't know what to do so I let a cough for her to know I was there, she ran out to me and we ran home, she begged and begged me to say nothing until I said ok. That night when I went to bed I was woken up by my stepmom and demanded to tell her everything as my cousin's mother had rang her telling her what happened at the old people's home. I told her I promised my cousin I would say nothing and had to keep my promise. I got the worst beating ever. I was made to get out of bed in the middle of the night and go to the old people's home and pick this man out. I said I wouldn't remember what he looked like but I was told I had to pick someone, anyone. I was so afraid of her so I did, I still to this day never forgave myself for doing this as an innocent man could have been moved from that home because of me. I ask forgiveness every day.

She was a lady that would be home one Minute and gone the next. I would come home from school to find no one home, one day I came home from school and no one there. I had to go upstairs to the neighbor's flat which was the 4th block up, the two lads in the flat thought it would be funny to chain me up over the balcony with a big chain and padlock, I was so scared and just cried and cried. I couldn't say anything as I would not have been taken serious and would be afraid it would happen again.

I went to school one day and my knickers fell down, I had to get someone in the hairdressers to put a hair clip in them to hold them up till I got home. I was beaten up in school, head flushed down toilets and beaten in the stomach. I ended up in hospital with a very bad case of shingles from the age of 12. I never received presents for Christmas or birthdays and when I found myself a Saturday job which was 5 pounds every Saturday I had to save it to buy my uniform. When I was 16, I was not allowed to stay on at school to do my exams I was made to go out to work and they took my money as soon as I was paid. I met this lad. I started going out with him from the age of 16 and when I was 17 we wanted to get married. It was an escape route for me, my father accepted and let us get married.

I was married for 5 years, and 5 years of hell. I thought my life would be so much better but ended up even worse. He changed when we got married, he lost his job, got very drunk most of the time and beat me up regular, and I would be black and blue. He always led me to believe it was my fault and that I deserved it, he smashed a glass table over my head when I tried to run under the table to get away from him, he then pulled me up by my neck and kept smashing my head from the wall with my legs dangling of the ground. Thank God someone heard the noise and called the police as there was a knock on the door which made him stop.

The last straw was when he broke my jaw, I was outside entering my flat when he arrived home from the pub early one day to start punching me in the face. A neighbour ran out to pick me up of the ground bundle me in to his flat and rang the ambulance. I never went back after this I finally started to see the light. I stayed with a friend for a while and was invited to a blind date for my friend's 21st birthday, this was when my life started to change for the better.

I met this man called Finian, it was love at first site, I just knew he was meant to be for me, he knew all about my ex-husband as I told him everything, he paid of all my debts my ex left me to pay and I got divorced and then got married to Finian. He had his own house in Hertfordshire and we had 3 beautiful boys Sean, Brendan and Finian, we then decided to sell the house and move back to Ireland as that was where he was born Co Meath and their we bought a house and had our baby girl Lisamarie. When I was young I hung around with my cousin a lot, she was a daughter of my mum's sister and she decided to come over to Ireland one day to visit me.

As I said at the very start of this chapter I came from a very mixed up family back ground. My cousin never spoke to her sister for over 20 years and I never knew why, so I asked her when she came to see me, she told me she had a row with her sister one day that her sister told her that my Dad was her father, I was gob smacked, my cousin could be my sister, we decided to get a DNA done with ourselves. And to see if he was her father and if we were sisters. He agreed so we did it discreetly.

When the results came back I found out that she was his daughter but I was not his daughter. I was in shock as I did not think at all that this could happen as we was just thinking about my cousin at this stage. Now I needed to know who my father was So I was cheated of my life growing up, my mother walked out on me at the age of 2 and I was brought up by a man that was not my father.

I felt I could have had a better life if I was told at an early age but this never happened. I asked my mum about this and she denied point blank that she ever did anything with anyone else, I asked him about it and all he would say ask your mother. I felt they all knew something but would not tell me because if it came out in the open things would be worse. I knew he was seeing my mother's sister. As I found out my cousin was his daughter from the DNA we did. So, I decided to do my own detective work, I was thinking it had to be kept in the family as what I could remember when I was young they all fell out with each other and it didn't make sense. Now I know why so I would wait till I got a chance to do a DNA from all the uncles without them knowing.

When my mother got divorced from my father she decided to marry his brother. I told you it's a mixed-up family lol. He passed away and I did a DNA to see if he was my father but it came back negative. I was back to square one, where do I go next. I was going to try and pinch a toothbrush from my uncle Joe which was my cousin's Mum's husband but during that time les got sick and passed away. I went over to the funeral to find out my other uncle passed away around the same time my father did. I had to go to him I needed a DNA it was my only chance, I never met this man as I said they all fell out with each other when I was 2. So, I would have never remembered him. He was being buried two days after my father. So, I went to the funeral then went to the morgue which was 3-hour journey away the next day with my daughter Lisamarie.

I went in and seen this man for the first time in the coffin, he was 85 years old, loads of hair thank god as I needed hair to do a DNA, I had to pull loads of hair from his head by the roots as they need the roots to do the DNA test, I also cut his finger nails just in case, I put holy water on his head and put a set of rosary beads around his hands, he looked so peaceful and looked like he was going to wake up. I got the feeling he was my father and told him I was sorry for having to do this. I went back to Ireland the day after and sent the DNA away to be tested. I couldn't believe it he was my father. I was as mad as I asked my mother a year before he passed away and she said no she didn't.

She deprived me of having a bonding with him the last year of his life. But at least one good thing came out of it as it put closure to me having to keep looking, all the sisters was seeing the uncles and having each other's babies. It's so sad, my 3 older brothers and sister look nothing like me but myself and one of my brothers is a spitting image of each other. The sad thing was I buried two fathers in one week of each other and met my real father for the first time in his coffin.

I am so happy in my life now it's put closure on it all and now I have learnt to move on with my life with my new family. I am married now 27 years and have two beautiful granddaughters that I adore so much. I want them to remember me as the best nanny Linda ever. I just focus now on my family and show so much love also talk with my angels and guides and most of all just want to tell the world that you can change your life around even when you think it will never happen, as it did for me, just have faith, believe and you can achieve your dreams for the future. I live for my family; my family is very important to me; I have never cheated on my husband and would never wish too. I now live for today and achieve what I can for tomorrow.

About the Author

I have always from an early age of my childhood been very interested in Angels, and have always been keen to learn more. From the age of 10; I had to dig a bit deeper of the understanding of the concept of angels.

I have always believed in spiritual side and healing world, and how it makes a difference in our lives, I have learnt to use my own intuition and know it comes from the divine above for helping others.

I have achieved many courses starting from (IET) Integrated energy Healing

Angel/oracle and tarot cards

(CAP) Certified Angel Practioner

Certified Numerologist

Certified Psychic and Medium-ship

I am an experienced Intuitive card reader and healer for adults and pets. I am direct yet sensitive bringing comfort during readings and extremely clear and precise, offering guidance and support without tailoring the reading to fit the expectations of the client. I provide information based on the intuitive energies and higher guidance I receive from spirits as it is received. I frequently get consulted on matters of love & relationships as well as every day concerns and healing which allows me to guide you bringing clarity and hope into your life. Angel blessings from the realms above.

I also do Crystal Healings and the Sacred Wheel Energy Healings.

Kathy McCartney
The Maui Magical Mystical Tour
Home Is Where the Heart Is

Life is a spiritual experience. The signs are there when things need to change. My sign came suddenly one evening, quite by accident, and triggered a sequence of events that brought me back to Mother Maui sooner than expected. I was living with fiancé number three, Richard, a generous man who I thought was the complete package. I had never truly been physically attracted to him, even when we first met. He was eighteen years my senior, and it showed on occasion.

Richard was 5'6", though he told people he was three inches taller than he actually was. His light brown hair had streaks of white frost above his temples and was styled youthfully, spiking at the top. It was thinning slightly and receding, revealing a broad forehead. He was not the typical man who I felt attracted to. It was his mental acuity, creativity, and confidence that I liked. His generous heart, power, and jet-setting lifestyle didn't hurt either. Richard wined and dined me, sweeping me—a single mother—off my feet.

Things moved quickly once we became a couple. He lavished

me with designer clothing, a new Mercedes, trips to places like Sofia, Paris, Nice, Rome, Florence, Capri, Pompeii, London, Kingston, Brighton, Amsterdam, Brussels, Monaco and, of course, the Hawaiian Islands. We travelled in five-star luxury, and the lifestyle appealed to my free spirit. I guess men with money feel entitled to things from those around them. Richard's dark side crept up on me one day when he was in the shower and we were getting ready to go out to dinner. The revelation hit me like a tsunami hits a high rise. Richard's phone beeped and delivered the end of my world.

"Check my phone, won't you, honey?" His voice echoed from the bathroom.

I picked up his phone, and a message popped onto the screen—a message from a girl who worked as a barista at our local coffee shop. She looked like she was fresh out of high school, pink-cheeked and wild looking. As I read the text, my insides slid over themselves, forming a hard knot. I tasted betrayal, regret, and heartache in my mouth.

For a long while, I sat on the bed in Richard's beautiful house too hurt to cry and too angry to speak. Then, as it happens with selfish men, things got worse. He wanted me out. I suppose I felt that I would be safer with Richard as the younger, attractive one in our relationship, which obviously was not the case. Just like that, my plan for true love had imploded once again, much like the two relationships that had come before him. Were there no good men left?

I called a close friend of mine and retreated to her house for the night. Her husband was out of town on a business trip. For a while we sat together, drinking and despairing. All I could hear from her was how ruined I was now.

"What are you going to *do*?" she would ask me, as if the idea of being single at forty-seven was worse than a death sentence.

Inside, I felt my strength swell. I had raised Riley as a single mother. If I could do that, I could do anything. But there I was, my heart a mulch of colors swirled into a dark black abyss. The word I had been searching for was "trapped." I had trapped my spirituality, limited my freedoms, and caged my personal growth for the men who I believed were meant to fulfill me. I had sacrificed my artistic nature at the altar of finding my true mate. But I knew that I had left the path. For all of my creativity and love, I had lost myself. I had to return home to the one place where I felt happiest, where I could run free, as a woman without rules or limitations. I had to move back to the Islands. There, I could rekindle the fires that had once burned so brightly inside me as a young child.

With three failed relationships, I had fallen out of touch with myself. I needed to find my way back to happiness, the kind created by my spirit and not given to me by a man. That is partly why I decided to escape my imploded life and return to Mother Maui. For me, there is no lovelier, more beautiful, and more spiritual place than that island. Maui is a place of love and spiritual investigation. If I was ever going to find the love I believed I deserved, it would be back home on Maui. I decided to leave it all behind. I needed to journey back to rediscover the love in my life. I would have to dig deep to find love without the trappings of attraction and physical comfort ahead of me. At forty-seven, a new chapter of my life would begin.

I searched Google for places to stay on Maui. I came across a couple named Rama and Sita who owned the Lotus Retreat and Farm. The pitch on the website caught my attention: *A place for mature souls.* Unlike many other places on the island, this was a deeply spiritual area. I knew instantly it was the best place for me. I desperately needed to be reminded that I had something truly great to look forward to. If I watched enough of these positive programs on spirituality with guests from Maui, it might take me out of my funk.

At once, I was captivated by a rhythmic chant; it was Sita's beautiful Hawaiian melody, her feminine voice strong, steady, and poignant. The side of a pahu (drum) was beaten softly and in unison with her song, creating a pulse that was reminiscent of a heartbeat: *tick tock tick, tick tock, tick, tick tock.*

I was transported to a tropical destination in Haiku, Maui deep in the forest to a spiritual retreat that sits on towering emerald cliffs overlooking the Pacific Ocean. We were led down a driveway to an entrance lined with large gray rocks that held back flourishing vegetation from treading forward on a red walkway. Inviting colors of purple and green Ti leaves intermingled with wispy greenery sprinkled with dainty pink, white, and yellow flowers.

What a nice, welcome home bouquet. I can almost smell the flora! I thought while watching.

The camera revealed even more and took me beyond the path to a bright green lawn with waving coconut trees and sparkling, distant seas. Slowly, we were led to the cinnamon-color Bamboo Malu home; it looked inviting and warm. There were solar panels to catch the sun's energy and a water catchment system for the ponds. The community guest house was where I would eventually begin my stay; I would take daily strolls there in my near future.

The scene shifted to the interior of a home. Lucia and her guest, Sita, sat on a couch filled with red fluffy pillows. There were two large windows behind them that let in the green landscape. The beauty and serenity drew me in as much as the rhythmic Hawaiian chant. With microphone in hand, Lucia began the interview in her Italian accent. She had the enthusiasm of an inquisitive child.

"*Heeeloh*, my delicious co-creators. Lucia here on the beautiful island of Maui, Hawaii with scrumptious Sita . . . Thank you for hosting me on this gorgeous property. It is very nurturing . . . We are all the way up north on Maui next to Haiku." She lifted her free hand to the universe. "Really, how do you call this place?"

Sita smiled, and her deep blue eyes sparkled as she turned to look at the camera and speak in her Austrian accent. "It's the area of Huelo, and we are on the North Shore right where the sun rises, where the day begins. Most visitors who come to Maui stay where the sun descends, but we are where the morning light first appears."

I usually stay where the sun sets myself, I thought. *I should experience more of the sunrise . . .* How symbolic to start each day that way with new hope, new beginnings, rebirth, witnessing heavenly rays slowly color the earth, when all is quiet and peaceful, when the air is cool and comfortable. The only sounds to break the silence: the ocean and morning birds' chorus. Starting my day at dawn would probably be the best time to commune with God before the chatter of the day took over.

"If your emotional heart is not a part of creating it, it's not going anywhere . . . It is your heart that needs to be accessible, to be tender and kind . . . There is not one power or sexual energy; it is all merged. Do you make use of your sensual energy in an honored practice, using it with tantric and breathing practices, awareness, and meditation? And, of course, you need a loving partner—one who you can really bond with . . ."

Lucia continued, "This is a very, very special spot. The mana here is really pure and superb; I want to acknowledge you for that. Because you had a big dream . . . you have done so many things. You have been a tantric teacher for over twenty-five years, and you wrote a scrumptious book that is coming out soon, and you have record labels. Tell us, when did you decide to make the move and respond to the message of your heart to make this vision a reality? I mean, this is like out of thin air. You are the Queen of Manifestation."

I was mesmerized; she had my attention. I needed to know more. I wanted to stay at that place to resuscitate my depleted soul and jumpstart my heart. I needed a miracle, some guidance, to be surrounded by pristine nature and the positive energy of that home in the jungle. I was sure it would mend the broken heart of mine quickly. I continued to listen.

"Lucia, I'm just a vessel for God. We all are if we allow the holy spirit to move us . . . I have learned it from Rama, to listen to your heart sincerely if you take a moment, be in the present, and you place your hand on your heart and simply listen. Pay attention to what moves you and what gift you want to leave and what really makes you happy; there can only be good. This is luscious living. There can only be love . . ." She shook her head, teared up, and became speechless.

Lucia turned away, looked into the camera with her dark brown eyes sparkling, and became her animated self with a radiant smile. "Luscious, luscious, my wonderful co-creators, I told you *bellissimo*, *bellissimo*, there it is, all these wonderful stories from around the planet. I'm so grateful to be sitting here. Thank you for manifesting this magical place for mature, creative souls to come and rest. Thank you."

"*Mahalo* for being here, Lucia, and I would love for whoever sees this video to come. I'm really touched, and I know that spirit is working in all of us. *Aloha*."

Synchronicity is at work because Sita must know energetically that I will be calling her soon.

We never know how our prayers will be answered. I was sold on the inspiration of the land, that power spot for creative types, to be in a place where Mother Earth nurtured her children, providing them with her medicinal healing balm and her sweet rainbow nectar to the thirsty souls who visited. That was the Maui Magic I wanted to experience. I would start my journey there and figure out the details of where to move next. That was the most spontaneous I had been in a long time. I felt hopeful and inspired to take the leap of faith, trusting in God and in the Universe to catch me as I freefell and gently landed upon a billowy field of Maui green, overlooking Huelo and the Pacific Ocean.

I booked a one-way ticket to Maui and accommodations at the Lotus Retreat and Farm with Rama and Sita. They seemed like the free-spirited types I needed to be around. The day came when I had to leave for my Maui adventure. I was hopelessly nervous and excited beyond words. A new adventure, done alone, and done just for me. That was the beginning!

Maui would breathe new life into me; I just knew it. I was a pioneer striking out into a new world. With some savings that I had accrued, I was on my way. Somehow, I would make it happen for myself. I said my goodbyes to my family and left for the airport in a taxicab. The sun was setting on Maui, casting a pretty glow upon the sky. The road leading to Haiku was a two-lane highway that hugged the coastline. The farther I traveled, the more twists and turns there were in the road. It was the beginning route to the Road to Hana. The drive was beautiful.

So far, so good.

My cell phone stopped working when I passed the cemetery. Another fifteen minutes passed, and I came to a sharp turn in the road and passed mile marker three. I slowed down as instructed; my turnoff was coming up. I saw a crudely-built green sheltered area with a bench. I wondered if it was a bus stop. There were several rows of mail boxes that lined the corner. That was where I needed to turn.

The corner was sharp, and to cross over, I had to be careful for oncoming traffic and watch for cars that might be riding my tail. Luckily, the roads are never really congested there. I crossed over the two-lane highway and pulled onto The Door of Faith Church Road. One needed faith just to cross the two lanes and even more faith to continue on the partially paved lane that eventually turned into narrow dirt roads filled with pot holes. I wove to avoid them. I traveled deeper on the road, and it became muddy with more holes and rocks scattered about. I missed my blue Mercedes; the blueberry sedan I was driving enhanced the feel of every stone and twig in the road.

Then there it was: the entrance. I recognized it instantly from the online photos and videos. Tibetan prayer flags hung from the pole over the golden amber bamboo fence that sat behind a dark brown octagon gazebo also made of bamboo. *Aptly named*, I mused, craning my neck and pulling into a parking space. Inside the gazebo was Saraswati—an Indian deity. The videos online said that all people with artistic expression were welcome and that the goddess of creativity was there to inspire all. I winked at her, knowing that she might be the reason I'd get my book finished.

A red pathway with large stones held back bushels of flora with broad green and purple Ti leaves believed to ward off evil spirits. The colorful path took me all the way to the Bamboo Malu House—a four-bedroom home with two bedrooms' downstairs and two upstairs. The guests shared the main house together. I was greeted by Rama, who was six feet of wild black hair and dark brown recessed eyes in a skinny, pale frame. He seemed a little slow and dazed at first, but this suited the yoga pants and white flowing shirt he wore. He was straight out of a hippy drum circle.

"Katie! Glad you made it out here in one piece! We expected you a little earlier. Follow me." The moment Rama spoke, I liked him. His deep baritone voice washed over me. He led me to the Indian room, and it was everything I expected it to be, although it smelled like herbal essence.

"A few things as you settle in. This is sacred land because we are right next to Huelo, which is a vortex spot of great energy. If you want, you can make your way over to the Hanehoi waterfall where the energy is strongest. Watch out for the aliens, though. Every now and then we get a UFO wandering over the property, so keep your eyes peeled."

I laughed, but quickly cut it short when I realized he was deadly serious.

"Here is everything you need," he added, handing me a map of the property while looking nervously around the ceiling, as if at any moment we might be accosted by little green men. There was a clearly-marked waterfall on the map, along with the two meditating temples. The beach was about a thirty-minute hike. After signing a waiver that he hastily produced, I was ready to settle in.

"Oh, and there is only one bathroom here, as you know from the website. You may want to visit it before I give you your heart reading, if you want it."

Confused, I followed Rama's gesture to the back of my jeans. A wet slab of lettuce was pasted to my rear thigh.

"Don't worry about it, man," he said. "You should enjoy what you eat, no matter where it ends up."

Mortified, I nipped off to the communal bathroom to clean up before heading back into the kitchen for my heart reading. I was excited to hear what Rama had to say about me. I settled into a wooden chair next to the counter, and as I sat down, some young men waved to me from behind a sliding door. People were very friendly there.

I heard my mother's voice in my mind again: *Now you done it, Katie. You have joined a cult, and they will want you to do sex things with them!* I hoped that was not the case. At the same time, I could not help noticing how handsome the young men were. *Good thing I changed out of my Louboutins on the plane.*

Rama sat across from me and skidded his chair over until he was right up close. "Okay, do you mind if I put my hand on your skin, on top of your heart? It's not a sexual thing."

I can't explain why, but I trusted him. Here was a strange man that I had met only minutes before, and I was allowing him to touch me. *Should I be concerned?* I pushed the thought from my mind and nodded. His hand was big and warm, and we breathed together in unison.

"Please gaze into my eyes," he added, becoming very serious. For a few awkward minutes, all he did was look at me. Each time I wanted to speak, he shushed me. Then he spoke again. "Whoa, shit, man, you have a lot of stuff going on here . . . You have been through a lot recently, too."

Now it was my turn to be tongue-tied. I nodded, and my eyes watered.

"You are here to write your book about this place and your experience here," he continued. "All your life you have nurtured other people. It is time for you to do the same for yourself. You have a good heart. You will have fun here; I promise you that."

Rama pulled his hand away, and I felt connected to him somehow. I knew the healing had begun. In all my years, I had never felt an emotional release like that. Had I been so lacking in acknowledgement of myself that I was starved of real connection?

Rama explained to me that he had been doing heart readings for over thirty years. He explained how he takes the time to connect by placing his hand on a person's heart, flesh to flesh; it is like touching God. He allows his awareness to expand, to really *feel* the heart vibrationally; our bodies are made up of mostly water. He starts feeling the heart; he actually says hello to the heart, and then listens for the heart to say hello back. He takes what he gets—what attitude, state of mind that he feels, and whatever answers he gets, whatever emotions from the heart, and sees pictures from the past, present, and future. Some readings can be so overpowering with love, sometimes like a symphony coming at him.

That night, I took a sleeping pill and locked my bedroom door. It was my first evening in a strange place.

To read the rest of my novel *The Maui Magical Mystical Tour*, based on my true-life experiences, you may purchase it on Amazon.com in paperback copy or kindle. Walk the spiritual journey with me in love and light. *Mahalo.*

About the Author

Kathy McCartney originally lived on Oahu with her family but moved to Southern California when she was very young. In 2002, she bought a condo that would eventually become the launching point of her business career and the key to getting back to the home of her childhood and the place of her dreams, Maui, Hawaii. Prior to making that decision she had been working with friends in a vacation rental business and made the leap to start her own company. She has over twenty-five years of experience in both business administration and customer service. She merged her business ideas with her artistic and free-spirited hopes, and dreams that would eventually be realized.

Kathy now lives on Maui and is living her dream as a local

artist, writer and owns a vacation rental business called, Maui Vision Rentals: **http://mauivision.com**

She is a gifted artist who creates on canvas but most recently expanded her creative tropical expressions to include works on etched metal. These one-of-a-kind pieces are described as 3-D or holographic, with movement and a life of their own. For more information and to experience Kathy's art work, please visit: **http://www.mccartneyfineart.com**

The Maui Magical Mystical Tour is Kathy's first novel and certainly will not be her last as we know this book will inspire and touch the hearts of many readers that will want more of Kathy's 'feel good' storytelling based on her true life experiences The Maui Magical Mystical Tour is an uplifting must read that will make you laugh, cry, and ponder your own life choices. The Maui Magical Mystical Tour is a novel that will add to your personal collection of uplifting must reads Kathy's book is available in paperback or Kindle edition at **Amazon.com.**

Freyja P. Jensen
FROM THE ASHES, SHE GROWS
#TheRisenPhoenix

As a writer, sharing from my personal experiences has become my cathartic healing process. It has become a way for me to turn my pain into a pathway to bring others hope. If I could get through these difficult times, I believe I can be an encouragement to others and a catalyst for change. I am a strong believer that our voices matter. So herewith, I unravel yet another part of my journey that perhaps you can relate to or if anything, learn from.

I am named after the Norse Viking Goddess Freyja. If you are familiar with the television series the Vikings, her name is one of the characters. She is the Goddess of love and beauty among other things. She is a courageous, spirited, feisty warrior. I never knew of this meaning until in my late twenties. My Mother had passed away 20 years prior, tragically while my brothers and I watched. I knew from that time, that there was something different about me and that I needed to use my voice, and that what I had to say mattered. It wasn't until I was nearly 50 when I began to emulate my name as a fighter and a champion for others.

Self-esteem believe it or not has been an issue for me nearly my whole life. Very few would ever guess that by the way I carry and present myself. People make a lot of assumptions on the first impressions as we all know too well. I would walk like a boss. Inside though I'd still be having moments when I am plagued with self-doubt talk, like a literal devil on one shoulder – angel on the other scenario.

My past history plays deeply into my being, my psyche, and affects my behavior and outlook to this day. I suffer from early childhood PTSD. From that stems a series of other issues including high anxiety, panic attacks, depression, ADSD, adrenal fatigue and even suicidal thoughts among other things.

As a young girl being told that I was ugly, stupid and would amount to nothing carried huge weight into who I would become and it has taken endless personal development and growth to shoo away that history of abusive language. It had a significant impact on me. My learning never stops. I am a sponge for growth.

When I was 13 years old, I was told to strip naked and sit at the dinner table with my family, my 2 brothers, Dad and step-mom. It was humiliating, degrading and unfathomable that a Father would ask that of a daughter and that a woman would sit by and allow it to happen. I'm not even sure how I managed to get through it. But I always remember that it made me feel ashamed of my body. Another time I was made to strip from the waist down and my pubic hair was shaved. I was mortified and shut myself off from feeling anything. Near that time, I was raped by my step-brother, tied to the bed, gagged, blindfolded and raped. I was told that I would thank him for it later in life.

As a result, weight has been a real struggle for me. I have gained and lost large amounts of weight numerous times. The most detrimental loss was to my self-esteem. I would be ashamed of being naked. The weight allowed me to hide. Who would want me? I struggled from one relationship to another looking for someone that would love me for who I am on the inside rather than on the outside because I was not happy with the picture of me.

Sometimes things happen to us and at the time they may seem horrible, painful and unfair, but in reflection, we realize that without overcoming those obstacles we would have never realized our potential, strength, willpower and our hearts.

For those that have hurt me, I have forgiven them. I finally have let go of my suffering. It no longer owns me. I have been shown a Love like I have never known. I am loved for my whole being. I am not my body. I am heart and soul. My body is merely my vessel with wrapping.

I have discovered that I am unique and that by being myself I add something beautiful to the world that was not there before. I am on the pathway of surrender. I no longer give my head control but my heart.

It doesn't matter how we are perceived by others in the big picture. What matters is how we are perceiving ourselves.

Those who care to know who we are will get close enough to see what is on the inside.

I am that warrior Goddess and I am fierce. All those who have come through the fire, wear the armor of proof.

Since I am in the business of "Relationship Management" presentation is of optimum importance in being seen and valued. Then there is the core. How we interact and react, how we speak boldly and without fear, how we command our audience, how transparent we are in our authenticity. As a "Practitioner of Life" I have learned through my experiences that things aren't always what they seem or how they appear.

In my position as a head-hunter, it is my aim to identify and match up candidates with employers and have them be an ideal fit.

This takes a keen eye to see beyond the surface of what an individual has to offer and then becomes more of a search and find mission to the truth of what is being shared. It's very revealing to look beyond the surface of who a person truly is. Listening then, with an empathetic ear and a non-judgmental attitude will reveal a lot more about who someone is and speaks to their passion rather than a superficial presentation.

In life, we spend a lot of time schmoozing* to get what we want. How good you are at it determines how far you will get. It all goes back to the package, the wrapping. Tearing that all away to see the "real you" in someone.

Every day is a new day to rebuild on loving myself. As an adult, I have had employers and co-workers who have been mean, nasty, arrogant people whose critique and judgement, bullied and tore me apart. I have been in relationships that have battered my heart and soul and left me for dead. My saving grace is that I was born with that warrior courage and an intense will to survive and thrive. I fall and I get back up again out of the ashes. I have learned about self-love and the importance of planting it into ones' life.

We need to open ourselves up to allow that self-love to grow. "When we learn to love ourselves for who we are, we discover a whole new found sense of freedom which gives us courage and confidence to blossom, revealing our innermost beauty, the divine essence of who we truly are." ~Mary Ann Byrne

We invent ourselves, or re-invent ourselves if we are not happy with whom we grew up to be, based on our familial traditions. We become who we truly are once we choose to. Once we recognize that the being, the inner being, the person who exists inside is not meeting our needs, we can reach deeper and once we take off the masks that we wear to suit everyone else, to be pleasing and perfect in others eyes, to meet the status and the occasion, we can begin to find ourselves. Create who we truly feel and know we are our authentic selves. Most people see us only on the surface. Who are we then, authentically? That person inside of us that wants to truly live, live life passionately and spontaneously and is acknowledged and appreciated for who we are.

Love cannot come from the ego because the ego, like a pendulum, constantly swings between past and future. Love always happens in the present moment, in the Presence. Every moment of love is timeless and eternal. Love is the pure essence of Being Present." Borrowed from the book- (We Are Human Angels).

Your history does not determine your destiny. Until you become self-aware and REALLY get to know the inner you, you won't be able to connect to your true potential, and your life purpose will remain a mystery.

Build a new relationship with yourself just the way you would with a new friend. It's an INSIDE OUT job. What happens on the inside will in due course manifest itself on the outside?" What's on the outside is just wrapping and we can make it as pretty as we want, or not. That is how I have chosen to live my life, to the utmost, in full magnificent color like a "Rainbow" and so can you (in whatever way that looks to you). I wish you blessings in manifesting your destiny in this amazing time of your life. **#TheRisenPhoenix**

About the Author

Freyja P. Jensen aka **#TheRisenPhoenix** aka Rainbow, shares another powerful, moving chapter of triumph and persistence in the face of some of the most difficult hardships anyone should have to endure. Her true-life experiences of intense struggle, personal growth, empowerment, and ultimately success in claiming her life back, has given her a meaningful voice of courage that has become a shining beacon of hope to those caught in their own storms of life's challenges.

This is her 5th contribution to a compilation book. Freyja has put her trepidations aside and written heroically about her experiences in order to challenge others to speak out bravely and become a catalyst to making a difference in their own healing journeys.

All of the books Freyja has contributed to have climbed up to become International Best Sellers. Freyja's first compilation chapter in; "Inch By Inch Growing In Life" is about overcoming adversity as a child. The second; The Missing Piece in Forgiveness, is about Overcoming The Impossible, the third; The Missing Piece in Bouncing Back, is about inspiring others to not give up and the 4th; The Missing Piece in Self-Love, is about Loving Yourself from the Inside Out.

In this book's chapter, her contribution; "From The Ashes She Grows," Freyja shares some of the significant struggles of her powerful journey through relationship challenges that proves one can rise from the ashes no matter how harsh the circumstances.

As the Executive Ninja in her business-career, Freyja is a Consultant and Relationship Manager (Head-Hunter) working as a contract partner in the Recruitment Industry.

She considers herself a Practitioner of Life and her mission statement is to leave a legacy worthy of remembering that promotes peace and love for all of mankind. She believes that we make the choice to be the change we wish to see in the world. Freyja enjoys volunteering on committee's and for causes she is fierce about. She is an advocate for those who are afraid to use their voices and a force to assist them in finding them.

In her spare time when Freyja is not indulging in her passion for writing, she enjoys applying her skills as a make-up artist to those in need of a boost in their self-esteem. She enjoys applying her flair for image & wardrobe consulting to assist those that are struggling, to learn to shop on a dime and offers makeovers and practical information and knowledge for entering or re-entering the workforce.

Freyja is loved for her contagious smile and laughter, for her generous hospitality, her fine cooking skills and her fearlessness when it comes to picking up the microphone to belt out a song among other things.

Her ultimate joy comes through the love of her family. Having lost both of her Mothers and both of her Brothers, Freyja cherishes her close, personal friendships. Her Grand-Daughter, her Son, her Father and her Fiancé hold precious space in her heart as does the extended family she has now become a part of. **#TheRisenPhoenix.**

Bernadette Garvin
We Are Doing This for Daddy

Where do I begin? God only knows it's been a journey from the beginning growing up in a male-dominated family. I guess I was a tomboy always running wild and free with the animals and nature. Upon reflection, I see how innocent it all seemed with not a care in the world, just happy go lucky me. Nothing could have prepared me for the journey ahead. Honestly, that was my happiest time riding my horse bareback across the fields, jumping everything in sight. Rose, my black beauty, was the love of my life, my best friend. She understood me as I did her! Can't explain it, but I know many of you know exactly what I mean by a connection that I believe was made in heaven many lifetimes ago.

Growing up on a farm in the west of Ireland wasn't a bad thing; it gave me the appreciation for nature and wildlife that I have today. From an early age, I felt different being the only girl in a family of four male siblings, and by the age of four, I was sent to live with my granny—a tradition in Irish families at that time. No one would understand the impact that would have on me in later life, always seeking the attachment that was severed. I've been told I was very happy at that time, but all I felt was a sense of being left behind, missing out, and being different. Yes, my nana was really good to me, but it was not home and I missed my mother, although she was just across the fields. At four years of age, I didn't understand then what I do now.

You see, my mother lost her second child tragically. "A beautiful little girl" is how she described her. Marion got meningitis while my mother had been hospitalized for tuberculosis. Isolation had prevented her from seeing Marion, and she was dead and buried before they told her. As a mother, I can only try to understand my mother's grief and the reason she wasn't able to bond with me for fear that I would die too. Even then I had a huge sense that I was never alone, especially in nature. I felt protected and loved. There were nights over the years I would lay in my bed wondering if I was adopted or why my parents loved the boys more.

Addiction surrounded me, and I became adult at a very early age, taking on a parental role for my younger siblings and assisting in the care of two elderly ladies. Life wasn't easy back then, and being a child I guess never came into play. I completed my national school and my secondary school education, and it was during that time when I met my ex. He was a handsome, kind, caring man, and in my eyes, he was the love of my life, everything I wanted and more. They say "Love is blind," and so it is, because when he got jealous it was my perception that he truly loved me.

If anyone looked at me, it was World War III, so I always remained quiet and attentive, never giving rise to draw attention my way. To be honest, I paid dearly for that at a later date, because no matter what happened, it was my fault. Having completed my formal education, I went on to train as a nurse and continued to date my boyfriend. Times were happy, and we actually had some really happy years with only the occasional major outburst of jealousy, usually around his drinking. Ignorant to addictions at the time, and although it ran in the family, I did not see the dangers or warning signs. For me, it was out of the pan and into the fire when I decided to immigrate to the USA, not realizing I substituted one addictive person in my life for another.

Arriving in America excited, happy, and full of dreams seemed so magical, but it didn't last for long after Immigration said my boyfriend couldn't get proper work status. That was the beginning and the end of something beautiful; over time, things began to crumble while he continued falling deeper into despair and alcohol. Nothing in schools or college prepares one for toxic abuse in relationships. You learn the hard way through each punch, kick, and degrading remark. It's funny how bumps, bruises, fractures, and even scars fade away, but those haunting words scar you forever: "Look in the mirror, you big, fat, ugly cow," "You're nothing but a weakling," "Who would have you," "Everything's your fault!"

You begin to believe that everything is your fault. To be honest, you lose your identity, your true personality, and conform to keep safe or ultimately survive or stay alive. Nothing prepares one for this, and only those who have walked in similar footsteps can understand.

In many ways, it is like living on the edge or with a time bomb. For most, you never know what is going to happen or when there will be an outburst of rage, physical aggression, or injury. Reaching out for help is not an option initially, as you have already been told that you shall not live to tell the tale. So, you remain silent, broken, bruised, and a shell of the professional person you once were. Life is controlled, who you see, talk too or interact with, and eventually you don't invite anyone to your home in case they might be put in danger. You go to work, make excuses for bruises or black eyes, say you hit a door or your iron count is low, and just live a lie because you feel so ashamed that you're a failure.

Why? Because you believe everything is your fault! Growing up in the Roman Catholic family, it was drilled into us that we must stay in our marriages and make them work no matter what. In other words, you make your bed, so lie in it or sort it out!

Obtaining appropriate immigration status in the USA was a slow, drawn out process, and he had to work illegal jobs for peanuts as I continued to be the bread-winner working two and three jobs. To be honest, all I knew was work until I got pregnant, and that changed everything. It was then that I began to realise how dangerous he was and started praying to Our Lady Queen of the Angels to keep both our child and I safe. Nothing changed; the abuse continued, and he developed a dual addiction with marijuana and alcohol. Even though my prayers weren't answered, in some small way I felt supported and less alone.

At the time, all I had were prayers, as none of my family members were aware of the abuse. Our beautiful baby daughter was born, and for a time things actually improved, but it was short-lived. If anything, he was jealous of the attention I gave my daughter, and that made matters worse!

Today, I know he was a narcissistic or psychopathic-type personality where he could brutally beat you, and then expect you to make up and be intimate. If I resisted, the brutality continued until he got his needs met. On reflection, I see it was like a near-death experience where I left my body until I knew it was over and no longer had to pretend. Sick is the only word to describe the humiliation and psychological impact this behaviour has on someone. No one deserves it, and yet out of fear, victims remain, thinking that in some way it's their fault. It's as if you're a prisoner in your own body or life, but that isn't true for your spirit or soul! Thank God for Mother Mary the Queen of the Angels and prayer, as that is what kept me going and ultimately got me to safety.

Looking back now, I realise that for years I continued to accept the abuse, multiple calls to police, safe houses, social services, a barring order, and on one occasion, I went to court for a divorce. Yet I always kept running back, as it was ingrained in my mind that I was at fault and that I could not survive on my own without him. In hindsight, I see that all that time I was on my own and surviving.

Several years later, I got pregnant with our second child, and just after my beautiful daughter's birth, my uncle who helped raise me came to stay. At the time, I thought it would be difficult having my bachelor uncle around, fearing the worst that he too might get hurt. Looking back, I see that it was a blessing in disguise. Because of his presence, the abuse subsided, and he helped with the children and loved every minute of it. During his visit, he confided in me that he thought he had cancer, and one evening he took ill, was hospitalised, and told he had a terminal disease. So, he remained with us for the remainder of his holidays, returning to Ireland at the end of September.

He was admitted to hospital in serious condition to the intensive care where he passed away several days later, still believing he was in the USA with me. No words can express my grief, as I never got to speak to him after I put him on the flight or to say my goodbyes, and due to financial difficulties, I couldn't afford a flight home. Life reverted back to living again with a house-devil and street-angel.

During the weeks following my uncle's death, we noticed items moved, especially the vanity mirror in the car, and my oldest daughter would say, "Buddy (her nickname for him), is back." As time went on, I believed he was there looking out for us, as on many occasions when the violence erupted, some memory or item of his distracted my ex who actually loved him dearly. Today, I have no doubt that he was one of my guardian angels who came to protect me. During that time, I got my first deck of *Angel Cards* by Doreen Virtue called *Healing with the Angels* that I still use twenty-odd years later. They became my bible, my strength, and the one piece of sanity or comfort at the end of my days.

All my working life, I worked the graveyard shift so that I could attend to my daughters' needs for fear that something might happen to them. One evening prior to my night shift, my abuser hadn't had his fix and he got very agitated because I refused to give him the money for food. He became so enraged; he took a metal can of paint and aimed it for my head. Putting my hands up to protect my face, it hit my hand and took the nail completely off my thumb with the blow. The violence continued, and my four-year-old tried to fight him to protect me while the one-year-old tugged at his leg to protect her sister.

He lashed back, causing them to fly in the opposite directions, and it was there and then I decided I needed to leave. As a mother, I would die for my children. At the time, I didn't care what happened to me, but my girls were a different story. Today, I know that if the girls weren't there, I would never have had the courage to leave, and I believe that I'd be wearing my angel wings and flying around heaven.

Violence continued, and it took a lot more bruises and bumps before I got out. On one occasion, we were locked in a bathroom for several days until the neighbours missed us and notified the police. The stories are endless. During those times, I was given an Archangel Michael prayer, and it empowered me to have the courage to face my fears and leave.

Women in Crisis and my family were now aware of the abuse, and I had to make a decision to relocate to another state under a new identity or return home. Broken, bruised, tired, and fearful of trying to raise my children alone, I made the decision to return home to my extended family in Ireland. It was about that time that I found out I was pregnant with my third child, and it was devastating to me. Not that I didn't want the baby, the direct opposite was the case, but plans had to be rearranged and scheduled with friends and support services. It took weeks to plan and get things set up; as the abuser threatened he would kill me or kill all of us if I ever tried to leave. It was necessary for safety measures to keep my leaving a secret, and believe me, it was a frightening time.

Times were very stressful. I felt that my pregnancy was different than with the other two. I had terrible sickness and a very strange feeling like nothing I had felt before. It was difficult to live everyday knowing I was going to escape the only life I had known for so long. Self-worth or self-esteem were non-existent, as all I knew was a toxic love that was cruel and that treated me like a door mat, that my crime was that I was there. It was several weeks before I was set to leave when I started to have what seemed like labour pains. Devastated and frightened, I started to haemorrhage, and yes, I lost my baby, a pain that I carry with me to this day. It was my sense it was a baby boy, and I called him Michael Daniel. I was very much alone and perhaps angry with God for his choice to take my little angel.

Today, I believe it was divine intervention so my transition would be somewhat easier. To be honest, many people don't realise a mother's pain with losing a child, regardless of age, and especially a miscarriage.

As my baby grew inside me, I sensed him and loved him from day one. Nothing prepares you for the loss; you never get over it. Time is a healer, and you learn to live with the loss and carry their memory in your heart forever.

Finally, the day came for us to leave. Though it was a terrible, abusive relationship, I was still in love with my husband; it was the only love I knew! It was with great difficulty that I hugged him goodbye and held back the tears.

As he left, my oldest daughter said, "it's okay, Mummy, we are doing this for daddy, and he's going to get help." That morning, he went to an annual gun show with his friend. Having secretly packed the girls' clothes, I looked around my home for the last time. With tears running down my cheeks, I locked the door behind me, not realising I would never see it again. The drive to the airport seems so long ago, and I was so frightened and mixed up then that I worried he would stop us or follow us! I have no recollection of getting through immigration and onto that plane.

All I recall thinking was that my daughters were safe and my baby's words "Mummy, we are doing this for Daddy." Looking back, I know I got out for my daughters, but realise that it was also for me. I was so conditioned to take the blame and had no concept as to what love, respect, and tenderness felt like. It was a cold winter's morning at Shannon Airport, but being greeted by extended family with love hugs and kisses definitely raised the temperatures. My children embraced their grandparents and uncles, and the look in their eyes said it all. We were safe, and as I pulled my passport out of my bag, out fell my Archangel Michael's prayer affirming he was there protecting us.

During the weeks and years that followed, it took a long time for us to adjust. We all slept in the same bed, still living in fear. The girls had nightmares that eventually faded over time, and their father initially made aggressive contact and used threatening behaviour, but never sought support to get help and drifted out of our lives. My adjustment was slow, and many nights, like that young schoolgirl, I would lay in my bed wondering why or what had gone wrong. Feeling abandoned was a terrible but familiar, lonely pain in my heart. Fears and learning to trust took years to heal and release.

Today, I can honestly say it was thanks to the angelic influence in my life and to Mother Mary's caring ways that took me through it. They continue to be part of my journey as a nurse and psychotherapist, facilitating me to empower other victims of abuse to find their way into the light that I call Hope!

Looking back with forgiveness, I thank my abuser for empowering me to find my "Warrior" that facilitated me to earn my angel wings. The lived experience, my divine connection with the angels, and my spiritual journey or my life path, is never ending. It has provided me with gifts such as empathy, compassion and a non-judgmental genuineness to empower others to find their Warrior and get out.

If any who are reading this are living in an abusive relationship, be it family, partner, or friends, my message is to get support and get out. Life is short, and you have done nothing wrong. You deserve respect, tenderness, and love. Take your courage and face your fears. You can do this. Also, remember that you are never really alone, as your guardian angels watch over you. Just call them to support you during challenging times. May you remain safe and protected and find the courage to leave. Trust me, there is always Hope. Angel Blessings.

About the Author

Bernadette Garvin is a Registered Psychotherapist & Counsellor also a Registered Nurse in several Specialised Areas. Her expertise is in Oncology & Psycho – Oncology in addition to Bereavement & Loss, Sudden Death, & Suicide. Growing up as a child she always had a gift of knowing, a Divine Connection with Angels, nature and animals. Then following a Near Death Experience where she left her body and went to a tunnel of white light with tall beings that she now identifies as Angels: Following that experience her gifts began to develop more and continue to do so. Today she describes herself as an "Empathic Intuitive Medical Psychic, Medium and Healer. Her Angelic work comes from an open heart of unconditional love and compassion for all. She trained as a "Certified Angel Card Reader ", Angel Intuitive and Certified Angel Practitioner: In addition to being a Reiki Healer, Mindfulness Coach, Creative Art Therapist, Laughter Coach & Crystal Energy Healer. Today she combines all of the above in her work with the Angels by channelling messages and by giving Guidance & Healing. I am also an Artist and created my own deck of Angel Cards all Paintings and Messages are by me Called, " Angel Messages for Life Oracle Cards ". They are messages of Hope for everyday people. The Angelic Messages that are channelled through her by the Angels is:

"There Is Always Hope".

Angel Blessings,

Bernadette.

Dr. Neesa Ginger Mills
Water, Breath, and God-A Transformational Journey

Looking at the expansive view of the sparkling waters of Kealekua Bay from my Bali-style hut, I stood in awe at the shocking chain of events that had taken me from the working life I'd known in California to this pristine Hawaiian island view. It all happened so fast, a tidal wave of events that swept me away from my children, my home, and my business. There I was, living alone in a hut in the tropics, spending my days diving deep into prayer and meditation, my spiritual path unfolding more quickly than I could ever have imagined. While my spiritual practices were dismantling so many inner constructs and bringing me closer the Divine, I worried that there was an ocean between me and my girls living in Los Angeles, one just getting herself grounded as a first-year college student, the other traversing the very difficult terrain of changing gender.

What crazy timing that *he* would find *himself* getting real with her identity as a woman right then. Her transition came smack in the middle of my own, another earth-shattering change for our unconventional family. How was I to manage her many emotional needs when I could barely keep my own feet on the ground? My emotional state was fragile at best, and the spiritual practices that had brought me to Hawaii were a lifeline that literally felt like the only glue holding me together during that tender time.

I had no idea that the prayer to surrender to the Divine would mean dismantling my entire life! I had put a prayer in motion years earlier to be delivered to my deepest soul's path and live in alignment with God's will. And so there I was: face to face with the most powerful spiritual challenge of all—trust and surrender, to allow myself to be guided, knowing that God would always support my every step.

My edges were being stretched daily during this time. I received only nuggets of guidance to lead me to the next step, and *only* the next step. I felt like I was walking blind-folded off a plank into the ocean with no vision past the steps beneath my feet. I prayed. I made requests, but never received answers beyond what was right in front of me. Nerve-wracking for sure, but a powerful lesson in being fully present *now*!

Is this really what I wanted? I often wondered, as I found myself stumbling around in the darkness during my time of loss, the time of change that would eventually deliver me to the healing power of breath, the vast ocean waters of the Hawaiian Islands, and ultimately surrendering everything to the Divine.

As I practiced surrendering each day, I discovered my steps were indeed full of grace. I was on a tropical island, swimming with dolphins, spending hours each day deep in prayer and meditation.

I had been offered my own little house on the grounds of a retreat center in exchange for managing the retreat business. I picked fresh papayas outside my hut for breakfast and had a killer view of the bay from my bed. I was indeed being held. It was the perfect place to dive deep into my daily practices!

The downward spiral of the familiar life I had built over my twenty-five years in California had brought me to this. I could never have imagined that this is where life would take me at age fifty-five. Wasn't I supposed to be secure now with a house, a big bank account, and a solid life partner?

I felt myself melt a thousand times as the energies of truth bubbled up from the well within. I was in Hawaii, participating in a priestess training that guided my journey into the depths of my feminine womb wisdom, diving deeply into the mystical through breath and meditation practices. Countless hours with these precious and ancient practices cracked my heart open to new levels of love, to pain, and sadness. And to the bliss of God. With each day, emotion turned to devotion. I unearthed what felt like lifetimes of buried memories and feelings. Rivers of tears helped me to know more deeply the Divine Presence in all things, emotions vacillating quickly from fear and shame to elevated frequencies of Love, sometimes both present in the same breath.

I cried more that year than even when I went through a divorce from my husband and the dissolution of our nuclear family, for sure the most crushing event of my life. Amidst the flow of tears, I was being rocked by the powerful energies of Hawaii's Pele, the renowned Volcano Goddess. I was ever humbled and fell deeper into faith. The powerful natural forces of this volcanic island and the vortex of earth energy where the retreat center sits was no place for the faint of heart.

These tears were different than the profound grief I felt in the shattering of my family. They were flavored with a deeper presence, a sense of awe and an awakening to Divine Love.

I came to know myself more deeply each day over the many months in Pele's lap, the trials and tribulations of my humanity, alongside the emergence of knowing my Divine Self, and the merging of the two. Swimming with the dolphins and afternoons at a nearby reef in the soft, warm waters of the Pacific, cleansed and purified my heart and body. I snorkeled among the brightly colored tropical fish and was healed by swimming alongside the transcendent spinner dolphins. I surrendered each day to Divine Will, as the persona of who I thought I was continued to crumble.

Who was I, *really*, without this infrastructure and the identity I had built in my world all those years?

I began to understand that the roles and sense of self-identity in life are temporaneous. I *really* got it after receiving a guided message at the retreat that first brought me to the island that I was not to work with clients. Another wave of anxiety wanted to swallow me up. I had to keep breathing into my body to move past the questions swirling through my mind, the emotions that made me feel like I was disappearing. What would I do now? How would I make money, be of service in the world, and be a good mother to my children? Would I ever be able to share my healing gifts again?

There was only one answer: Water, breath, and God. Just let go and keep trusting, as I later read was true to the teachings of the spiritual surrender process. Spiritual surrender is not something that means giving up to a power that brings harm, as in human war. This kind of surrender is a merging of personal will with Divine Will, a process of becoming a vessel of light on a path of heart while the paradigm of mind struggle melts away.

It was a growth process, and I had not fully mastered the art of surrender. I was being stretched in Hawaii inside and out, a seeming conflict between my inner and outer worlds. I was missing my kids and wrestling with my sense of responsibility. Finances were edgy and unpredictable, and I'd feel myself go into angst. Again, it was back to my breath, listening to the subtle cues of divine guidance, observing synchronicities, and following the path of trust I had started walking the day I drove away from my home in California.

Regardless of what was happening then, or at any at other time along this journey of unraveling, I always found myself surrounded by beauty, with plenty of nourishing food, friendship, and shelter. My new operating instructions were encased in grace, and I moved only from guidance. My children were fine too, despite their concerns and uncertainties about what was happening with their mother.

In some ways, it seemed the physical distance strengthened all of us. When I saw them again six months later, they seemed more self-reliant, more solid in themselves. Besides connecting with them and my friends on the island, I found it difficult to stay connected with the world I had known in California and with my family of origin. I desired only to cocoon, to be with myself, and avoid the projections of others about what had happened to my life. Some seemed enamored by my new-found path of freedom, while others stood in judgement of my apparent lack of responsibility.

My inner landscape was delicate, and there was no room for the energies of what others might be thinking of me. Without a home, a profession, and my old identity, I felt like a caterpillar wrapped in a chrysalis. All I knew was that it was, and is now still, a breath at a time, as I witness the unfolding of my new life path, my wings still held closely to my back. When I try to push, I fall. When I surrender, relax, and listen, magical gifts always appear in my path.

 I knew I would know when the walls of the chrysalis were ready for me to emerge and take flight from the comfort of the retreat center, as would the steps after that. As I reflected from my lanai, looking at the vast ocean from my hut in Hawaii, it had been eighteen months since that fateful winter day in my office back in the San Francisco area when the voice of Spirit spoke to me. I shuddered, knowing that the few times I'd received such a clear message, there would be no negotiating. I really was "going to have to give all of this up?"

I knew in an instant that radical change was coming. I had been deeply enjoying that day, sitting comfortably in the stylish, peacock-blue chair in my beautiful chiropractic office. I was listening to a guest perspective on the topic of energy healing to the group I was teaching. I was full inside, feeling as though my work life had delivered me right where I wanted to be: sharing my gifts with my wonderful clients in daily practice, running workshops, and leading sacred ceremonial circles. I could have never imagined on that prophetic day that in a matter of months, I'd be closing my office, losing my house, and filing bankruptcy with no clear picture of what was to come. I found myself breathless more than I ever had over the coming months, overcome by the rapture of my expanding heart, as often as I stood in the face of fear.

This wildly unexpected turn of events moved very quickly. It was scary. I fretted and worried, overcome with guilt and sadness, and wondered if I had done something wrong to dismantle the sense of security I had built for myself and my two beautiful children. I was frightened, my self-esteem shaken and my sense of who I was in the world had vanished. I had spent more than twenty years building this life I thought was pretty solid. My healing practice supported me in having a home for myself and the children. There was not much fluff in our lifestyle, but we lived comfortably in a big house with an ocean view, just a short walk from a beautiful beach on the Pacific Ocean south of San Francisco.

It was devastating losing our home, our sanctuary that provided a spacious place for the kids to bring their friends, a nourishing nest for my chosen lifestyle, dedicated to creating sacred space, hiking, yoga, meditation, painting, drumming, and running my business. Suddenly, it was gone, all of it, my worst fears realized. I had no home, and my youngest daughter, then a junior in high school, would go to live full-time with her dad. For months, I felt lost and confused with only the occasional flashes of insight needed to keep going as I stumbled along, living with friends and working just enough to meet base survival needs.

I wondered then if maybe this was the end of a successful, vibrant existence and that maybe I would die this way, with a great hole in my heart. It had been about a year since receiving the Spirit message in my office, pointing toward this pivotal change. Although the message couldn't have been any clearer, I would spend the next several months arguing, pleading with the universe, hoping there had been some mistake.
I loved my office, my clients, and I had been expanding my work with groups. I had even hired an expensive business

coach that year to guide my professional offerings to the next level, but true to the flavor of the Spirit message, as the year continued, the ways I'd always marketed my practice stopped working and my zest for putting myself out in the world faded. Within a few months of that prophetic message, I felt myself feeling depressed and shaky, losing my drive to market and keep my office going. Things had gotten testy with the coach, and I began to see the writing on the wall. My life as I knew it was crashing. This really was happening.

As difficult as it was, I should have known that by that time of my life when Spirit delivers such an articulate message, it *would* most certainly be for my highest good, and there would be no turning back. It has been that way for my transgender daughter, too. She found the courage to claim her identity, and life has never been the same since. Our journey together through this time was anxious and teary when she first realized this about herself, just a couple short months after we had lost our home.

She was in Los Angeles, and we spent hours on the phone trying to sort it all out. Although it was not completely unexpected, knowing her as I did, it was still tremendously difficult to come to terms with the loss of my son. I worried for her body and how it would be affected by hormones and surgeries, and I worried for her safety and the wrath she could face from ignorant people who never will understand choices like this. Her life path as a boy had been tough enough.

Her transition, like my own, has proven to be breathtakingly beautiful. The moment her father and I saw her standing in the doorway at his home after she'd been away for a few months, our concerns began to melt away. She was radiant and beautiful. My mama heart is full, as I watch her find her footing in her changing body, with more confidence, joy, and ease than I had ever seen.

This new chapter of life for both of us has continued to unfold with ease, devoid of the ways of pushing and trying that I had so often known negotiating life and business. Since the beginning of this surrender process, starting with my professional practice, I was continually met with invitations from earth angels, friends with offers of places to live, and leads that would connect me right where I needed to be next. As I stay true to my inner work and follow the guidance that whispers to me in the stillness, there is always a powerful synchronistic meeting or event that leads me unequivocally to the next right step. The excited feelings that come with synchronicity continue to assure me that all is well.

During these two years, synchronicity and guidance took me to Maui twice and to the unexpected gift of spending three months with family where I was raised in Pennsylvania. There was an alchemy during that visit that I still don't completely understand.

I feel it though. From the day, I arrived, memories of my mother's funeral flooded my heart as I watched a herd of deer foraging in the winter rain through the window of my sister's home. I later discovered that we had buried her that exact day, forty years earlier. I found healing in the unexpressed grief of my teenage years when my chronically ill mother left too soon, and I supported my loved ones there with my own brand of medicine.

I feel changed after all of this, softer, happier, living with greater ease and flow. I'm excited as I wait in anticipation for what's to come. People say I look younger and are curious about my gypsy lifestyle. I always try to leave a trail of goodness behind wherever I go.

It still feels scary sometimes, but I continue to surrender and pray to be aligned with God's will. I still receive answers only for the short term, and I breathe into the place of not knowing where I'll be in another few months. When I feel stressed and uncertain, I return to find answers where I always find them; Breath, Prayer, Meditation and Time in nature.

As I finish this chapter, I am in California again to be with my children, still uncertain of what's to come. Coming full circle, I've come back to offering healing services with a uniquely different flavor from what I had done in the past. I had barely gotten off the plane when I was greeted by a series of opportunities to offer private soul journeys and healing intensives to others, which has been as profound for the clients as it has been for me.

As I open myself to this new lifestyle, I feel I am part of a shift that is much larger than me, a consciousness change that is awakening many souls on this planet for a healthier, happier, new Earth. My journey has served to illuminate more clearly the unhealthy design of the world of false power in which we live—a world that keeps people in boxes and running on stress hormones, making it difficult to follow the new directions naturally elicited by the nature of our evolving souls. Becoming free to be self-expressed and fully aligned with the Divine is a trust walk that requires stepping on some slippery slopes. With the lightness, I've come to know in my being, I see no other way.

About the Author

Dr. Neesa Ginger Mills practiced as a chiropractic doctor for 22 years and was busy raising her two children in a coastal town near San Francisco until a series of events propelled her into a time of deep discovery of her divine connection that changed everything. Now, after more than two years without a solid home, during a time one may call a dark night of the soul, she is redefining her newly-awakened work in the mystical healing arts and resurrecting her professional journalistic skills as on online blogger.

Neesa offers a new model for healing, guiding clients through life blocks in health and spirituality at a distance and through intensive, intimate, ceremonial settings. Throughout her career, she has supported thousands of clients in finding balance and awakening through holistic health counsel, chiropractic, medical intuition, shamanism, energy healing, and the use of sacred space.

She is currently writing a book with her daughter about altars to cultivate soul purpose and divine presence. Personally, she is a dedicated mother, painter, writer, yogi, meditator, and mystical traveler.

Neesa's blog *Healthy Solutions for the Awakening Soul* and her professional website can be found online at www.Soulfulalignment.life.

Teresa McBeth-Gwartney
Cowgirl T's Inspiration

Let me introduce myself, I'm Teresa Gwartney, I am 56 yrs. old Cowgirl & I'm a widow! I never dreamed that my life would turn out like this, with me being made a widow at 35! I guess I was like most little girls, in the fact that I had dreams of what my life would be like when I grew up! I had it all planned out! I was going to graduate high school and college and become a Veterinarian, and open up my own Vet Clinic and then marry my soul mate. We were going to have a large horse and cattle ranch where we lived happily ever after!

It is funny how we think we are in control of our lives; when in reality we have very little control, at least once we are born. I believe that we sign a Soul/life contract before we are born with certain life lessons that we need to learn to be better spiritual beings and more like God! I believe we are sent to Earth to learn unconditional love for one another & to help lift each other up to grow spiritually!

I had a very difficult childhood, had a lot emotional trauma that I lived through and I never felt special or truly loved; so, when I met my late husband Steve in November 1977, he became my Knight in Shining armor; He was the first person that I ever felt unconditional love from with no strings attached.

My best friend at the time was LuAnn and she was dating Mark, Steve's best friend, so they decided to fix us up! Best friends dating best friends, Perfect, right? Steve and I were both really shy at that age! Our first date was to the Snowball Dance my junior year! It's funny how some things in life we can remember every detail of and then we can totally forget other things. I can close my eyes and remember our first kiss, just like it was yesterday. I remember him asking me to dance to a slow song, but I can't remember the song. I can remember what it felt like when he put his arms around me and we started slow dancing; then he leaned down and kissed me; at that very moment I fell head over heels in love with him. We actually talked about getting married that night, about what type of life we wanted to live! We both wanted to have a horse & cattle ranch and from that moment on we spent every minute we could with each other.

In January, we asked my parents if we could get married; they said no, that I had to graduate high school first and I was planning on going to college so we would have to wait; neither one of us was happy with that, but I was underage and we had no choice. Well in March I found out I was pregnant and I was terrified to tell my parents! I remember we told them on the front porch. My Dad got up and walked into the house, probably to get control of his emotions. I was so scared he was going after his gun to shoot Steve! But thank God he didn't! They told us, "yes that we could married" but, I had to promise

I would graduate High School; so, Steve promised if I wanted to go to college that he would make sure I went!

So, on May 23, 1978 at 7pm I became Mrs. Steve Gwartney! That was the 2nd happiest days of my life! The only day that could beat it is the day our son, Jimmy Don (JD) was born! We were still inseparable after 18yrs; we went and did everything together! I swore Steve could read my mind! Someone once told me that they could see how much Steve loved me because whenever I walked in a room or said something Steve would stop whatever he was doing and I'd have his total attention! Funny, I never noticed it; that was just how we were with each other!

We were happily married for a little over 18yrs when he was tragically killed in an auto-accident on his way to work! Another day I will never forget, it was the day my whole world completely shattered into a million pieces! It was July 12, 1996 at 6:30 am! How can I find all the pieces to put my life back together and even if I do, will they all fit? I had always felt that we were so connected that if anything ever happened to him I would know the very moment it happened; but I'm here to tell you that I didn't!   It was just like any other day, except that it wasn't!

Steve would always tell me he was going to die young and that I would out live him! The night before he died, I can remember when he made love to me that he had such a serious look on his face! I remember asking him, "Why do you look so serious, where's your smile?" He looked at me and said "I want to do this right; I want it to be perfect!" I found that strange because it was out of character for him! He was more the joking around type! Our usual routine was talking about our day till we fell asleep with me snuggled up in his arm! That night was a little different! It was like he knew something was fixing to happen to him!

They had a Company Health Screening at his Job earlier that week! He wouldn't tell JD or me what they had told him; all he would say is they told him to get a Doctor appointment ASAP; he needed to go on a diet and start exercising. That night before he was killed, He wanted to make sure I knew "if something should ever happen to him, that he didn't want me to be alone and that it was ok to remarry. I told him that I didn't want anyone else except him and I'd never remarry! He laughed saying yes you will, I give you 2 weeks! I remember getting upset because he was talking about dying and me remarrying, I didn't want to consider that possibility! I turned over not realizing this would be our last night together! I couldn't imagine my life without him! He then said He "was sorry, he would change the subject because he didn't want to upset me." Then he pulled me up close to him and we fell asleep in each other arms as always! Everything was perfect!

Steve had always told me that he was going to die young and I refused to believe it! One of my biggest regrets was not listening to everything that he had to tell me that night and that I hadn't told him that it was ok for him to move on and remarry if something ever happened to me! I didn't want to see him with someone else! Boy wasn't that selfish? If I could go back, I would hang on every word, etching them forever in my brain; I would have told him it was ok for him to remarry if something should ever happen to me! I just never imagined anything happening to him! That was not in my plans! This was not how my life was supposed to be! We were going to die together, be buried together in one casket, because I was scared of the dark and I couldn't imagine my life without him by my side!

When we went to bed that night, we had made plans for him to take a change of clothes with him, because we had plans after work that evening! He was going to load our 4-wheeler in the back of my pickup and drive it! I was going to have his Mom, Winnie to drive us to work in her van! She worked with me on Fridays at the beauty shop; I'm a licensed Beautician. He told me before he left for work that he had decided to take his pickup and us meet back at our house instead! That morning he left 20 minutes early, if he had only taken the time to load the 4-wheeler in the back of my pickup and drive it; he would have missed crossing paths with vehicle that killed him! If he had left at his regular time he could have missed the wreck! I asked him why he was going in early and he told me he had to do some paper work before the 7am meeting at work. He normally always would stop at Haircuts store on his way into work to get some snuff and a coffee, but he didn't; if only he would have stopped he could have missed the wreck! But, God had other plans!

I know God was preparing me for Steve's death when I look back! Leah and I, becoming friends, her getting me to start doing things without Steve, up till then we had done everything together! We were inseparable; he was my best friend, my husband, my lover, & my soul-mate! He was the only person that made me feel loved and special! He was my other half that completed me, made me feel whole, loved, and safe. I can now look back at that whole year and see how God was preparing me for this horrible tragedy. A few weeks before Steve died, Clara, Leah's Mom, gave me a book to read called- Embraced by the Light, by Bettye J. Eaddie; she told of her near-death experience and of her dying two times, and being brought back and how wonderful Heaven is. How she didn't want to return back to her life, she wanted to stay in heaven with God! That made me feel better about the dying process that he was in a beautiful place and healed; I just wasn't ready to let him go!

I look back now and remember that day, I wish I could forget! When they told me that he was killed in an auto-accident; I refused to a believe them, I even tried to argue that it wasn't him and that it was someone else! I told them that he had pickup trouble; someone was driving into work stopped and gave him a lift; that it was someone else who got killed, not my Steve! He was always my anchor, my calm, my guiding light in the storms of my life. Steve just hadn't heard this terrible rumor that was going around and as soon as he hears it, he will call me to let me know he is ok; but that call never came!

I can't tell you how I was able to convince myself that he didn't really died that day! I woke up every morning for 6 months, before I opened my eyes, thinking that I had this horrible nightmare where Steve was killed in a bad car wreck; but when I did open my eyes, it wasn't a dream, it was a living nightmare and then I'd fall apart again; then somehow I decided it was a nightmare, "all I have to do is survive this nightmare and on 7/12/97, I was going to wake up that morning and I would be snuggled up beside Steve, yes, it was only a bad nightmare! It was going to be like on the show Dallas, when Pam Ewing woke up to Bobby Ewing just being in the shower and it had just been a bad dream!

I couldn't eat, I couldn't sleep and my hair started falling out by the handfuls. I felt like a shell of a person, just stumbling around, trying to find a reason to go on. Needless to say, when I woke up 7/12/97, nothing had changed; Steve wasn't there and I needed to except that this was my new reality. I got up took care of my cattle and my horses.

Then I went out dancing and got drunk; this was my new reality for I couldn't pretend anymore. I had 2 choices, I could feel sorry for myself and give up or I could be brave and try to live; that right there was the hardest part, trying to live without him!

All our friends were from his job and we spent a lot of time together; but that all stopped when Steve died! Now the wives saw me as threat, now they were afraid I would go after their husbands! How stupid were they? I didn't want their husbands. I wanted my husband, Steve back! I was totally consumed with soul shattering pain! All I wanted to do was to die and be with Steve! When I needed them the most they turned their backs on me; but Leah didn't, she is who kept me going, she was there for me, when I was so shattered I couldn't be there for myself!

My son graduated high school in May 1997. The older men were telling JD, my son that he was the man of the house now, he needed to step up & take care of me! I was so mad when I found out! I told JD, that I was a grown, independent woman that could take care of me! That if I needed him all I had to do was pick up the phone and call! That was probably one of the hardest things I ever had to do! All the while inside I was thinking please don't go, I'm so scared I don't know what to do; I've never been alone and I've always been a Mom, I raised my sister and brother, then my Son; now I'm not only an empty nester but a Widow too! The pain in my heart was almost unbearable!

I told him to go onto college because I didn't want to be the reason he didn't follow his dreams and live the life he deserved! I didn't want in 15-20yrs him saying that he had to give up everything to take care of his Mom because his Dad had died! So, in Aug 97, he loaded his pickup, moved to

Stillwater & basically never came back home! My plan at that point was to commit suicide as soon as he left for college! I even had a Living Will made that said they couldn't do anything to save my life or keep me a live with machines! I even planned my funeral and paid for it completely; but family put me on suicide watch.

Who am I? I'm no longer Steve's wife, I'm his Widow and my son didn't need me anymore, my whole world revolved around them. What do I do now? Well, I've always had a gift with animals, especially horses and I loved cattle. I worked with cattle and horses all my life, they are where I find my center, peace and joy; so, I focused on my quarter horse and cattle ranch. I really miss it a lot especially foaling and calving season. I was blessed with 3 little nieces' that became my shadows; I'm not real sure how things would've turned out if they hadn't been there. They were more like my daughters than nieces. Stacia and I are still real close, I look at her as my daughter!

The girls, my Dad and I competed in barrel-racing, team penning and cattle sorting until I was injured in a team penning accident. I ran full speed into my Dad on his horse during a competition; we didn't find out till later the full extent of my injuries; I fractured 3 vertebrae, ruptured a disc, herniated disc, broke my left hip, my left knee and ruptured the left piriformis muscle and so that required back surgery, leaving me in a lot of pain. This forced me to quit competing; I couldn't train horses anymore. Now what am I going to do? This was basically the only thing that had kept me going after Steve's death and now God was taking this away from me too!

That was my breaking point; I was still in pain from the loss of Steve, from the surgery and not being able to ride anymore was more than I could handle; I felt that I didn't have anything left to live for. That was when I decided to end my life; I remember telling God that "he had way over estimated me! I'm not as strong as you think I am! If you want me to live, it is all up to you because I give up!" Then I took as many pills as I could, till I nearly threw up, stepped into a hot shower and when I got out, I took the rest of the pills; then I went in the living room, laid down on the daybed and went to sleep; then a friend found me, He said that I wasn't making any sense, acting weird and he asked me if I had taken any pills. He said I told him yes and he asks what I took, because he knew I didn't do drugs of any kind! I don't remember anything after I went to sleep!

The Doctors said I flat lined 3xs & they were able bring me back; that's when I realized that I was here on Earth until I had fulfilled my purpose. I could keep trying to die and chance being left crippled or brain damaged; I thank God that I was not left with any noticeable damage. The only problem I seem to have is trouble with my blood pressure and with my heart rate, so I've been really blessed. I'm not exactly sure what God has planned for me, other than I'm supposed to help other people from the traumas' that I have survived and I believe this is my first step!

I know you're probably wondering who I am; If you had asked me before the age of 35, I would have told you that I was a Cowgirl that was blessed to be happily married to my soul mate, Steve for a little over 18yrs and that we have an amazing son together! I was a wife, a mother, a daughter, a sister & a granddaughter! I loved my life, it was MY perfect life! July 12, 1996 at 6:30am my life was turned upside down, forever changed! Today, if you were to ask me who I am now, I would have to tell you that I am a 56yr old Cowgirl who was made a

Widow at the age of 35! I never dreamed my life would change like this! What little girl grows up wanting to be a Widow?

My life was shattered into a million pieces! Can you recover enough pieces to put a life back together? That one day is forever etched in my memory, never to be forgotten! I'm afraid that the biggest and maybe even the best part of me died that day as well! Who am I? How do you start putting the pieces of a shattered life back together again! I would tell you one breathe, one step, and one day at a time! Now, I can say I am still a Widow, Cowgirl, but I am also a creative Artist, a mother, a grandmother, a sister, and a daughter, who is strong and independent!

About the Author

I know you're probably wondering who am I? If you had asked me before the age of 35, I would have told you that I was a Cowgirl that was blessed to be happily married to my soulmate, Steve for a little over 18yrs and that we have an amazing son together! I was a wife, a mother, a daughter, a sister & a granddaughter! I loved my life, it was MY perfect life! July 12, 1996 at 6:30am my life was turned upside down, forever changed! Today, if you were to ask me who I am now, I would have to tell you that I am a 56-yr. old Cowgirl who was made a Widow at the age of 35! I never dreamed my life would change like this!

What little girl grows up wanting to be a Widow? My life was shattered into a million pieces! Can you recover enough pieces to put a life back together? That one day is forever etched in my memory, never to be forgotten! I'm afraid that the biggest and maybe even the best part of me died that day as well! Who am I? How do you start putting the pieces of a shattered life back together again! I would tell you one breathe, one step, one day at a time! Now, I can say I am still a Widow, Cowgirl, but I am also a creative Artist, a mother, a grandmother, a sister, a daughter, who is strong & independent! I AM A SURVIVOR! If you would like to know more about me, you can find me on Facebook under Cowgirl T's Inspiration or by email Tlgwartney@gmail.com

Elizabeth Blade
Angels and Warriors

The feeling of loss is in my heart at the moment. Life can bring you struggles and pain, but we walk through the tougher times with love in our hearts and the faith to carry on. I have lost people that I have loved so very dearly. I watched my mother take her last breath. I was with her during her final moments. *That final heartbreaking, earth-shattering hour; and everything in my world turned sour.*

It wasn't like the movies where sentimental music played; there were no do-over's or a shining light. Darkness consumed my world. I was so lost. It was as if my heart was ripped from my chest. I looked over to my dad who was standing across for me, and I had to tell him that his devoted wife who he loved so much was gone. My mother was gone! How could I ever succumb to the thought of her not being with me for the rest of my life? A life I had to live without her. I contemplated all kinds of things after she passed away. My mind constantly ticked over that I needed to be with her, to give everything up and just *be with her.*

My mind turned into a dark place. It had gone there many times before, even before the passing of my dear mother, but the urge seemed stronger. I feared for myself, as I wasn't thinking rationally. But then again, I had never been through anything like that before. I mean, yes, I had lost loved ones and friends in my life, but my mother was my rock. My mother was someone to whom I always ran and told my feelings. That was all gone now. A part of myself was gone, and a part of myself would never truly be whole again. But piece by piece, I try and glue myself together, even though no matter how hard I try, I know I will never fully be whole again.

I believe when you love someone that much and they are no longer of this earth, pieces of yourself go with them too. She made me. I am accomplishing things now I can no longer physically share with her, though every night I talk to a photo of her. It's how I cope. We all cope in different ways and continuing to talk to her is how I cope. I tell her things before I go to sleep. I always wonder if where she is now being safe, and I hope she's not frightened or confused. I wonder if she's safe and not torn between the worlds of here and now and where spirits roam.

The amazing thing is that I believe when we leave this world, we take the love and memories we shared with us. I hold that belief near and dear to my mind and heart. She was here, and in some way, she still is. We are angels and warriors, and every day we fight a battle. We get through life, we get through sadness, and we get through experiences that I am unsure how we ever get through, but somehow, we just do. I think of her every day along with everyone I have ever loved and lost.

I miss them, and I hope that they are looking over me now. I hope they can see how I am at present.

I look to the skies at night and see the stars' twinkle and shine; memories and thoughts we shared are forever mine; thoughts and memories so divine.

We are the angels and warriors of life. We are the warriors who roam the land and try to find people who understand us and what we're all about.

We are the angels and the voices that people long to hear; we have a message, and we say it loud and clear.

We are here for a time and we must make that time matter. I know I try and do that with words. Words of importance and utter inspiration are what the world needs more of. I miss the voices of my mother and grandparents and what they use to tell me, but I close my eyes and visualize hearing what they use to say. Perhaps I can recreate those moments in time over in my mind, those memories I tend to live in always.

I run to moments of you and I; the sheer thought of those times makes me want to cry; but we are the warriors and angels of the heaven and skies.

We are part of this world and we have stories that need to be told; we are young and brave and bold.

I don't believe in getting old. I believe we just get wiser with time. Whenever someone says, "I am old," I tell that person that he/she is wise, that wrinkles and grey hair are just part of time passing. We are wise. We are always young. We never grow old. Time just passes us by. I am not a mother, but I long to be one. But if it's not meant to be, then I will turn my wisdom to those who need it. I will share the love and things I have learned along the way.

Thoughts of you and everything you have taught me will never go away; how I love you, how I miss you.

A lover's hand takes you and guides you through life, offering you someone to share your world with. A gift is more than a gift; it's the ultimate thing we are given. Love is a splendid thing, and the joy and everything that is connected with it brings so much to our lives. I am a daughter, aunty, granddaughter, friend, and wife. I am a poet and writer of words. I am an angel and warrior all at once. We can be so many things rolled into one. We start when we breathe our first breath, and it all ends when we die.

Does it? Do we carry on? Do we leave our marks in the sand?

We carry on in our names, our passions, and fields. Love is everything. Passion for what we love is real. We create so much in our everyday lives.

We create friendships, bonds, and ties that forever bind us to this life. Our lives are not in vain. We don't just end.

We keep on running, and we run on forever; life, love, inspiration are all our endeavors.

We lift our voices to the sun; we lift our voices as one; we are the ultimate ones.

We are the angels and warriors of the world.

We are so many things rolled into one; we each find our setting sun; life is never over; it's only just begun.

Let the stars and moon shine on down. Put on our crowns and become the kings and queens of life. The angels and warriors shall live forever more.

About the Author

Elizabeth Blade is from Adelaide, Australia. A writer and poet, she has co-authored several pieces, two of which became international best sellers. She has branched herself into freelance writing and has a branded name especially for her writing called Moondance Word Artistry. Elizabeth writes poems, lyrics, articles, and blog pieces. Her writing is inspirational and uplifting; she writes for the needs of the people. She writes with her soul and puts her heart into everything. Her following, though small in numbers, is growing larger by the day. She is expanding her horizons and making connections with people all over the word.

Elizabeth is available for magazines, publications, events, special occasions, artists, musicians, individuals creating memories for loved ones, and much more! Her new book, *A Rising Moon on Domestic Violence*, is available in paperback and eBook format. For more, please visit:

Website: *http://elizabethblade.com*

Facebook: *http://facebook.com/elizabethbladewriter*

Twitter: *twitter.com/moondance_81* (@Moondance_81)

Email: moondance_81@me.com

Gail Dawn Fisher
Northern Storms to Starry Nights
Overcoming Hopelessness
by Lifting the Spirits of Others

Six years into an incredibly abusive and emotionally draining marriage, there wasn't much left of me. I felt like a tattered, empty shell clinging to life by my love for my little girl. She had become the only light that I could see, and that light helped to navigate both of us to a brand-new world. I married a man and we lived on acreage in Northern Alberta. I quickly came to understand that being married to him was much more like being a single mother who also took care of a man, a house, a farm, canning and preserving, a garden, a band, his gravel truck business, all of the errands, bookkeeping, etc. Much more than a full-time mom, I worked from early morning until late at night every day. He rarely helped me with anything, and he demanded that I serve him and perform sexual acts for him no matter how sick or tired I was. My life became a meaningless drudgery that I could never dream of escaping.

Two years into the marriage, I was diagnosed with cervical

cancer and subsequently had a hysterectomy. After the surgery, I was told that the cancer was actually an STD. It wasn't until a few years after I had left my husband that I found out he was having affairs with many other women during our marriage and that the cancer was given to me by him. While living on the farm I also trained and rehabilitated abused horses, re-homing them with loving families. However, one mare that had been particularly abused by her owners was very unpredictable and emotionally scarred. I underestimated her state of total fear, and the moment I was seated in the saddle, she began to buck like a professional bronco. I stayed on as long as I could while trying to calm her down, but in the end, she threw me, and the fall injured my neck and lower back. For more than a year I could barely walk, and I couldn't lift my little girl at all. My husband still would not help me, and I continued to serve him, on my knees if I had to.

In addition to the farm and my husband's gravel truck business, we also had a six-piece classic rock and country band. We practiced every week, and I learned to play bass and sing harmony, which was in many ways like learning to sing all over again. The band was called Northern Storm, and I developed the backdrop and all of the promo for us. We played all over Northern Alberta until inflated egos blew the band apart. I'm not sure why, but losing the band absolutely broke my heart; there was so much of me invested in it that it took a long time to let go.

A very dear friend of mine offered to take me to see her chiropractor. I started going with her every week, and although I didn't see very much improvement with my back, the conversations that I had with her saved my life. She had a way of reflecting back the words I spoke, and when she did, it reconnected me to my own emotions.

Listening to her talk about my life as though it was her own aroused the protector and warrior in me. I began to realize that I had to leave my marriage both for me and for the sake of my little girl. I saved up what little I could and slowly stowed away our most personal belongings in our motor home. Every summer I drove down to Chilliwack to spend time with my older daughter who was living with her dad. I decided that I would take the motor home and my little girl and try a temporary separation from my husband. I was hoping that it would get his attention and cause some much-needed change in our relationship. I drove as far as I could on the first day and stopped in a quiet campground for the night. I got my little girl settled and went online to tell my older daughter how far we'd driven that day. I noticed an unread message on Face book, and when I checked it, I saw that it was from a woman my husband used to live with.

The message was clearly intended for him, but she obviously didn't realize that our Face book account was shared. She wanted to know if I was gone and if it was safe for her to come over. At that very moment, I knew I would never return to him. I spent the next several hours watching and copying the conversation that they had. The next day I sent it to him with a long letter explaining that I wouldn't be returning and why. He was very upset with me, but with the proof I had there was very little he could say. We continued our journey, and with every mile, I could feel the life coming back into me! I picked up my daughter from Chilliwack, and we drove to Penticton and spent a couple of weeks on the beach, just the three of us. It was glorious to feel such freedom and peace and be able to rest and enjoy my girls.

My mother was living in Vernon and invited us to come and

stay with her. We had always lived so far apart that she rarely got to see my girls. I wanted to give her the opportunity to spend time with her grandchildren, so we drove to Vernon to spend the rest of the summer with her. The visit went so well that even after my oldest went home at the end of the summer, I decided to stay with her. We lived in the motor home at my mother's place and began looking for shared accommodations with her. At the beginning of September when my little girl started school, the motor home was broken into and everything of value was stolen. The police came and dusted for prints, but nothing ever came of it. I had brought enough equipment with me to perform solo in order to support us. However, after everything was stolen, it left me scrambling to come up with a way to work enough to get by. Due to the significant injuries to my back, I was not able to work in a conventional way. However, I had accumulated many skills over the years in art, computers, networking, advertising, costuming, etc., and cumulatively they all came together to help shape my future.

A plan began to emerge while talking to a friend one day. I told him about a dream I'd had before I left my husband. In the dream, I was standing on a stage by myself performing my favorite warm-up song "At Last" by Etta James.

When I turned to look at my band mates, I realized I was on stage alone in front of a crowd that was applauding very enthusiastically, and I felt very confused. Then I told him about a past experience with some friends at a little pub that had karaoke. When they called me up to sing, I had my back to the audience, could not hear the music, and had to look at the screen through the bars of the dance floor to see the words. After singing, I really thought that it was the worst performance I had ever given and seriously questioned

138

whether I should be singing at all! He also told me about his experiences with karaoke, and we thought it be wonderful if karaoke could be similar to performing professionally with a live band, and that was the very beginning of Superstar Karaoke!

I got to work designing a logo, backdrop, promo packs, and lists of what kinds of equipment would be needed to put the show together. My friend had a trailer full of speakers and said that I could rent them from him. I had to find and make some of the other equipment as well. He also offered to MC the show for me, and after about two months of collecting music, programs, stage production, lights, etc., we were finally ready to launch. I went to every bar, pub, night-club, and social house in the entire Okanagan, and had every single door slammed in my face. I couldn't seem to adequately share the vision of what the show would be like with the owners. All they could see was that it was karaoke, which most of them didn't like, and that I was charging twice as much as they would be willing to pay, even if they wanted karaoke.

Finally, a pub owner in Armstrong, BC decided to give us a chance. He had recently reacquired a bar after some problems with the owners to whom he had sold it. He was looking for something unique to bring business in, and that was exactly what we gave him. We had a twenty-foot backdrop that was painted like stage lights, and when the spotlights were directed at the painted lights, the whole thing looked 3D. That, combined with huge professional speakers and audio equipment, made for the biggest karaoke show anyone had ever seen! On opening night, there were only a handful of very drunk people in the bar, but in no time at all, our night made more money for the bar than the rest of the week combined and has continued that way for nearly seven years.

Eventually, my friend went on to other pursuits and I upgraded my equipment for the show. I secured another long-term venue in Vernon, which subsequently became their busiest night as well. Slowly, the stigma of karaoke started to change, and people who would usually run for the door the second karaoke began stayed to hear the carousel of talent that was attracted by this one-of-a-kind professionally-produced show. For me, the show was a perfect opportunity to make ordinary people feel special and appreciated. From the very moment that they walked in the door until they left at the end of the night, they were the superstars of the show!

One night, a man came to the show and quietly came up to me and gave me his song selection. It was a country song, and I was surprised because he didn't look like a country guy at all. He got up to sing the Alan Jackson song that he had selected, and I thought if Alan was ever sick, he should get this guy to stand in for him!

My sister was at the show that night and got some great pictures of him. She came whenever she could to get pictures of all of the singers as keepsakes for them. I could not tag him in his pictures on Face book because I did not know who he was. However, he knew a lady that I had recently connected with, so I was able to contact him and ask if it would be all right if I added him as a friend and tagged his pictures.

After talking many times, we decided to go for coffee, and I was so impressed by the story of his life and how he had grown up in Northern BC like I had. He was raising his three children himself and working very hard, but I could tell that he was a caring father and loved his children very much. When I left our coffee date I remember thinking how wonderful it was that there were still gentlemen in the world!

We were very committed to remaining single, but during our conversations we both admitted that it would be nice to have someone special to share memorable moments with. I asked him over to watch a movie with me one night, and when I sat down beside him, I accidentally brushed his hand with mine. I have always heard people talk about "sparks flying", but I had never experienced it myself. I knew at once we had both felt it, and we cautiously began to explore the sensation of just holding hands. It felt better than anything I could imagine! We have spoken every single day since that day. He is the most incredible man—warm, loving, and kind. I am so blessed that he is a part of my life. After several months of him coming with me to the show, I asked him to be my co-host, and now his beautiful, warm country voice can be heard every night.

Superstar has given me the opportunity to make so many wonderful connections and relationships with people, and to witness the building of a very warm and caring family of singers who are always there for each other. They come week after week to perform, to support each other, and to escape the drudgery of their own lives. It gives me tremendous pleasure to produce this show for all of them; there is nothing in this world like seeing each of them shines in their own way nightly under the stars.

When I look back now, it's hard to imagine the brokenness that I came from just seven years ago and how my life has become mostly about lifting the spirits of so many people through the universal language of music. I would not change a single day in my life, as I am completely confident that I am right where I am meant to be. Experiencing their happiness is one of my greatest joys.

About the Author

Gail Dawn Fisher was born in Burnaby British Columbia on December 16th 1968. When she was two years old, her parents moved the family to Northern B.C. and became homesteaders. They grew and raised their own food, built shops & barns, dug wells by hand, and played under the dim light of oil lamps at night. Gail grew up much more like her great grandparents than her peers at school. As a result, she had difficulty relating to other children and spent much of her time daydreaming and going for long walks alone collecting wildflowers and pretty stones.

When she was just 15 she left home to complete high-school and post-secondary LTCA, CPR, & Esthetics programs. She sought out many different types of work; janitorial, geriatric & respite care, selling limited edition art, all levels of restaurant services, and even owned a salon on Granville Street in Vancouver.

Ever seeking new experiences, she lived on a large acreage in northern Albert and retrained abused horses, raised chickens, turkeys, and often had the opportunity to rescue wildlife including two orphaned mule deer that she successfully raised and returned to the wild!

Gail has always been drawn to helping and encouraging others, she is a gypsy at heart, quirky, eclectic and artistic, she wears glitter in her hair and just about everywhere else! She loves owls, butterfly's and anything shiny! She leads with her heart because she chooses to see the best in people, she will take you as you are and expects the same in return!

She is a devoted mother of two beautiful daughters and partner to a loving man with three children of his own! They live in Coldstream B.C. and enjoy long peaceful walks and spirited conversations!

She is self-employed as a DJ/KJ, an Artist of all thinks that glitter, and a Graphic Designer.

Lizbeth Russell
An Angel's Touch – Deciding to Live
Deciding to live was the hardest decision of my life.

My husband walked out, leaving me with our three children, the youngest not even two years old. I felt abandoned by him, by his family, and by my own family. His family blamed me, and I think, to an extent, my family did, too.

I rarely asked for help, because the responses I always seemed to get were, "Things are so hectic right now," or "You're strong, you can handle it," or (my personal favorite) "Just try to be more positive!" These responses are the worst things you can say. They are defeating. My anger built, my depression deepened. But I hid it very well.

My job as a high school Spanish teacher was stressful. My contract required 35 hours a week, I often put in 60+ hours. I had health issues stemming from perfume & chemical allergies, and was continually exposed to both at work.

Add to that the stress of moving to a new home, selling the old one, two pre-teens reeling from their father's departure, a high-needs toddler, and a divorce leaving me in serious debt. It was a recipe for disaster.

For the first two years after the split, I managed to keep things together.

I did, however, start pulling away from people. I stopped visiting family, I didn't go out with friends, decreased my extra-curricular involvement at work. My focus was to keep my family together as best I could. I watched my eldest get more depressed as my middle child tried to be the rock for everyone. The youngest continued to be the wild child, who sometimes took 4-5 weeks to emotionally recover from his father going back overseas for work.

Then came the carbon monoxide poisoning; from a gas dryer incorrectly installed in the new house. It took months to figure out why my middle child was getting so sick, and by the time I did figure it out, there were severe physical and academic consequences. The next two years were full of doctor's visits for him, including a neurologist 2 hours away, and a week spent in the hospital because of self-harming, plus counseling sessions. I felt like a complete failure as a parent because I couldn't help my child, I hadn't seen what was happening, and was so sick myself that I could barely function.

I broke down and asked my family for help.

Again, I was told "You're strong, you can handle it. Just try to be more positive about things." They've always thought that I was just a drama queen, wanting attention, and living just over an hour away was "too far" for them to visit. They were busy helping with my sister's kids, volunteering with their church, and other things. No time to help me out. Honestly, I felt more abandoned than ever.

After several bouts of bronchitis, I ended up with a severe case of pneumonia. The doctor wanted to put me in the hospital for the pneumonia, but my ex was out of the country and there weren't any family members available to take the kids. So, I refused to be admitted. It took several months for me to feel "human" again.

I spiraled down, and crawled into myself. I avoided anything that didn't have to do with my own children. I gave up helping with the school theater group, I went back to advising only one club, stopped going to church, and declined all invitations. If it didn't involve my kids, I was a recluse.

Was going through all this pain really worth it?

It hurt too much. Emotionally, I felt devastated; and the physical pain was getting unbearable. Even breathing was difficult. I was crying all the time because movement was excruciating, but I knew if I stopped that I would probably not start again and I had three children that needed me. They didn't understand what was going on with their father. I was the only consistent in their life, and I had to keep it together, regardless of the cost to myself.

When I bought a new house (less expensive than renting) for the kids and myself, I was left with the task of sorting through everything in the old house to get it ready to sell. Packing up, moving my own things, putting his things aside for him to sort through, taking things to good will, or to the dump. I found myself working my full-time teaching job, and then spending evenings at the old house sorting, packing, and stacking. The kids were bored, nothing for them to do, except help sort things - and we all know how kids enjoy that! Weekends were more of the same. The only break in routine was soccer practice, games, court dates and appointments.

When I didn't have, everything completed inside a month, and found myself in court with the county judge yelling at me to get this finished so the house could go on the market. He didn't care that my teaching schedule had an added 20+ hours a week spent in trying to get the house ready, plus being a mom. His suggestion was to take time off of work to get this done, or hire a babysitter for the evenings and weekend.

This wasn't the first time I'd been yelled at by the judge.

He favored my ex over me because my ex is an engineer with a local high profile business. I was "just a teacher". My ex's career was more important than mine, and it was unreasonable for me to expect him to help with getting the house ready because his work took him overseas frequently. Mind you, my ex could have asked for time off, or to stay state-side for a month or two to help me do this; and this was the house we had shared for 15 years.

After the divorce, I was left with over $30K in debt. I managed to pay this off within 6 years, but had to dip into my retirement to do so. But it was paid off, and I could breathe a little.

My health continued to decline. I was in constant pain; my joints were so swollen it was difficult to move. Food didn't sit well, and I found myself taking 3600mg of Tylenol just to get out of bed in the morning (with another 3600mg taken by the time I went to bed that night). There were also other issues that required medication, including my blood pressure, which was very high. Well, high for me. I'd always had ~100/60, and with the divorce, it went up to ~140/90 (or worse).

I would try to ask for help.

The pain made climbing stairs increasingly difficult and other activities nearly un-bearable and I was only in my mid 40's but

I was used to it, I continued to persevere, and did my best to ignore all the jokes and harassment from colleagues and administration at work about my mobility issues. I had a classroom on the 2nd floor, that would be 60º in the winter, and 90º+ in the warm weather, there was mold in the ceiling from roof leaks, all of which contributed to the health issues. I look back and wonder how I even managed to do *any*thing.

At that time, I had a doctor who told me; "Its stress, just de-stress your life and you'll be fine," when informed her of my migraines, bloody noses, and chest pains. I was in the middle of a divorce, and told her the stress wasn't going away, she rolled her eyes and asked me what I thought she should do about it. I felt defeated.

Because of the joint inflammation and pain, she kept testing for Lupus, Lyme, Hypothyroidism, and Rheumatoid Arthritis. My tests all kept coming back negative, which only reinforced her view that I was imagining things. I tried to talk to her about my GI issues, which were getting worse, and with a disgusted look, she told me "It's probably something you ate; I don't want to hear about it." My doctor then told me I was a hypochondriac, and that it was all in my head. She never looked beyond the four things she kept testing me for, *even when I asked what else the symptoms might relate to*.

I would lie in bed at night, in too much pain to sleep.

I was lucky if I got 3 hours. Most nights it was 2-2.5. This went on for several years, even after I switched doctors. My new doctor was as puzzled as my first doctor, but she did help me deal with my blood pressure, and sent me to a neurologist & rheumatologist to see if they could figure out why I was getting these symptoms. These doctors were also stumped, but at least they were looking beyond the four things I'd been tested for repeatedly. The rheumatologist wanted to put me on narcotics to manage the pain, because I was damaging my liver with all the Tylenol, but I'm allergic to narcotics, so I refused.

THEN CAME THE FIRST VISIBLE ANGELIC ENCOUNTER OF MY ADULT LIFE: ARCHANGEL RAPHAEL

I was going through my darkest period. I had essentially lost the will to live, and only went through the motions for the sake of my children. They were already devastated by their father leaving; I couldn't do the same thing to them. Breathing became a chore. I would often wake up after dozing off; gasping for breath because I'd stopped breathing. Not your normal sleep apnea, this was full out stopping.

One night in particular, I lay in bed, focused on breathing. Just breathing, one breath in, one breath out; Just breathe, I would tell myself; *and began to wonder if it was even worth it.* How easy it would be to just let it go. To just. stop. breathing. My kids would understand, some day.

As I lay there, I saw a glow in my bedroom. I was puzzled because my room is as dark as I can make it for sleep, because light wakes me up. But there was a growing light in my room. It was bright enough that when I sat up in bed, I could see my shadow cast on the wall.

But the light wasn't coming from any place in particular. I could not find the source of the light.

It was welcoming, warm, soft, comforting and I felt safe, loved.

I was lulled into a sound sleep, and told that *I couldn't give up, I was here for a purpose, and still had work to do.* That night I slept for over 4 hours. Later I learned that it was the Archangel Raphael who had been with me that night. Upon waking the next morning, I knew something was different. I knew I didn't want to give up. But *something* had to be done. As I was already under chiropractic care for my back, and my chiropractor's office had just brought in an acupuncturist, I decided to try that route before agreeing to pain medication.

This was life altering. The first thing my acupuncturist did was muscle testing for food allergies. What came up were wheat, eggs, oranges, and a few other things. No one had ever brought up food allergies. I'd never been tested for any, although they knew I was allergic to bees, certain medications, and a few other things; and I have several family members with food allergies. This also indicated severe gluten sensitivity (though I do not have Celiac Disease).

Within three months I was pain free, and stopped taking any pain medication - *just from cutting out wheat and gluten!* In addition to losing chronic pain, my GI problems cleared up, along with the neurological issues, the cystic acne, the hair & eyelash loss, the splintering fingernails, the inflammation...all of the symptoms I had been experiencing for over 20 years. It turns out I was not a hypochondriac after all. It turns out that my first doctor, in her sarcasm, was right; It *was* something I ate.

THIS PATH, HOWEVER, WAS NOT WITHOUT ITS ROADBLOCKS AND CHASMS.

It took me over two years to get my blood pressure under control, and I still have to work to maintain it without medication, and my doctor keeps a close eye on it. Every time I get "glutened", it takes weeks to get it out of my system, during which many of the symptoms return. I am now very strict about my diet, because it's just not worth it to "cheat."

When my life is too stressful, I tend to get nightmares. Whether it's zombie (these are the worst!), or apocalyptic dreams, they are awful, and sometimes wake me up in total panic, reaching for my inhaler because a panic attack can precipitate an asthma attack.

One night, after a particularly bad nightmare, I found myself waking up to see a glowing figure by my closet door. The quality of the light was the same as the first experience, with Archangel Raphael. But this time I could see a figure in the light: tall, slender, glowing. I was told to not worry, that I was safe, protected, and much loved. *They* would watch over me, and be with me through all the changes coming. I remember replying "Oh, okay, thank you," in total wonderment right before I fell into a peaceful sleep.

Yet another time, when I woke from a nightmare, the Archangel Michael was there. I heard and felt him, as he stepped between me and someone (ethereal) standing at the end of my bed, telling them they couldn't have me, that I was of the light. I felt no fear, only gratitude and love for AA Michael.

Once these changes in my life were set in motion, it was like a snowball.

I started taking control, refusing to be a doormat. I changed my daily routine to include time for meditation and other self-care. I learned how to say "no." This didn't sit well with some people, including family, resulting in a lot of changes in my social circle. While I have felt more alone than ever, I do not feel *lonely*.

It took working through a lot of fear to be able to embrace who I truly am. I see, hear, and speak with Angels, as well as other spirits, including unicorns and dragons. The Archangels Michael and Raphael are always with me, as are many more. ***They have always been with me.***

As a baby and toddler, I used to see them clearly. My family did not. I remember getting teased incessantly about my 'Imaginary friends.' My parents used to get frustrated when they'd come into my room in the morning and I would be asleep under my bed or behind my door. When they would ask why, I would tell them "because that's where they said I would be safe from the witch in the attic."

The house we lived in had a walk-up attic, and the door was directly across from my bedroom door. There was something not quite right about the energy of the attic. I was terrified of it. My parents kept the attic locked but would often find the door unlocked and open, and would yell at both my brother and myself for opening it, even though the lock (a hook and eye) was too high for us to reach, even with a chair. Whatever was in that attic is what the angels were protecting me from.

We moved when I was four, to the countryside, where I learned to speak to trees, and plants, and fell in love with Mother Earth. It was a safe and magical place where I could lose myself in the forest and fields, but never be "lost." Growing up, I learned to not speak about what I saw, heard, and felt. That was the kind of talk that got you branded as crazy. Instead, I lost myself in books with magic, dragons, reincarnation, science fiction – anything I could get my hands on that was "acceptably esoteric." Anne McCaffrey, Mercedes Lackey, JRR Tolkein, CS Lewis, Ray Bradbury, and Isaac Asimov continue to be my favorite authors, even into adulthood.

THIS SENSE OF COMMUNITY, MAGIC, AND ANGELS IS WHAT I HAVE RETURNED TO.

I know that I am not alone, that I work with incredible beings of light, and that I am a healer on many levels. I am also a warrior. I love working with angels, ascended masters, my ancestors, and any being of light who believes that we can help heal the world. Because I believe the world is worth saving.

One of my favorite messages from the Angels is: **"Be the Beacon, Be the Light that helps others find their way home."**

About the Author

Elizabeth (Lizbeth) Russell is an Intuitive Holistic Wellness Coach, Angelic Herbalist, Kundalini Reiki Master-Teacher, and Certified Angel Practitioner™. She has a Master's in Education, with over 25 years' classroom experience; and as a graduate with Honors from the American College of Healthcare Sciences, where she obtained diplomas in Holistic Health Practice, Natural Products Manufacturing, and Herbal Retail Management.

As an Intuitive Holistic Wellness Coach, Lizbeth works with clients in "facilitating finding the wellness within", through improving their daily lives naturally, addressing issues with body, mind, and spirit. Lizbeth also has over 30 years' experience reading Tarot and Oracle cards, helping to bring guidance, insight, clarity, and angelic advice to life's challenges. She is the owner of Linden Tree Intuitive and Lizbeth's Botanicals.

Lizbeth makes her home in Corning, NY, where she teaches workshops and classes on wellness, herbal preparations, wildcrafting and gardening. She also meets with clients in person (or via the internet) for wellness coaching, angel and tarot readings and group angel gatherings.

Additionally, she has a line of organically-based, all-natural, wheat & gluten free body care products, herbal teas, and perfume oils that are hand-crafted in small batches. In her spare time, she enjoys being with her three children, hanging out with the fairies and gnomes while practicing full-contact gardening, and hugging trees.

You can connect with Lizbeth through social media (Facebook, Instagram, & Twitter: @LindenTreeIntuitive), via email: lindentreeintuitive@gmail.com, or on her website: www.lindentreeintuitive.com)

Karen Tants
The Power of the Divine Presence

What is a warrior? My definition of a warrior is someone who has the courage to stand alone in their own power, and by power, I do not mean control over others, power over others, or violence. What it does mean to me is to maintain control over our own lower base instincts; self-mastery; the power that comes from God; being in our own truth, willing to be a catalyst for change and transmutation through *compassion-in-action*; being willing to face the shadow aspects of our own creation and those imprinted on our psyches; holding to faith, courage, forgiveness, and unconditional love; and to face the unseen and the unknown with faith and trust in the Higher Power that moves beyond time and is in us all, both manifested and un-manifested. We can only manifest our inner warrior when we are standing in our own truth, looking out into the world rather than in our own little bubble with no care, compassion, consideration for others, or thoughts of helping anyone other than own little self with a limited view of reality.

Angel wings allow us to fly high, to fly above the drama of life, giving us wings while we are counter-balanced by our warrior who has his/her feet firmly planted on the earth. Like Archangel Michael with his sword of protection and mastery as the warrior, our angel wings are in spirit as faith, and they are Archangel Michael's counterpart. One day, I was talking with some friends at work when I instantly noticed each of their faces were symbolic of an angel. I saw that the third eye area was the face of the angel, the eyebrows were the angel's wings, and the eyes and nose, the body of the angel and duality experience. I felt I was shown this for my own understanding and that it was not meant to be shared with those concerned, so I didn't say anything to them about my experience.

God is always listening, and His angels are always around and within us just waiting to be acknowledged, to enable us to consciously receive their signs, guidance, and support as we journey through life, and that a myriad of potential encounters are available to us at every turn. Angels guide us on our paths towards God and always work for the highest good. There have been documented cases of angels intervening unasked when we are in dire danger and our time is not yet finished. Sometimes, this happens to *awaken* us and guide us to follow our purpose for being here. When we open up to the angelic realms, there is no end to the help and assistance that we can receive as we go about our daily lives. Angels are with everyone; they are beyond time and can be with us all at the same time simply because they are omnipresent, everywhere, just as God is ever-present.

Our individual selves cannot comprehend the fact we never left God because we have bodies that are separate and we appear apart from everyone else. It is the processes of the mind, our two eyes seeing, and our bodies beholden to the senses that trick us into believing that what our five senses are telling us is our only true reality.

I will bring you angels.

Holding my clear quartz laser point in my hands, I asked the angelic light beings and my guidance for clarity concerning what to write for this chapter. I then went to bed, taking the quartz crystal with me. The following morning as I lay in bed, I picked up my quartz point and meditated with it, holding it in both hands at my chest area. I, again, inwardly asked for clarity, and lay there experiencing a flow of energies. As I held the quartz point in my left hand, I began to feel the presence of a feminine flow of warmth from my left side.

I felt guided to place the crystal point at my higher heart and lay that way, experiencing feelings of unconditional love and joy. After a while, I sensed the presence of a masculine energy at my right. My right hand was placed over my left, which held the crystal, and I felt a *melding* of the energies and such warmth and love and cocooning, acceptance, honour, and trust. I felt a blending, a sense of finding space in honour, and a sense of entwining. I suddenly noticed that it felt spirally and that my left foot was over the top of my right. At this point, my left hand was still covered by my right with such warmth and a feeling of being allowed to *just be*, and with my feminine energy safely held in this space of trust, honour, and faith, I received a vision of the symbol of the caduceus—the healing symbol used in the medical field—with the angel wings and spiral.

I finally relinquished the hold on the crystal by my divine feminine and allowed my divine masculine to hold the crystal in a hand-over-hand swap. Now, my left hand was placed over my right with my right hand holding the crystal at my higher heart. I felt like I was held in the arms of angels, of Faith and Archangel Michael. As the feeling of this realisation manifested, to my amazement, I instantly felt my quartz laser point buzzing through my hands in validation. The thought *it's the wand of Archangel Michael* entered my head, and I questioned this, as he carries a sword not a wand, but then I reasoned that I was to now use the crystal as my healing, prayer, and meditation wand for use in my connection and work with the angelic realms to help bring me clarity of purpose.

My understanding from this was the importance of balance and polarity to enable us to do our best work in service to God, and for the highest good that also helps us to remain with our feet on the ground to be able to manifest from spirit to the physical experience and vice versa. It is also a perfect example of being a warrior with angel wings and embodying the Divine Feminine and Masculine within, which can keep us in truth and authenticity and from being swayed by the many misinformed and deluded ideas that are prevalent, especially with social media and television media that can mislead and breed fear, hatred, and violence.

It helps us to stand alone in our own truth, and to rise above the dramas of life. The masculine principle corresponding with the sun is a creative force, active and *doing*, and manifests in the world of action and getting things done. The feminine principle, corresponding with the moon, is a passive force and *being*; it is nurturing, loving, and receptive. The masculine part of us and the feminine part of us, whether we are incarnated as either a man or a woman, complement each other and are representative of the Divine Principles of the God and Goddess within us. If everyone worked on their own inner being, understanding the wisdom of these teachings, imagine what miracles would be manifested in the outside world!

Awakening to the idea that our bodies are literally the bridge between heaven and earth with angelic light beings moving up and down it like a ladder to God is very empowering and uplifting. Just knowing this can awaken the joy that is within you. It can sweep away depression and anxiety in an instant, enabling you to lead a more fulfilling life by feeling whole and complete within yourself and attracting relationships into your life based on love and respect and honouring of your own space rather than getting into relationships in order to fill a need, which fills the space with all manner of ills!

About the Author

Karen Tants is a wife, mother, and grandmother who lives in Central Victoria, Australia. Karen is also a Reiki and Seichim Master Teacher, as well as a self-published author. Karen is a member of the Self-Realisation Fellowship founded by Paramahansa Yogananda. Having attended many courses, it was while journaling during a psychic development course when the floodgates opened, allowing her intuition to flow through the medium of writing. After documenting countless dreams, visions, and past life experiences, a deep desire was awakened to express and to flow God's wisdom, teachings, and guidance towards self-mastery, empowerment, and healing in order to open up to a higher heart unconditional love and joyful being.

Karen Tants is the author of *Soul Magic-Spiritual Alchemy, In Silence Your Garden Grows, and In the Presence of Angels.* She is also a co-author in the anthology *From Fear to Freedom.*

Facebook Author Page: Soulful Pen-reflections, guidance and healing.

Website: *www.bluelotusangelicreiki.weebly.com*
Inspirational Facebook community pages: Heaven's Healing Angels; The Wisdom Portal

Rushingspirit
The Bravest Thing I Have Ever Done

It started with a phone call I *never* thought I'd receive from my brother, Tim. It went something like, "So, Tammy, if I told you Dad was going to be at Scott's house and everyone thinks it is a clever idea that you see him, would you go?"

Imagine dead air and the penny dropping at the same time. I guess Tim got stuck with that part of the weekend my brothers had been plotting to put together. I hadn't seen Al in about thirty years. The air had gone out of my lungs. Time stood still. Twenty-nine years, four months, and fifteen days washed away like they never existed. The two amazing children I had without him around, the *many* years of searching for ways to heal and become whole, all washed away. There I was, standing before someone who took away what I use to think of as my own personal happily-ever-after, which included a white picket fence and Prince Charming, or at least my ability to believe that white-picket-fence theory or any hope of being successful or loving someone, maybe even loving myself.

Who was I kidding? I never even got to experience the thought of happily-ever-after. I had no clue what that meant because, apparently, I wasn't special enough to get it. My sperm donor abused me sexually, mentally, and emotionally. Sperm donor. My ex-boyfriend hated that definition, but in my world, all he did was provide the sperm. He didn't raise me, he didn't love me, and he sure as hell didn't shape me or show me what I should have in life.

I grew up being asked why I was laughing. "You have nothing to laugh about. Why are you crying? You have nothing to cry about. Why this? Why that, and you have nothing to back up what you're feeling right now, so you need to not be feeling it." In addition to being told I would never amount to anything, I also grew up having sex with someone who was supposed to protect, love, and guide me.

I remember the first time it happened as if was happening right now. Sperm Donor had just gotten home, my three brothers and I were watching *The Apple Dumpling Gang Rides Again*. Or maybe it was the original movie. It was 1975 and I was seven years old. He walked into the house and said, "Load up the truck. We're going to the flea market."

It was in Wisconsin; I can't remember exactly where. We lived in Saint Paul, MN on 5th Street next to a Church (the irony is not lost on me). The boys got excited and Mom got to work doing whatever she did. He stopped and said, "Boys, I am taking Tammy."

They were crushed, and because I was still *pure*, I was excited. Super excited that I now got to see what the big deal was about all of this "flea market" stuff! So, with truck loaded and camper readied, off we went. It was raining, but off we went anyway. We stopped at 7-11 on the way out of town, and he purchased some Pabst Blue Ribbon beer, otherwise known as PBR. On our way, again, we started to cross over into Wisconsin just before the bridge that takes you into Hudson. We pulled over, he gets a green blanket out of the back, and then he gives me a beer. *Huh?* I am seven! As he hands the drink to me, he says, "You can, Chickadee (his nickname for me). It's okay." It tasted *nasty*, and since then I have never touched that crap again.

My whole life changed. That is when my first experience with sex began. He wanted a blow job. I was way too young, and of course, my mouth was too small. He showed me how to give him a hand job instead. That is why he grabbed the blanket— to hide what we were doing as we drove down the road to our destination, even though it was dark and rainy. When we arrived at the flea market, he had sex with me. Then he got up, told me to clean myself up, and left. Just left me in the trailer alone in a strange place loaded with *strangers* and went to see his girlfriend. Yup, he was cheating on my mom.

I don't think I need to elaborate any more than that. I was told it was my fault, that no one would believe me. I was treated like a second-class citizen and left at home to clean the house while they all went fishing. A note on the table told me to clean while they were out. Never asked if I wanted to go. Guess what? I wanted to be fishing too! Nothing I said was considered, nothing I wanted mattered, and anything I felt was demoralized. I was ten years old when he and my mom won $5,000 at bingo. My two older brothers got dirt bikes. I got a $20.00 (if that) transistor radio. It was ugly green with a strap to carry it over my shoulder. The strap was orange, green, and white, I think, and had terrible reception.

That was around the time I almost died from my appendix bursting. "Five hours to live," the doctor told my Mom, "if she hadn't gotten to the hospital." That was how long I had, and that was scary. They had put a tube in my pelvis area to drain the fluids from the appendix. It had to be taken out due to an infection, and they put in a new one. No medicine, no surgery. Nothing! I felt like they were pulling a tennis ball through my stomach. Then they took hemostats and pushed another one in through the incision. You know the bands they use to tie around your arm when they are taking blood? It was one of those. I was holding onto my mom's hands so tightly, she had to release them and have me grab onto the railings. I can see her standing at my bedside so scared and white as a ghost from my grip. Al must have been home with the boys because I don't remember seeing him there.

I started drinking when I was seven and started smoking pot and cigarettes when I was nine. It's a logical conclusion, right? If I can drink at seven, I can smoke at nine. I also started wetting the bed. Mortified is all I can say about that turn of events.

I also became withdrawn and quiet. *Ya think!* When I finally went to my school counselor and told her what was going on, my whole life changed again. I finally spoke up when a movie came on that I wanted to watch called *Something for Amelia*. Al wouldn't let me watch it due to the content of the show. It was about sexual abuse. We ended up watching *The Pod People* instead. Google *Something for Amelia*.

Fast forward thirteen years, and I was quickly becoming a drug addict, alcoholic, and a bitch with an attitude. I was also a new mom and ruining my life and that of my adorable baby girl's. Her dad fought me for custody and won, and what an a-hole he was. However, I was the biggest loser. I lost the first person who ever showed me what unconditional love meant on both sides, the one who cracked that petrified tree of mine. You know that thing they call the heart? I got every other weekend for quite a few years, and eventually, she came back to live with me full-time because her dad treated her like Cinderella. I had to heal her from that. Of course, that is a whole other story. We have also concurred on that. *Yay, us!*

I vowed to face whatever I could to change my victim status into an "I can survive, no matter what you said or did" status. It took some time to really start diving into the healing. I didn't know that was what I was doing back then. I do now. My first healing moment came when I realized I was reacting to everything and everyone as if the sperm donor was *still* standing in front of me, telling me what I could laugh at, cry at, or even like. Telling me that I was no better than my cousin, Mary Therese, who, at the time, was lazy and four hundred pounds. Saying I would never amount to anything.

I needed to stop and really look at a situation and think *how do I* really *feel about this? What* do *I want from this?* Believe it or not, that first healing came from a Tarot card reading I was giving to a friend of mine, Tara Davidson. I was doing the Celtic Cross layout, and I could *never* remember what the #7 position meant until that day. It signified how you felt about the situation you were inquiring about. I truly had no idea what I felt about anything. I interrupted the reading to tell her all about it. She loved it, and we continued on with the reading. That was the most freeing day of my life. I started participating in my life, asking questions I really wanted to know the answers to.

I was court-ordered to go to Alcoholics Anonymous. I did go, but I hated it. I ended up going to Narcotics Anonymous and stayed in the program for about eleven years. I was there due to crank; it was the speed before meth. I still allowed it to mess up my life. I have not gone back to doing drugs, but I do drink. Drinking was never my problem, although if you asked someone in the program, they would say alcohol is a drug. Period. Whatever works for them. It worked for me for eleven years. Then I decided it no longer worked for me. I can do that, you know? I am an adult.

My biggest battle at that time was to *connect*. I mean really connect with people other than my kids. I can tell you I broke the "abuse pattern" and cherished, ruled, and raised my kids with *love, love*, and more *love*. I showed them I was the boss while still cherishing everything they were and everything I knew they could be. *I love you, brats!* But I have major intimacy issues. I trust no one with my feelings or anything else personal. I still attract people who blame me, all because they can't take responsibility for their own actions. The severity of the blame has diminished tremendously over the years.

Nonetheless, there is still work to be done. I look at it like a gauge of how far I have come. Also, so that I can speak up and tell them to shove it, basically. I had to learn how to speak up for myself. I had to stop giving Al the power. He had been out of my life for years, which is why when the penny dropped; I agreed to go to the *next* step in my freedom phase, a phase that had been going on for thirty years.

Fast forward another sixteen years, four months, and twenty-three days. I am face to face with *him*, and I was going to be around *him* until the 6th of July 2013. I was worried about the bed wetting more than anything. Because as soon as I reported him, I stopped until I wore his favorite pajamas. I threw those away, and it never happened again. I arrived in Ohio at Scott's house. The first three days, I was very distant, working *really* hard to not make my brother, his wonderful wife, and my nieces pay the consequences. My mind whirled, spun, and basically wouldn't stop. I had no idea *how* to open my mouth to ask for what I needed. At one point, I asked my brother to start the conversation.

 That was not going to help me at all. If I really wanted any sort of healing out of this, I needed to initiate the conversation by myself. Friday afternoon rolled around to about 3:00 or 4:00. We were sitting on the front porch, Scott, Mary Ann, Al (sperm donor), and I. I finally thought *now or never*, so I leaned forward and said, "You know, Al, I need two things from you: an apology and to hear that it is not my fault."

Win! Just as I leaned forward, this cocoon of love and peace enveloped us. My brother would say it was God, but this healing wasn't for him and his beliefs (no offense, Brother). It was the angels, it was Spirit, and all beings of love and light, with my mom playing a loving role in it as well. Al said that he couldn't differentiate between a child and a woman. That he got his ass kicked in prison. He got his brow beat into believing that what he did was wrong. He said he was sorry, that it wasn't my fault. There was a bit more to the discussion, however I don't remember everything that was said. Shortly into it, though, Mary Ann had gotten up and went into the living room (she has a very sensitive soul, truly can't handle the pain of others). Quite frankly, I had at one point wanted to do the same thing.

I couldn't though, for the simple reason that I needed to finish it once and for all. My brother said I had to leave there forgiving him and calling him Dad, so I might as well do it then. I said that I didn't have to do anything I wasn't ready for. Actually, my exact words were, "No, I don't." Al said he couldn't make me do any of that; I needed to do it on my own. The only thing we ever agreed on. And another story of meeting someone in the middle of Sturgis (the big bike rally) who was in prison with him, knew my grandma (his mom) and loved her, worked with her at the Cambridge State Mental Hospital, but felt bad about her having to have one son in prison. Not for Al being there, but because no mother should have to go through that.

I had a lot to process. Did I believe what he said? *Yes and no.* Did I *really* want to believe? *Yes!* Did what he said make sense? *More yes than no.* I had *a lot* of growing I needed to do, and I wasn't exactly sure what the benefits (for me) and side effects (for others) were going to be. I looked forward to what it would bring. I had suffered from fear of success, fear of abandonment, and downright *fear* of personal connections, addictions, afflictions, and trauma drama.

What I neglected to tell you was that on 4/12/04, I lost my *amazing* gay mother. She told us kids after I turned in my sperm donor that she was gay, and she had known she was gay since she was young. I was so hurt, mad, and confused. I blamed her for a while. If she came out of the closet, I never would have been damaged or even born. Yet, I realized the world would have been denied of my awesomeness and my two "amazingly wonderful brats" who are my world, life, my *true loves* and the *light* of my darkness! My brothers and I would have also been denied getting to know Anna Banana, her widow. We love her; she is very much a part of this family.

I originally wrote these four years ago. Since then in 2015, he mailed me a rosary. I finally responded to that and wrote him a letter. It took me a few months. After his stint in prison, he became a born-again Christian. *Hey, whatever helps him sleep at night.* I am not a Christian. I call myself a recovering Catholic or a spiritual person, witch, and psychic medium. I have no issues with born-again Christians or any religion, for that matter. We are allowed to have our own beliefs.

When I wrote the letter, I informed him about my beliefs, what had happened in my life due to *his* actions, and what happened because of mine. I wasn't accusing or blaming, merely stating facts. I also stated that if he wanted any kind of relationship with me, he needed to keep religion out of it. I included my phone number.

He didn't listen, started sending me all kinds of religious things, and even said I worshiped the wrong God. I never judged his God. I just asked him to be real. Again, it took me a few months to respond, but when I did, I told him to *never* contact me again. That I could believe in whatever God I wanted, and that he wasn't religious in his soul, only in his ego.

I also told him that he didn't care what he did to me as a child, and he didn't care now. Otherwise, he would have respected me enough to start with something simple, something real, like, "How's the weather down there," or, "What are you doing for work? Do you like Florida? What are my grandkids like?"

Since he couldn't do that, I chose to make the healthy decision and cut him out of my life. I tried, he failed. Again. I refused to be ignored or berated for what I was given at birth. My right to say this is okay, and this is not! What is the bravest thing you have ever done? Every story of bravery is different. Not harder than mine or easier. Just Different.

In Love & Light, Rushingspirit

About the Author

My name is Tammy Rush; I have 2 AMAZING children. An adorable Grandson and I am a survivor, of Sexual, and emotional abuse. I am a Psychic Medium, a warrior and now an Author. I am also writing an Auto-Biography; as well as co-creating a website called Rushingspirit.com for readings. I do have a day job, but soon that won't be a part of my life. Therefore, I won't include it in my general information. I work a lot with the Angels, Spirit & the Dearly Departed. One of my earliest childhood memories, is seeing my Uncle Ray moments after he had passed. He came to let me know that he will take care of me. While I traversed the abuse, I was about to endure.

Jess Kawecki Adams is my SOUL Sister, one of the other Authors in this book. I hope you enjoy the book as much as we loved writing it.

Danielle Alaina Ellis
Divine Inspiration

It was a Saturday morning, and I awoke in a relatively good mood. I could not believe how fast time had gone. It was my daughter's fourth birthday already, and I had a party to organise. After waking both my son and daughter up to the sound of me singing "Happy Birthday," I had two very excited children.

After the opening of presents and breakfast, it was time to get a move on, as I was expecting guests. So, with both children happily settled and my little cat, Jasper, fed and watered and off on his travels, I made a start. Within a few hours, I had everything ready for the party with just the banners and balloons to go up. I decided to put some on the front door, as well as on the gate outside my house. On the way, back in, I saw my little cat attempting to play with the balloons on the gate, and I tried to call him in, but he refused.

I left him to it, but how I wish I would have made him come in.

Within ten minutes, I heard lots of screaming outside and someone calling my name. I looked out the living room window, and my heart sunk. It was my poor little Jasper. My neighbour was crying, saying she loved that little cat. I lived in a house on a very busy road, and it looked as though a driver had been speeding, hit my cat, and drove off. So, there he was on the pavement outside taking his last breaths. He was only nineteen-months old. What was I going to say to the children, or more challenging, what was I going to do with him? In less than an hour I was going to have a house full of adults and children arriving for my daughter's party.

My neighbour was kind enough to assist me and kept him until after the party, I had to pull myself together the best I could for the sake of the children. The rest of the day passed in a blur, and with everything packed up, my son with my sister and my daughter with their father, I had to find out where I could take my cat to be laid to rest. He was my first cat; I never grew up around many animals, so what to do with him puzzled me, and I was still so upset.

I had to calm myself down, as I did not want to make myself sick. Eight years earlier, I had been diagnosed with epilepsy at the age of twenty-eight. It occurred later in life for me and pretty much put an end to my career back then. It regulated itself over time with the right medication, and I believe my positive attitude. My seizures reduced, and then only started happening in my sleep, and those got less and less, but stress and tiredness was a big trigger for me. They could quite easily cause me to have a seizure, which physically puts me out of action for up to three days until I feel myself again.

With this in mind, I tried to pace myself and get a handle on my emotions. I did not have to explain anything to the children until they came back the following day. I knew, like me, they would miss Jasper, especially my five-year-old son who is autistic and had a close attachment to his friend. The year had not been the best for us with an educational tribunal in relation to his schooling needs and right placement, which I did win, though I paid for it with how I was personally treated.

I'd had a meeting only a few weeks beforehand, as he was still only attending for a limited number of hours per week and with a schedule that was all over the place. After five months, we were still not happy, and the way the whole ordeal was making me feel was having an impact on my health. I had my first seizure in over a year due to the stress the situation caused, and now the situation with our cat added more stress. I would just have to explain to the children that he was in heaven with their grandfather when they came home. For now, I had to try to clear my head and think logically.

I prayed and asked for guidance, and before I knew it, I was doing an internet search and up popped an animal crematorium on a farm very close to home. I went and collected my cat from my neighbour, and my two best friends along with my brother assisted me in taking him to his final resting place. On the way, there, we somehow got onto the topic of psychics and mediums. I had been reading Tarot cards for a hobby for nearly nineteen years, and had always had a keen interest in the metaphysical and angelic realms, and was also a firm believer in the Law of Attraction, Law of Spirit, and Law of Service.

My friend pulled up to the farm, which was such a beautiful place, and I knew I had been guided to the perfect location. It was getting late by then—the day had faded into night—and I could see a lady standing at the doorway, and then she walked over to the car to greet us. Presumably, this was the lady I had spoken to on the phone.

She offered to take my cat from the car, which I allowed, and then I slowly followed her inside on my own with the others waiting. I was not expecting what happened next. The first thing this lady had said to me when I walked inside was that she had a recommendation for a medium she had seen. Considering that less than ten minutes before, I was talking about the same thing with the others on the way over, I knew it was a sign, and that I would be booking an appointment with this medium.

I said my final goodbyes and paid the lady. Heartbroken and overwhelmed with the day I'd had, I made my way back to the car, and my friend drove me home. At least I did not have the children that night, as they were with family overnight, but walking through my front door with no little friend to greet me made me sad. As the days moved forward, I learned to accept what had happened even though I could not figure out why. I had a great urge over the next week to buy myself several new oracle and Tarot card decks, with the love I had for crystals also increasing. My little Jasper used to sit on the end of my bed, watching me with my cards, and I always said he was different. He used to look at me like he knew something I didn't, and I said a few times to others that I thought he was an old soul and had been here before. I also booked an appointment with the psychic medium that had been suggested to me by the lady on that very sad day. She had a three-month waiting list, but I knew I had to see her and was willing to wait.

It was the week of my birthday, so I thought I'd treat myself, and that is what I did. Along with my new purchases, I booked a hotel for the night before a Mind, Body and Spirit

Event at a conference centre that I had randomly seen advertised. I felt pushed to go and figured it would be perfect, so when the day arrived, I was excited. I knew I would find something that would assist me on my path moving forward.

Walking into the venue, I remember thinking how great it would be to put on an event like this. I had a previous background in sales and marketing from the age of eighteen, and had even lived and worked in a few different countries in my twenties. I'd had a few roles that involved events, business events as well as property, and thought how fantastic it would be. I suppose I was allowed to dream. When I entered the event, I noticed there was a mediumship demo taking place in five minutes, so off I went to the room holding the workshop.

Within a few minutes of taking a seat and sitting down with all the other people who were wondering if they would get a message from spirit, the psychic medium approached me and straight away told me I'd find what I was looking for today and that my connection was earth. She also said that things were going to move for me very fast, and she really did not know how I was going to do it. I looked at her slightly puzzled, as she was doing the same, but it did make sense inside what she was saying to me, due to my being an earth sign and my great love of crystals.

Regarding things moving fast for me, I guess only time would tell. She then stated there was a very smartly-dressed man in spirit with shiny shoes who was very proud of me. He had passed suddenly and was not ready to leave yet. I knew instantly this was my father. He had passed away from cancer a few years earlier, and I knew he was not ready to leave this life because he wanted to see his grandchildren get older. This was a lovely message that gave me such warmth, and even though I knew and could feel my father with me in spirit, it was nice getting a message to confirm he was still very much around me.

Over the course of next few hours, I found myself buying crystals I was drawn to, and I attended an angel workshop and one on shamanism. I also had two readings that were very interesting, one with a palm and card reader, and the other with a medium. They both made a lot of sense and picked up a lot on what was going on around me. I was also informed, like I had been plenty of times in the past, that I had a gift, and in the future, I would use that gift to assist a large number of people with love, and that it was part of my life's purpose. At the end of the day, I checked into the hotel and treated myself to room service. I felt a great sense of purpose and knew I had to carry on listening to the divine guidance I was currently receiving. And as the months went on, that is exactly what I did.

I found myself drawn to several courses that I completed. First, I got my certification as a Tarot Master, so now I was certified after reading Tarot as a hobby for nineteen years. Then something guided me toward a course in lithomancy, which is Crystal Oracle reading. This was of great interest, as I was already doing an online course in crystal healing, and my knowledge of crystals and their healing and metaphysical properties was increasing fast. Within a few months, I had completed these courses and was then guided to a Certified Crystal Practitioner course in London that I booked. I also started a course to enable me to be a Certified Angel and Oracle Card Reader. I found myself receiving more and more messages from the divine, not only from the pushes I'd feel, the excitement when guided to find certain courses, and the feelings that I had to be at a certain place, but I also started receiving ideas and inspirations sent to me late at night, and I found myself writing, writing, writing. I was surprising myself with the divine inspiration I was receiving and continued to trust where I was being led.

The number of card decks and crystals I owned increased, and so did my thirst for more knowledge. Before I knew it, I had four certifications, and was then drawn to do a Certified Fairyologist online course. I was on a constant high vibration and excited for what the future held. I was drawn to an online crystal summit, consisting of a number of crystal experts speaking of their experiences and working with crystals, and there was one expert in particular who I felt drawn to. This all seemed a little different, and I really could not explain why I felt the way I did, but I had an overwhelming urge to contact this particular crystal expert. After doing some research, I found out he was also based here in the UK.

I had found his email address and felt very much guided to send him a message to introduce myself. I sent him pictures of my certifications and card decks. Why, I did not know, I just continued to follow my intuition and what my inner voice was telling me. It did cross my mind that he might think I was crazy, but hey, I was learning fast and knew if I felt guided to do something, then that was what I had to do.

Within a week, I found myself travelling over three hours away from home to attend a crystal workshop by the same expert I had contacted. I booked myself a hotel nearby and was excited to see what the following day held for me. The hotel was based in a small seaside town I had never heard of before, and whilst walking down toward the sea front, I had a feeling come over me that I had been there before. I just could not shift the feeling. I continued to walk past a very old fairground that was closed and made my way up to the sea wall where I found openings and steps leading down to a walkway with several benches placed along it that looked out over some fantastic natural pools and a sea view. I sat on a bench for a while; it was very quiet with not many people around. I felt calm, connected, and free. I watched the sun go down, and then made my way back to my hotel for dinner followed by an early night ready for the crystal workshop the following day.

The workshop was fantastic, and the day went by very fast. I met some fantastic people who shared my passion for crystals, and it confirmed to me that I was on the right path and that being a Crystal Therapist was also very much part of my life's purpose, which was evolving slowly in front of my eyes. The crystal expert was also of great assistance. I told him a few ideas that I had, and he encouraged me to follow my heart, giving me the kick I needed to move forward with the inspiration I was receiving. The time had come for me to have courage and faith that I was here to assist others, to set up a social media account, and share my gifts and inspirations to the world.

I was guided to use my cards and crystals, as I saw many others were on social media assisting others, and I was guided to a number of groups where I would be allowed to spread my love and light daily. I really did not know what to expect, but continued to do what I was being guided to do. The name Divine Inspiration was very much around me. Fifteen years earlier, I had actually put a business plan together with the name of Divine Inspiration. It was going to be set up as an online shop to sell cards, crystals, and dream catchers, while also offering Tarot readings. This never happened due to life taking me in a different direction. I had lived and worked in three different countries by the time I reached my late twenties, and I gained a lot of not only work experience, but life experience too. I was very much a traveler, had visited a number of different countries throughout the years. Different cultures, origins, and beliefs intrigued me. Over the years, I could see how that also assisted with the person I became.

Divine Inspiration - Angelic Crystal Therapy and Guidance was the name that was very much in my head and what I used along with a picture of some crystals for a cover page. I picked a picture of an angel I was drawn to for a profile picture, and after several guided trips to Glastonbury, the chalice well in particular with its healing waters. That place had also happened to be my happy place. I found myself taking the guidance of the Magician Tarot card that kept popping up. I had to stop procrastinating. I knew I had all the tools in my toolbox to move forward, so with strength and determination, I made a start.

After one month of simply posting a daily pick of a card, crystal readings, shared posts that I related to, and some posts of my own, I was feeling blessed. I had over a thousand friends and a thousand page likes. I gave a few free personal email psychic readings and was stunned by the response. It looked as though I really did have a gift to assist a lot of people, as I had always been told by readers. So, I had to stop pinching myself and start believing in myself and what I had to offer the world. I kept following the divine guidance that I knew all too well now, and trusted what I was being shown through feelings, inspirations, signs, numbers, and synchronicities.

Little did I know it was really only the beginning.

About the Author

Danielle Alaina Ellis: Certified Angel Therapist, Crystal Therapist, Psychic Consultant, Certified Tarot Master, intuitively reading for 20 years, Certified Angel and Oracle Card Reader, Fairyologist and Crystal Oracle Reader.

Being Claircognizant she is highly intuitive, and very much divinely guided in all areas of her life. The divine connect with her through thoughts, feelings, ideas, and inspirations. Being inspired to combine Angels and Crystals together within her therapy treatments, and psychic readings, Danielle offers the perfect healing and guidance, bringing heaven and earth together as one, to bring much needed balance, clarity, and insight into all areas of the lives of others.

With a strong belief in the Law of Attraction, Spirit and Service. She is very much an Earth Angel, and Light worker. With a large worldwide following, she spreads Love, Light, and shares her Gifts, and experiences with the World, which she thrives on.

With a back ground in sales, and marketing for many years; Events and Property in particular, she also uses her business skills to assist others with spiritually based businesses. Danielle is also in the process of organising a Mind, Body, and Spirit Event offering assistance to those locally on their spiritual Journey, whilst also supporting a Local Autism Charity close to her heart.

Danielle is deeply grateful, and feels blessed to be able to assist so many with her gifts, and states that it really is an honour, and will continue to follow her inner guidance with nothing but Trust, Faith, and the purest unconditional love.

Always sending out: "Love, Crystal Light and Angel Blessings!!"

Danielle Alaina Ellis

www.divineinspiration.me.uk
www.facebook.com/divineinspiration444

Pamela Lott Campbell
The Truth Changed Me-No More Chains

As far back as I can remember, I have been exposed to violence. I remember things all the way back to the age of three. It was nothing short of a miracle that I did not lose my mind. I watched my dad abuse my mom mentally and physically, and in turn, inflict mental abuse on his three children. I don't know about how my brother and sister feel, but I've resented him for that up to this day. My parents' relationship was so volatile that it left its footprints on the lives of their children. My brother became abusive towards me. He grew up treating me like I was a stranger. He'd punch me in the face, stomach, arms, etc., and did it hard enough to make someone think he was fighting another boy. My sister never liked me either. She did vindictive things towards me that were so disgusting, I don't want to mention them. All and all, I fault my parents for the three of us growing up angry. I, too, wasn't exempt from the anger bug. I grew up in defense mode. I fought my brother back like I was a boy. My sister would get the same treatment for acting ugly towards me. She and I have never been close. Still today, she calls all of her friends her sisters and not once acknowledges me except as her crazy sister.

At the age of sixteen, I ventured out on my own. By then, I had been affected mentally, physically, and sexually, and I could not stand the thought of being around my family any longer. Life got hard for me. I cannot remember a day when the sun shined in my life. I walked around mad at the world. I had so much rage bottled up inside, I could have exploded at the drop of a hat. But I stayed in school, kept my grades up, graduated, and moved onto the next difficult phase of my life.

I was pregnant and a mother at eighteen years old. My son's father was a serial cheater, and by the time I was twenty-two, I had had enough. I moved on from him and fell into the arms of a one-night-stand that would prove to be a nightmare. I got pregnant again. Now, I had two children at the age of nineteen and no one to turn to. Both fathers were absent, and I was lost. Things went further downhill from there. I ended up shacked up with a very abusive narcissist just to have a roof over our heads. He made no bones about cheating on me, as he told me to my face. What could I do? I was dependent upon him. There was nothing I could do about it.

Not long after the one-year lease was termed, I left him and moved into a shelter for women and kids. I was embarrassed, to say the least. However, that did not stop me from feeling empowered. I finally got away from an abusive situation that I would never return to. Living in a homeless shelter was extremely depressing. My mind was all over the place. I had nothing and no one except the two children who depended solely upon me—a teenage mother who felt like a failure and who hopelessly wanted to die. Where did I go wrong and why? I never wanted kids. I never wanted to walk the path I was walking, but there I was, treading not so lightly towards destruction. A personal destruction that no one could fathom.

As the years went by, my life began to spiral out of control. I would love to say that everything is a blur, but that would be the biggest lie ever told. By the time I was twenty-three, I'd given birth to two more children. I became a single mother with four growing, needy babies and nothing in the world to call my own.

What is really going on with me?

I was determined to find someone who loved me and would keep me because I had no one and neither did my children. Sure, I was physically present, but mentally I was a basket case. My life was a rollercoaster, and the ride was as rough as it could ever get. I had to do a serious reality check, and when I started to do that, I did not like what came up. There I was, a young, beautiful, smart, talented, and extremely intelligent girl, living a life as if I'd been raised by a pack of wolves.

Who am I? What have I become? I had dreams and aspirations while I was growing up. Where did they all go?

By the time I was twenty-five, I'd had enough. I buckled down and decided to pray as fast and hard and consistently as I could. The night I made that decision changed my life forever. I prayed for life. I prayed for the generational curse to come off me and my children. I prayed for peace. I prayed for hope. I prayed for new beginnings. I prayed for everything and anything positive, and before I knew it, three hours had passed.

When I got up off the floor, I felt as if I was in a time warp. The room wasn't the same room in my apartment. There were no walls, no furniture, no windows, just a bright consistent light. To my amazement, I wasn't afraid. I was calm, as if I knew I was supposed to be in this moment waiting patiently for what was about to occur.

I remember as clear as the sound of a bell a voice saying to me, "Go upstairs and shower."

I did just that, and as I showered, the low, gentle voice said, "You have done well. You have not disappointed me." The voice explained how to clean old soul ties from my spirit and how to be free to live with no shame or regrets from the choices I'd made up to that point.

I knew I would never be the same after that night, and that the truth of it all would be my truth. I learned that words have power, and whatever you speak to the universe from your heart, mind, soul and/or spirit, the universe will give back to you exactly the way you intended. To me, that is what karma is. If you do or speak wrong, you reap that wrongness, and the same goes for doing good.

The old me died that night, and I woke up ready for the next phase of my life. Words can't express the entirety of my gratitude for having this awakening. I can say with certainty that the laws of attraction gave birth to something remarkable inside me, and from that point on, I started to remind myself to always expect great things. Nothing anyone could ever say would move me the way this remarkable experience had.

I was faced with my family turning their backs on me, no friends to be found, mean and judgmental stares from people who knew my past, and got the worst of it all from the woman who gave birth to me. No one ever understood why I was estranged from my family or why I never let anyone get close to me, and as far as I was concerned, it wasn't for them to understand. My journey was mine. It was tailored just for me. There is not one person in this world who could come up against the trials that I have had and match my exact experience. For that I am grateful. I am unique in a sense that there is only one me, and the best person to tell my story is me. No harmful, spiteful, despicable words could ever harm me again.

All of this transpired after I attempted suicide with my kids in the next room. There was someone watching over me who would not allow me to die. Those three hours when I lay on the floor praying was revealed to me when I rose and found the room different. It was as if I was talking while drifting away. It wasn't Heaven or Hell; it was the void between the two. I wasn't given a choice; I was reborn—new—in mind, body, soul and spirit.

That voice/the spirit guide/the angels/God was not allowing me to be successful in dying because my purpose was far from being fulfilled, and I was worth saving. I felt no side effects, no pain or anguish from dying. It was as if I was in a dream, and the experience left me when I woke. From that point on, I have given my time and effort to mentoring the young people and women who I meet. Being in a job position dealing with people is a great point of contact to initiate true community service. Not in the worldly sense, but the spiritual sense. I have reached and touched many lives. Is it overwhelming to take on other folk's problems? Indeed, but with all that I realized through the frustration, I would not have changed one encounter. Life is all about choices.

Even though I died that night, I was given a second chance at being the best me I could possibly be, and I went through great lengths to do so. I spoke *life* to everyone I talked to, I gave encouragement for downtrodden young mothers and young men headed down the wrong paths, I even gave myself resuscitation a few times after being totally exhausted with the service that I took on. God expects us to be brothers and sisters and treat one another with the respect and honor that He does. It's taken me baby steps, of course, but I have grown and matured to see life from a different perspective. I am far from perfect and will always have flaws, but I will continue to speak *life*, expect great things, and be the best me I can possibly be.

Being great and expecting great things is extremely complicated. I get tired and weary of "complicated" things, people, and situations, but I realize God wouldn't have it any other way, and because of that one truth, I came to crave greatness and continue to expect great things from life and the people with whom I surround myself. With all of this happening, I can honestly say that I have grown from things set in place to break me. I've gotten stronger and wiser by the day, and I owe it all to God for ordering my steps and listening to me with an always-understanding ear. I will never look back over my life and assume that where I came from up to where I am now is all there is. I must tell myself constantly that this is life. It's a journey down a road less traveled by many, simply because the footprints in the dirt are authentically mine.

I tell myself that I am a strong, beautiful black woman, and I walk with my head in the air because I am wondrously made. There is something to be said about the strength, essence, and beauty of a black woman. There is not one thing on this planet that compares to her. Some women are born with strength. The essence and beauty flourishes effortlessly through their DNA. Others work hard to maintain and possess their strength. In doing that, pure essence, *earned* essence, flows and shows as transparent as the color of their skin. That hard work and perseverance displays a beauty unimaginable to her even after she has obtained it. That particular woman who I am speaking of would be me.

Before this awakening as far back as I can remember, I had never thought very much of myself. I had always thought and felt like my very existence was questionable, and there was no real reason to be alive. There is nothing more refreshing than knowing that I have become a much more enlightened and aware woman. I am aware that God has blessed me in ways that I never thought possible. I have my health and strength intact, and I am accomplishing things that I had only dreamed of. I can actually see the results of the words that I speak, the thoughts that I have, and the feelings tied into both. I am much more aware of how to speak, when to speak, and what to speak about.

Nothing can damage a person's spirit more than the powerful words that roll off their tongue. I haven't become completely delivered from cursing, but I can honestly say that I think more now before I speak than I ever have in my life. I have known that somebody has been watching over me for a very long time, and I am not about to go back to that negative spirit that I groomed from a child with a broken spirit and a broken, lonely heart.

All of this that I write about is my truth. This is my testimony for the chapter that I am about to close. As I close it, I will continue to remember that this is not who I am anymore, but a vital part of the journey that has gotten me in a better state of mind and a more grateful spirit than I have ever had in my life. If I never do or say anything else, I will say that I lived because God wants me to. I will continue to live this blessed life according to His purpose and His plans for me.

There is a lot more work to do, and I am not about to let anything disturb my peace and wellbeing. I think happy because I am happy. Am I rich with millions of dollars? Not at all, but I am rich with a spirit of thanksgiving and gratitude, and I will continue to spread that in the space that I am in. I have learned to love myself, treat myself well with meditation, healthy eating, and healthy relationships. Life has not been easy for me, but I will honor the years I have left by being better to myself than I ever have before. I have learned to be convicted and passionate about what is right and just, and I do that with ease.

No more turmoil or strife will occupy this one body that I must continue to reside in until God calls me home. Seeing is believing, and I believe with every fiber of my being that life has just begun for me, and I won't take it for granted. I will live a blessed and spiritually, financially, morally, mentally, and physically abundant life because it is God's will for me, and I will join Him in that. I deserve to be happy and to live a life of abundance, and I will go to the ends of the earth to ensure that it happens just like that. I speak *life*. I will live. I will be happy and joyous and all because I am grateful for the new lease on life that God has afforded me.

I am a woman. A woman of strength, love, and character. A woman who makes no quarrels about good and bad or right and wrong. I am an empath on a journey of unchartered waters. A journey that is new to me, but perfect for me. I have a zest for life that has caused me to thirst for knowledge of self and the world around me. Unbeknownst to me, I have embarked on a venture down a road I must travel alone. I know that this could be a life-changing journey, but I also know that it is necessary for me so that I can appreciate where God is about to take me and what He is about to bless me with.

To end this chapter, I would like to add that I am now clear on what life is about. I know that life is to be lived in abundance paired with joy, love, and happiness. I am grateful for being alive and well because I am happiest when I am healthy and can focus more on living life in all its splendor. I am grateful for a good night's sleep because I have grown to appreciate being still and the importance of listening for God to speak to me. I am grateful for the manifestation of a higher vibration because I can attract more positive things and people as I face the challenges and hurdles that I may encounter to strengthen me. There is absolutely no end to the things I am grateful for, and for that, I am also grateful.

I love the woman that I have become. Because of her, I hold no grudges and no ill will toward anyone who has hurt or harmed me. I love me because I am in tune with who God has created me to be, and I am on a path to greatness. The only thing that can ever stop me from reaching my full potential in life is me, and I don't plan to go backwards. I'm moving full speed ahead toward my purpose in life so that I can fulfill my purpose and live a healthy and abundantly prosperous life while doing so. I end this chapter of my life with love, peace, blessings, and glory as I declare all things great and wonderful. This is my absolute truth. This is my "now."

About the Author

Pamela J. Campbell is a native of Memphis, TN, a single mother of four adult children, and a proud nana of five grandchildren with another on the way. She is extremely family oriented and wants nothing but the best for her loved ones. She studied Business at Draughn's Jr. College in 1994 and proceeded to work in a flourishing housing market as a Leasing Agent, ensuring potential tenants got the best lease for their dollar. Passionate about housing and people, Pamela worked diligently to be promoted to a Property Manager position. In 2009, she decided to be more diligent in an effort to help people. She landed a job position as a Certified Housing Specialist, working in the Section 8 (HCVP) program with the Housing Authority in Memphis, TN. Grateful for an amazing career, Pamela made a transition from the Housing Authority and combined her education and experience to land a position as a Certified Tax Credit Property Manager with a SCHM (specialist in housing credit managements) designation issued by NAHMA (National Affordable Housing Association).

Currently, she is pursuing her childhood passions of writing and becoming a published author.

Melinda D. Carver
Stepping Boldly Out of the Shadows

I was born with the ability to see Spirits (loved ones, guides angels and more), Auras of people and the future events which would happen to them. Attending a wake or funeral meant seeing the recently departed flit about the room among the living. Going to the woods or park meant playing with fairies. Walking into a hospital meant seeing ghosts. Starting kindergarten meant seeing colors and energies of new classmates and the teacher. Vacationing at historical sites meant seeing and hearing what happened there in the bleed-through energies. Talking with my Spirit Guide was an almost everyday occurrence.

Being born with these abilities did not always make my life easier as a child. Sometimes I was hushed by family when I spoke out loud. Other times I was not believed when I said I didn't want to be somewhere because the energy of the place or the people inside made me sick. Sometimes I was teased in school for being "freaky" for saying what I saw would happen to a friend. Other times these friends would look at me in fear when these things came true. Learning quickly that speaking out meant being met with disbelief, fear, anger or mockery, I stopped talking about what I saw, felt, or connected with.

I stopped talking about Spirits, auras and future events to the people in my life. Just because I stopped talking about it, that did not mean that my abilities also ended. It was a shadow side, a hidden side, of my being. This movement into the shadows lasted most of my life. Occasionally things would slip out. I would peek out of the shadows every now and then to family or friends, but would quickly recede once more when I was met with jeering or fear.

Even though I hid what I could do from people, I would still use my abilities and I could speak with my Spirit Guide, Claudius. He was always around me. When I was a kid, I thought he was a deceased family member – like an uncle. He never changed his appearance; he was always calm, telling little jokes, and even explaining in detail what I "saw" when I was unsure. He would comfort me when I was not believed or was teased. Claudius would assure me that I was "normal". He would declare that one day people would not run in fear from me.

Being aware of a Spirit Guide from childhood has sometimes been like Pinocchio having Jiminy Cricket on his shoulder. Jiminy Cricket was Pinocchio's conscious, attempting to guide him through his new "alive" status. I remember as a child watching that Disney movie and understanding what Claudius was to me. Claudius commented on the choices that

I made all during my childhood and teen life: the friends I spent time with, the boyfriends I chose, all these other little decisions. He would always make some sort of quick observation, running commentary or hand gesture while I was growing up. Sometimes I tuned him out or blocked him, especially in my teen years. I would do what I wanted and would refuse guidance. Other times I would ask him what my other options were. I was very rebellious as a teen with my parents, and just as headstrong with Claudius.

Hiding my abilities in the shadows became easier as I grew into adulthood. For a long while, I completely tuned Claudius out. I wanted to be more like other people, not having to be half way in this world and half way in the Spirit world at the same time. During this darkest period of my time in the shadows, not hearing or speaking with Claudius became my new normal. It was weird to have silence around me, for I had become accustomed to his guidance and observations. Occasionally, he would fill my vision or try to communicate with me, but I would double down on blocking him. Silence. I wanted silence from all Spirits and for a short time I had it.

I did not want interference or guidance; I wanted to choose people, jobs and things on my own. New friends, boyfriends or coworkers were not aware of my abilities. I stayed firmly in the shadows so that I did not scare them away. Bosses were never told for fear I would be fired. Sometimes though, they would look at me and say that I was too insightful, or too independent in the way that I thought or acted. Numerous times I had to hear that I seemed older or more knowledgeable than those around me. My abilities would come peeking out again, meeting fear or anger – so I would scurry back into the shadows. Silence. I thought silence would bring acceptance.

After a while, I no longer felt whole. I felt that I was missing something living so deeply in the shadow side. I was not happy, trying to deny a part of my own soul. It felt darker and colder and I was tired of always hiding what I was and a large part of what I could do. I was exhausted from not speaking up. Sometimes it took great effort to juggle what I was actually told by a person and what I knew psychically about them. I was worn out from not living fully. Something was missing from my life; I just did not know what I needed. I began to hate living in the shadows.

One night, I sat at home by myself contemplating making some personal changes. I did not know what I wanted to do. Decisions are usually very easy for me, but I grew frustrated. As I sat there, I stated out loud "I just want some answers!" A few minutes later, I heard a knock on the door. I answered the door and no one was there. Sitting back down, the knocking began again. One more time to the door, and again no one was there. Then I heard a loud male voice ask "are you going to let me in?" Ah! Recognition kicked in. I knew that voice, one I refused to listen to for a couple of years. It was Claudius. He greeted me like old friends normally do after a long absence apart.

When you open the door back to your Spirit Guide, things begin to move quickly. One of the first questions out of Claudius' mouth was "are you ready to step out of the shadows?" That was a loaded question for me to hear. Did I want to put myself out there as seeing future events for people, seeing their dead relatives, or knowing more about them through their colors and energies? Could I handle people's disbelief, fear, teasing or anger? With my guide by my side once more, I felt more in control of my life. Claudius told me it was time to move forward in living my destiny – I needed to choose.

I stepped out of the shadows slowly at first. I began by letting close family and friends know that I could read Tarot and loved to attend psychic fairs and expos. Small steps, but doable. Not everyone ran screaming from fear out of my life; only one friend. For a couple of years this was my new normal. Showing my true self bit by bit to those I was closest too. Claudius applauded these steps as well as urging me to stride further out.

Eight years ago, I stepped fully out of that shadow world. I declared in public that I was Psychic and Tarot reader by working my first large expo – a women's lifestyle expo – in my very own booth. I was the only psychic there among the retail stores, salons, and service industry providers. Of course, Claudius was right by my side. I remember how nervous and worried I was as I waited to hear the reaction from the general public. He told me not to worry; I would help some people and provided amazing help to those that needed it throughout the two-day show. Only two women ran from me, while other ladies I spoke with were excited to meet a real psychic. I provided readings to about 25 women that first show. Claudius said "see, this isn't so bad!"

A week after the women's expo, I was providing readings at my booth at my first metaphysical expo. I had finally stepped firmly onto my path, embracing my destiny. I was in the world that I belonged, helping others out in public. Since that first week eight years ago participating in two large expos, I have never looked backwards. I announce loudly and proudly to people who and what I am. I am a Light Warrior.

I embrace all that I am: an author, a psychic medium, Tarot reader, teacher, energy healer and radio host.

My guide Claudius cheers me on, proud of me for shifting firmly into my power as a Light Warrior. The shadows no longer call to me. I do not need them. Allowing my true self to shine, to feel whole, to prosper and to be in a state of happiness was a huge step from living in those shadows. I serve those that need spiritual guidance and healing. I serve both my human and Spirit communities. Life is beautiful in the sunshine.

As a Light Warrior, I no longer dread other people's reactions to what I am. Their fear, dismay, mockery, and anger are their own, not mine. Yes, some people may scatter when they learn I am a psychic medium, but I no longer allow them to push me into that shadow space. I have declared my victory over the shadow realm.

Claudius protects me as I tread forward boldly, waving the banner of Light Warriors from the past, the present and the future. He has never receded from my everyday life; he is no longer blocked from my life. My new normal is a life filled with abundance: new people, opportunities, travel and happiness. My light shines forth around me. Claudius holds my hand as I stride forward confidently, successfully and in pure joy. These abilities that I have were mine in many lifetimes, and returned once more in this one. They grow stronger each day that I work within the Light. I am a Light Warrior; I vanquish the darkness. It is my calling, my fate.

Do you hear the call of your Spirit Guide? Will you move willingly out of the shadows? Are you eager to embrace living as a Light Warrior? I urge you to step out of that half-life you have been living in the shadows.

Now is the time across the Universe for us to create love, harmony and peace. It is time to raise awareness. It is time for the evolution of our souls. Those living right now on Earth are hearing that call to action. This energy strums within you, aching to be released. Are you ready to leave the shadows?

Grasp onto your Spirit Guide's hand firmly. Take a deep breath, and march out upon the battlefield. Your guide will not release your hand. Step boldly from the darkness that you have been hiding within. Allow yourself to stride into the radiance as a Light Warrior. Vanquish the darkness of the shadows. We welcome you! Shine on you; beautiful being of light!

About the Author

Melinda Carver is the Official Psychic of the Tarot Guild and hosts Positive Perspectives Radio. She is the author of Get Positive Live Positive; Clearing the Negativity from Your Life. Melinda has appeared on TV, radio, magazines, expos, conferences and corporate events. She is the creator of an award-winning magical product line, Melinda's Positive Products. She stars in 13 titles of the Holistic Highway to Wisdom DVD Series and is featured in two books Eternal Magick and Reflections through the Veil.

Maria Cefalo
Activate Now

"Have you ever sat at your desk, facing your printer that doesn't fully work wirelessly, but it is printing and copying and scanning? It's awesome, right? And you find yourself looking at your computer that was given as gift from the Commission of The Blind in Boston, MA. A wonderful and beautiful state. A state that represents the blue for hope and will."

Maria Raffaela Cefalo is a warrior and the glue of her family. She received her Masters of Education and Creative Arts in Cambridge, MA at Lesley University. Her passions in life are to grow, learn, and create. As a girl who turned into a warrior woman, she is always looking for ways to allow her heart to grow and for ways to challenge her brain to problem solve.

Maria lives in the Boston area and is grateful for all of the resources and services around her. As an author and illustrator of the children's book *If Dreams Could Talk*, she is here to tell others that anything is possible and to believe in yourselves and never give up hope. To be a warrior and female in this world means putting your pineal gland into therapy mode.

"Allow yourself to be challenged, don't give up, and allow the unknown to not sway you from who you are."

The Author wants to Allow you to Activate NOW in the space provided below:

_____

_____

_____

_____

_____

_____

_____

_____

Use this space to Draw your dreams, visions and life!

About the Author

Maria is also known as Zia Raffi. Zia Raffi inspires all the children to be majestic rainbow creations, and she gave her nieces names, such as Rose Light and Rose Heart. Maria has been a teacher for over twenty years, and she teaches compassion and unconditional love. Her message to the world is to be in the now, breathe, and ask yourselves what you can do in this moment; be present.

 Remember that people who cannot see need a friend to see, so be there for them. She believes that we are all here to work with each other; that is our highest purpose. Her message is to stay strong, don't give up, activate *now*, and be an elemental dreamer. "Practice self-love and dream your dream."

Maria is a female warrior, Zia elemental dreamer, sister, daughter, teacher, author, student, creator of majestic rainbow creations, friend, and soulful person on this journey we call life!

A. Sibyl
Reality Slap

Marla had made the house beautiful. She had spent a wonderful morning in the rainbow-colored rooms of her home in Iran. Every year she would paint the walls different colors to keep life new and fresh. This year brought canary yellow into the living room, purple for the girls' rooms, orange for her son, and her own bedroom had turned sky blue, pleasing her immensely with a calming influence on her emotions. She walked among the rooms in a state of gratitude and serenity.

She was burning incense to mimic the perfume of the sacred temples and mosques she loved so much. Now that she had lived in Iran for eight years, she had found numerous positive points to cherish in the strange new country. The scents and sights of the religious experience had captured her interest from the moment her plane landed in Tehran. Everything was new and completely unlike her life in Northern California, but she felt welcomed wherever she went.

Spending her first twenty-five years in the USA had not prepared her for her future adventures in Iran, but she had found much in the country to enjoy. From freshly baked bread on every street corner to the unparalleled religious fervor during sacred ceremonies, she had been wooed by Iran. At age twenty-four she had fallen in love with her Iranian husband, but the love affair with the country had come unexpectedly and with much gratitude. Among the various treasures Iran had offered her, her husband's house in the northern province of Iran was one of the greatest gifts.

She arrived at her new dwelling in the middle of the night. With no pictures of the house beforehand, she was totally unprepared for her first encounter with the wonderful space. The house was enormous, all covered in a gentle crème-colored stone and surrounded by a stone wall, as are most homes in Iran. The stone wall connected to a front and side metal gate opening to the street and alley. The house had two stories with an underneath courtyard and parking space under the second floor. The ground level apartment had a bathroom, kitchen, one bedroom and one sitting room that were later remodeled into Marla's teaching classroom. The second floor was huge with ten-foot-high ceilings, stained glass doors, and a wonderful kitchen full of cabinets. She was wonderfully surprised and pleased when she first arrived at her new house in Iran.

Now, eight years had passed by and life had happened. Unfortunately, the walls had not seen much peace and pleasure in that house, yet as Marla looked around her home, she felt proud. Her morning had been spent dusting and sweeping. She had picked flowers from the garden and spread them around each of the rooms. The children's bedrooms were organized and tidy with clean sheets and bedding. The rooms smelled like sunshine and fresh air. The windows of every room were adorned with red and white curtains she had sewn using local fabrics. The entire house spoke of her love and devotion to her first home in a country far from her native homeland. She sat on the couch, full of pillows she had made, and inhaled the delicious smell of home.

She had prepared a traditional lunch of potatoes with fried chicken in a tomato sauce, rice, and salad. It was not a special occasion, but Marla was someone who looked for opportunities to have fun. She was in a cheerful mood because of her gratitude for the little things in life. She had been alone all morning and she was pleased to have had the time to herself. Most of her waking hours were usually spent caring for her three young children and attending to the needs of her husband, Alborz. So today, with an entire morning of time, she thoroughly devoted her heart to filling the space of her home with love.

As she took a few moments to admire the work of her hands, she began to ponder time. So many hours of her day were always devoted to the service of her family. She woke at 5:00 a.m. every day of the week. She prepared breakfast and then drove her three children to three different schools around the city. Once she returned from dropping off her children, she would clean up the morning mess in the kitchen, prepare for lunch, and head downstairs to teach her private English classes. After her classes, she would prepare lunch, go to pick up the children, and then the afternoon tasks would begin: homework, sports, exercise, art class, language class, and many more as ages and desires changed. On hundreds of occasions, Marla would look at the clock at 10:00 p.m. and be shocked at the passage of time.

Today, she had no classes and her husband had driven the children to school because he had some business with which to attend. He rarely woke before 10:00 a.m. on typical mornings, so to have an entire morning of peace was a rare gift. As she closed her eyes to bask in the fulfillment of her clean and much-adored home, she heard the front gate open. Alborz had returned for lunch. She stepped to the front door and opened it for her husband. He peered into her eyes with anger and slapped her in the face with his left hand.

"I heard you talking on the phone to someone. A man! I know! Give me your cell phone!" he yelled and went to search for her purse.

"You must be hearing things, Alborz. I wasn't talking to anyone, perhaps my own self." Marla contained her tears. She worked to inhale a breath, to recover her composure, when suddenly, in a moment of intense sensitivity, she heard a voice speak directly to her heart:

Turn your other cheek to him. You are no longer afraid of this man. Fear will no longer exist in your body. All of your fears are now washed away as you forgive this soul and offer your other cheek. You feel no anger or frustration. For the first time in all these years, you feel nothing but unconditional love without any anger or resentment. You will soon be free from this man and this life. You will soon be completely free because fear is no longer with you. You have passed this part of your soul's test. You are free. Fear has gone from you forever.

These words passed into Marla as a beam of white light hit her in the back of the

head. She felt the voice to be from Jesus. In that instant of revelation, she felt loved beyond any sensation she had ever known of love. Internally, she was revolutionized in that moment. Externally, she stared silently at the man she called husband.

"Shut up, you whore. I know who you are. I know you hate me. I know you want to get away from me." He pushed her away, grabbed her purse, and was dumping out the contents to look for her cell phone.

Marla quietly reached into her pants pocket, pulled out the cell phone, and threw it onto the couch next to all of the odds and ends of her purse.

"Is this what you want?" she asked and turned to walk into the kitchen.

"Where the hell are you going?"

"I need to turn off the stove or else lunch is going to burn." She spoke as if he were a stranger and a guest. She was unbelievably calm. After years of hearing abusive words, which had usually disturbed and cracked her inner peace, she now only felt detached and distant as he continued to harass her.

"Fuck lunch and fuck you!" he yelled and grabbed the collar of her shirt. Alborz pushed Marla down onto the couch.

"Now, tell me who you were talking to! Tell me who the hell you were talking to!" Alborz sat with one knee pushed against Marla's chest. After a few seconds, he pushed her away as she maintained a strange calm silence.

Upon her release, Marla crawled over and slouched down on the couch. She focused on her breath and her prayers to be released from her husband's unfounded jealousy. She knew that this was only the beginning of the harassment. She had experienced her husband's paranoia before on many occasions. Many times, she had been forced to hold tight to her spiritual rope of faith while he continued with his chaos and violence. She knew it was only a matter of time, and she felt more patient than she had ever remembered feeling. Now that fear had flown away from her heart, she decided to speak.

"I spoke to no one. We can sit here for days and the same answer is going to come your way. Just look at my cell phone and you can see that I have made no phone calls over the past two hours." She spoke evenly, managing to sound almost friendly.

"You could have deleted your calls. I don't trust you, Marla. I will never trust you after the iron pill incident." He looked at her as if she were a criminal.

"Are you kidding me? That happened ten years ago. Why do you insist on bringing that up again and again?" She felt the angels watching. Years prior, she had not obeyed her husband and had taken an iron pill while pregnant for the baby. She felt justified, but he used it to prove her a liar forever after.

"I'll drop it this time because I'm hungry. Now get up and serve my lunch." He took off his pants and went to wash up for lunch.

Marla stood from the couch and went into the kitchen. Unlike other slaps, she had not experienced the shattering of her heart with this one. She quickly set up the table for lunch. The children would not return from school for another two hours. This gave her some relief as she sat down to eat. She remembered the joy and happiness she had been experiencing only moments before her husband's arrival. She thought of that time and realized how oddly opposite to the moment of now, her current state of unforeseen pain, and a new awakening to fearlessness.

They ate in silence. Marla could not bring herself to look at her husband. The sound of his chewing food had always bothered her as she felt him defiling the food with disrespect. Perhaps she was merely feeling her own suffering in the helpless bites of food in his mouth. She was sorry for the food entering his body. She didn't wish to be anywhere near his body, yet she stayed for her children and for her marriage vows.

They had married seventeen years earlier. They had met in the states during university studies. She had seen the distant future of adventure in his eyes and had fallen in love. She had changed her entire life to please Alborz, yet satisfaction never came. He was never truly pleased with her. Marla, on the other hand, had found much satisfaction in her children, her religion, and in her fortitude over the years. Never had she thought it would be possible to become so patient and disciplined. She had not once imagined she'd marry a Muslim man and become a submissive Muslim wife. Everything had been accepted by Marla, and she had submitted to countless forms of abuse.

Yet now, a revolutionary sensation settled into her consciousness. After seventeen years, she tasted no fear. She had lived every moment of her married life afraid of her husband. Yet now, all such thoughts had left her. She chewed the food in her mouth with the greatest satisfaction she'd ever known. As she sat staring at her empty plate, her soul began to fly joyfully and wildly with the knowledge that these words would guide her to freedom:

Turn your other cheek to him. You are no longer afraid of this man. Fear will no longer exist in your body. All of your fears are now washed away as you forgive this soul and offer your other cheek. You feel no anger or frustration. For the first time in all these years, you feel nothing but unconditional love without any anger or resentment. You will soon be free from this man and this life. You will soon be completely free because fear is no longer with you. You have passed this part of your soul's test. You are free. Fear has gone from you forever.

About the Author

Born and raised in Northern California, A. Sibyl developed an intimate relationship with the natural world. She experienced a typical American upbringing with much freedom and fun. Her childhood and adolescence did not prepare her for the alternate reality she would enter upon marriage. At age 24, during a short hiatus from her university work, she met and married an Iranian Muslim man. Upon taking her marriage vows she became a Muslim and remained one for the duration of her married life. She finished her M.A. in English Language and Literature at Central Michigan University during the spring of 2004 and traveled to Iran the following summer. She and her husband had three children during their marriage.

These three children were the glue which kept her in an abusive relationship for seventeen years. April 7, 2014 A. Sibyl fled the country of Iran leaving her entire life, children, and all she had acquired during her marriage. She currently teaches English Writing and Reading courses at the University of Hawaii Maui College. She is currently writing a book about her experiences in Iran titled, "Unveiling Your Strength" and she is thrilled to be sharing a bit of her story in this anthology.

Susan Hook
The Broken Angel-O-Meter

I have spent the last two years in my bedroom. The only reason why I have ever had to come out is if I want to make some food. Otherwise, my husband brings me meals. The bathroom is attached to the bedroom. Therefore I don't have to walk far. In this time, I have gained 50 pounds, which is a surprisingly small amount given the lack of exercise and my calorie intake. The weight gain would not have been a critical issue had I been at a healthy weight, to begin with. But as of today, in fact right this minute, I will go weigh myself - hold on - I weigh 310 pounds.

I have spent the last two weeks in Montana. I drove there from my home in Colorado, by myself, as the first act of breaking free of this self-imposed prison. I visited a friend from Facebook, where all of my friends gather. As I grew more and more isolated, I found a solace in starting an online business as well as developing a close-knit community of friends. My doctor had suggested that I start out by taking short walks to the mailbox and back each day, to break my isolation, leave the bedroom, and get some fresh air daily. Because I don't know how to do anything "small" I decided instead to drive to Montana.

Now, I am home from my amazing trip, and I have a lot to tell you about courage and Angels. When I first had the idea to write this story based on my trip, I had second thoughts. I was sure that you would want to read some hair-raising tale from my shady past, and perhaps you would! Who knows? Maybe I will have time for both stories.

The Montana story doesn't lack in courage just because it is rather mundane. If I broke down my vacation into its basic components, there was a lot of driving, staying in hotels, staying at my friend's apartment, eating, and shopping. You might be asking yourself, "What do those things have to do with Angels? Or courage?" I have asked myself the same question. It's why I was having a really hard time getting started on this story. I connected with my Guardian Angel in prayer and meditation, and the message that was coming through to me loud and clear is that Angels desire to help us in every situation of our lives. It is we who make the decision that a situation is "too easy" for the help of Angels.

When I decide, a situation is "too easy" for their help, I try to do it myself and find that often I can't accomplish what I thought was so "easy." In the "hard" situations, I generally forget to call on the angels until I'm exhausted or pushed to the brink. Apparently, inside of me, I have an "Angel-O-Meter" that measures which situations call for Angels and which ones don't. I am being told by my Guardian Angel,

Stella, that my Angel-O-Meter is broken! I wouldn't doubt that one bit.

She is also telling me that it isn't fair to bring up talking to Guardian Angels without telling you how to do it. Everyone has a Guardian Angel, regardless of religious affiliation or lack thereof. Angels are completely non-denominational.

They have absolutely no judgment about what you believe or don't believe. They are only motivated by love and a desire to help any human being that calls on them. It is important to keep things simple when it comes to Angels, not for their sake, but for ours. To meet your guardian angel, the first thing to do is ask. They are with you at this very moment while you are reading these words. When I first asked to meet my Guardian Angel, took about three weeks for us to make contact. Keep in mind that your Guardian Angel is with you all the time around the clock.

 However, we often do not have eyes to see things that are happening spiritually. The first time I became aware of my Guardian Angel was when I kept seeing the color yellow in my peripheral vision. I kept thinking someone was walking next to me wearing a yellow shirt or perhaps a sweater, but when I would look no one was there. It slowly dawned on me that this could be my Guardian Angel.

Step two of meeting your Guardian Angel consists of talking to them. I tend to talk to myself, the older I get, and so this was not a big problem for me. If you are not prone to talking to yourself and concerned about how it might look, put a Bluetooth headset in your ear, and everyone will think you are talking on your cell phone!

When I first started talking to my Guardian Angel, it was awkward. I wasn't receiving any response, so it was like talking to me, except I kept waiting to hear back from someone! If I had, I probably would have jumped out of my skin. Do I hear from my Guardian Angel now? Yes, I do. It usually comes as a thought or an idea and then I realize hours later, "Oh! That thought was much too clever for me to have come up with it! I bet that was Stella!"

Another thing that comes to me at this moment (probably from Stella as well!) is that you might be wondering, "How does she know her Guardian Angel is named Stella?" The truth is I don't. The other truth is, Guardian Angels don't particularly care what we call them, and they are fine with any name that we feel comfortable with. You would be surprised at how laid-back Guardian Angels are!

Let me wrap up my journey to Montana story so I can tell you the other story as well. How did a person that was house-bound make it to Montana and back, alone? Angels. Straight up, I talked to them every mile that I drove. I asked the Angels for so many things I felt like a kid in a candy store asking, "Can I have this? Can I have this? Can I?" When we are asking, Angels are at their best. They love it when we ask, ask, ask because they want to give, give, give. They really are here to help us. They understand that being a human is difficult.

We deal with dense energy here on this planet; so much negativity and suffering floating in the energy around us. They are here to lift us and guide us – to always hold out hope and help to us whenever we ask. "Believe," I am hearing. That is the message I have to share with you. "Believe."

I promised that I would give you a really dramatic story about my Guardian Angel, and of course, I will. But I have to admit; it took many, many years even to realize that my Guardian Angel had been there for me. I wonder, if you look into your past, will you see times that you received supernatural assistance but maybe didn't realize it was an Angel?

This particular incident happened over twenty-five years ago, but it is still as vivid as the night it took place.

I was eighteen years old and dating a dangerous man. I didn't realize how dangerous he was when I met him. He was charming and handsome and funny. To me, he was just Dan. The fact that he had a bald head, swastika tattoos and wore clothes as if they were a uniform, all of that escaped me; I was ignorant and admittedly naïve when it came to the reality of prejudice in its most vile forms. Dan was a "white-power skinhead" – a white supremacist who was deeply aggressive and full of hate toward any race other than Caucasian.

It wasn't long before his true colors showed, but by then, he had become deeply attached to me. I attempted to break up with him, but it was difficult to shake him. He was not a solo skinhead; he belonged to a group. He had his friends follow me and keep tabs on my whereabouts day and night. They left dead animals on my front porch, exploded firecrackers in my window wells, spray painted graffiti on the exterior of anything I owned. Of course, I called the police but was told that unless he hurt me, there was nothing they could do. That was quite discouraging!

As you can imagine from the people I was hanging out with (like Dan), I wasn't exactly as pure as the driven snow! I was into the punk rock movement, and I think that my Mohawk and black leather jacket might have sent the wrong message to the police when I met with them. As you can also imagine, going to church was not on my to-do list. But when Dan's predatory behavior increased, I slipped into the big Catholic Church in my neighborhood. Taking the back row and sitting alone, a single tear fell onto my lap. I remember praying for my life. I was truly scared and had no one to protect me. It was one week from the day I sat in the church that Dan attacked me. I was walking home from work in the evening. I rode the city bus, got off on a busy street, and then had a hike of about 12 blocks through the darkened side streets of downtown Denver, Colorado.

He came out of the shadows, and I didn't see him until he was on top of me. I fought him the best I could, but he had a hundred pounds on me and was all muscle. No could hear me struggle; no one could hear my screams as he muffled my mouth with his large hand. At first, I thought he wanted to rape me, and in my head, I had made peace with that until I realized he had his hands around my throat and was intent on killing me. I thrashed and struggled beneath him as kaleidoscopes of color swirled in front of my eyes. I clawed at his hands which only tightened his grip. Right before I passed out, I saw a bright light above me. It was directly above my head.

I remember being very confused, thinking that the police had arrived, but wondering how in the world they were hovering above me. My last thought as I lost consciousness was that a helicopter must be landing, but it really made no sense to me, even as everything went dark.

I woke up several hours later; in the same place, he attacked me. My throat was painfully sore and swollen, but I was alive. I was breathing! I tried not to move my head while I glanced around. Where was he? Where were the police?

A woman arrived by my side. She had a cool cloth, and she laid it across my forehead. She spoke gently to me and told me that I was safe. She said she would take me home and I wondered how she was planning on getting me there. She didn't seem to have anyone with her, and there were no cars or any transportation that I could see. Besides, she didn't even know where I lived. I dropped off to sleep again, with her stroking my hair and telling me that it would all be OK.

The next time I woke up, I saw flashing lights and felt myself being lifted onto something, then rolled – it was the back of an ambulance! How did they get here? Who called them? Then I fell asleep again.

She came to me one more time in the hospital. She had that cool cloth again and laid it on my head. How had she known that my parents had always done that for me when I was little and felt sick? She was the most comforting presence I had ever known. She told me I was deeply loved and that I was saved. I thanked her for calling the ambulance, and she laughed quietly. She said all was well and encouraged me to go back to sleep. I found out later from the doctor that I had been in a coma for three days. All of the things that I had "seen" well, he says they were just dreams. But I know better.

My Guardian Angel was there with me. My prayers were answered. Whatever happened to Dan, I don't know. No one ever heard from him again. He wasn't in Denver any longer. When I was released from the hospital, it was as if he never existed. That was fine by me. Here I am now. I'm fifty years old, and my life is not nearly as exciting (thank goodness!) But I still depend on my Guardian Angel and the Archangels, primarily Michael (for protection) and Raphael (for healing). It is a wonderful life living with the Angels. They love me, and

I love them. I am protected, cared for and never alone in this big world. Oh, and one more message before I end my story. You are never alone either.

Whether you need an Angel to help you get out of bed in the morning (when I lived with depression, that was often a big act of courage!) or you need their help as you drive across country to a place you've never been before, or you need their help in a life-threatening situation, they are always near, always ready to help. Just ask. Don't let a broken Angel-O-Meter tell you that your situation is too small – or that it is too big! They love you more than you know and are here to help you in any way possible. Being human is hard sometimes. They are here to help it go easier.

About the Author

Susan Hook is an experienced intuitive and energy healer. She has been trained in multiple modalities and utilizes all the spiritual gifts of clairvoyance, clairaudience, clairsentience, and claircognizance in her private practice. She excels at helping people live in alignment with their soul purpose and most enjoys coaching relationships where she can work one on one with women and men who want to improve their lives. She holds certifications in numerous areas of study such as Angel and Oracle card reading, Tarot reading, Life Coaching, and more. She is skilled at Akashic record reading, where she is able to discover her client's soul origin, divine gifting, and how to remove the blocks and restrictions that are keeping them from operating from their divine nature. She received training and certification from Doreen and Charles Virtue and is an Angel Therapy Practitioner® and an Archangel Life Coach. Susan has twenty-five years of experience working with the Angels and using her spiritual gifts. She has helped many people break destructive patterns, heal relationships, and set their feet on the path toward fulfilling, productive lives. She is the founder of a support group on Facebook called "Spiritual Support for Intuitive Women," which has become a thriving community of close-knit women. She teaches and leads discussions weekly, sharing life, love, and her gifts with the group. In addition to facilitating the women's group and running her business, she enjoys reading, meditating, journaling, and Pinterest. She has been married to her wonderfully supportive husband for twenty-nine years and they have five grown children and three beautiful grandchildren. If you would like to connect to Susan, there are numerous ways to find her on the Internet. She enjoys hanging out on Facebook and Pinterest and always welcomes friends and followers. She also enjoys Instagram and of course, is a member of LinkedIn and Twitter. If you want to experience a breakthrough in your personal life, she highly recommends starting by meeting your guardian angel and scheduling an Akashic reading. You can contact her through her website or her business page on Facebook for more information on all her services.

Facebook: https://facebook.com/oracleofthespirit
Twitter: https://twitter.com/oracle_spirit
LinkedIn: https://linkedin.com/in/oracleofthespirit
Pinterest: https://pinterest.com/oracle_spirit
Instagram: oracleofthespirit
Website: http://oracleofthespirit.com
Email: oracleofthespirit@gmail.com

Jessica Kawecki-Adams
The Light in the Dark

I had a happy childhood in suburban Southern California; sunshine, citrus trees, the ocean a few miles away and only the cares of a seven-year-old to concern me. I had a hardworking, divorced father who loved me and cared enough for two parents. Since my mother was gone, I think he felt he needed to always give. I never felt the absence of a parent, ever. He encouraged creativity, art and thinking "outside of the box". At the same time, he was also strict and expected tidiness, good grades and was pretty conservative with his thinking, especially in the realm of education, religion and spirituality. He was never a fan of organized religion so that stuff was never discussed in our home, which goes back to his baby boomer childhood in the church back in Pennsylvania.

As for me, I was very sensitive for as far back as I can remember I used to hear things, see things, and smell things and sense things. I always seemed to have the innate ability to feel what others were feeling, even if I didn't always know what I was feeling myself. But that was life, right? At least to me it was. Everywhere around us, something was happening. *Life* was happening. Another life living, breathing and existing; another soul on its path to places I scarcely understood. I never thought this was abnormal or that I was different; because if I was aware of all these things, then surely everyone else must be aware as well, right? Of course, at that age my mind didn't rationalize it like that. It was just the way that it was...and I was open to it all. Young and innocent and open, this was just how I lived my life in those days. But it was difficult being so aware. It would leave me drained of energy and my emotions seemed to be all over the place at any given moment, like fallen leaves being blown about by a cool, autumn breeze.

As far back as I can remember my dreams have always been very vivid. I would be able to tell a complete story, leaving no details out, when sharing my dreams with others. So, when I awoke one night in my pitch-black room and saw a shadowy figure standing mute at the foot of my bed, letting my eyes slowly adjust to the silent darkness, I wasn't initially shocked or scared. I remember thinking that this was all just another dream. While keeping my eyes steadily on the figure, I slowly reached my arm over to my nightstand and pulled the chain cord to turn on my bedside lamp. Light flooded the room and the figure was gone, much to my relief. Smiling bashfully to myself, I decided that it must have obviously been a dream. Nevertheless, I noticed that my body had become unconsciously tense with unseen apprehension. After silently chastising myself for being silly and with only the sound of my heart beating in my ears, I sighed and reached back over to my lamp and pulled the cord and prepared myself to settle back into a peaceful sleep.

After the light went off I glanced back towards my feet and there he was; the shadowy figure at the foot of my bed...only now he seemed larger. Darker, *Closer,* Closer to me! I froze my body heavy with the weight of fear as the undertow of dread began wrapping its cold fingers around my heart. My stunned seven-year-old mind could not comprehend what was going on, but something deep and primal inside of me was utterly terrified. He wasn't there a moment ago when the light was on...and yet here he stood. Here *something* stood. Shaking myself free from the cold grip of fear and struggling to regain the use of my body, I grasped blindly for the safety of my light as fast as I could and pulled. Just like before...he was gone and I was alone.

As the warm light of my personal salvation flooded the room with both light and relief, my mind raced to come to terms with what I had just seen, how something so surreal could be true. "Ok, you must still be dreaming," I thought to myself. "Turn the light back off one more time, just to see." So, I did, albeit with my eyes closed. Still holding the chain in my hand like a lifeline to safety, I slowly loosened my grip and felt the cool metal begin to glide silently across my fingers. I felt a chill come over me and told myself it was the cold, hard metal, nothing more. With a deep breath born of faith and fear, and a pounding in my chest I only vaguely recognized as my heart; I slowly opened my eyes and looked to the foot of my bed. Enveloped in the darkness was a deeper shade of dark. A shadow in the shape of a man, only this time, he was leaning over the bed with one solitary arm reaching out.

He's looking at me. HE SEES ME.

Stifling a scream, I yanked the light back on so fast that I nearly broke the chain and jumped out of my bed in blind fear, bolting out of my room completely numb. I stood outside of my bedroom door, looking down the hall to my dad's room...a room that had never seemed so far away before. I contemplated running in there, but what would I tell him? There is a shadow, or that there was a *ghost* in my room? He didn't entertain those kinds of things; ghosts weren't real in his mind.

They didn't exist, except for in the movies. I thought to myself that he would probably think I was just having a bad dream. I was even second guessing myself. So, I waited for what seemed like forever and once I finally regained the courage to go back into my room, I crept quietly back in. My heart was pounding in my ears; my throat was dry and my senses were electric from the terror that seemed like a lifetime ago. Gathering what little composure I had left, I began to apprehensively look all around - in my closet, under my bed, behind my curtains...nothing. With not a sign of anyone or anything in my room, I carefully crawled back into my bed and studiously began to tuck myself under every blanket that I had. Not daring to turn off my light and the safety of its illumination, I slowly fell back into an uneasy sleep thankfully devoid of dreams.

Morning came, as mornings do, and when I awoke I lay in my bed just looking around and thinking. Eyes heavy with the memory of sleep and thoughts weighed down by the uncomfortable gravity of my situation, still unsure if what I saw was reality or a *very* vivid dream. I sighed deeply to myself as I came to a decision and I got out of bed and decided to go find my dad. I wanted to tell him about everything. I went into our den; my favorite room of our house. It was a big room with a projector TV and a large double chase to watch movies on. One wall was full of brightly lit windows and a door that looked out over our covered patio in the backyard.

When I entered the den, I noticed the door was open and heard noises outside on the patio. I padded out through the door and got a good morning and a smile from my dad as he was watering our plants. Before I could mention anything about what happened last night, he asked me if I had just woken up. "Yes," I replied. "Why?" And his reply is something I won't ever forget, as I can still feel the chill deep in my soul to this very day. "While I was out here watering the plants there was a knocking on the window, coming from inside the den. I thought you had gotten up, so I asked what you wanted but didn't get a reply," he said, still watering the plants. "Then I heard the knocking again, so I repeated the question and still no answer.

I heard the knocking one more time, so I opened the screen door and took a look to see what you were doing...but no one was there. Did you come out and try to trick me?" he asked with a warm smile on his face. I stood frozen in place as my heart began to hammer, my face a mortified mask of shock and dread. In a hollow voice that sounded distant and small, I told him that it wasn't me and that I had just woken up and come to see him. I was too scared to mention what I had just seen in my room that night; I was so confused and dazed. It was at that moment that the realization began to dawn on me that there was something in our house, something that was trying to get our attention...something that dwelled in the dark. But what was it and what did it want?

The rest of the day went by as usual, and after a time I began to settle once more into the calm complacency of childhood activities. We had a very large backyard with a pool and fruit trees. I would spend most of my days running through the trees and pretending that I belonged among them and then jumping into the pool, swimming as deep as I could, moving my body as if I were a mermaid exploring a new undersea world all to myself.

My imagination seemed to know no bounds! I was part of another world, at least until I was called to dinner by my dad. At the dinner table, I was so busy daydreaming and humming contentedly to myself that I hardly remembered to eat. But after I finished, I headed into the bathroom to shower and start getting ready for bed, like any other night.

As I was brushing my teeth and absently wondering how mermaids brushed theirs underwater, I caught a glimpse of something out of the corner of my eye - a shadow! It was large and startling and almost managed to scare me right out of my skin.

I dropped the toothbrush with a clatter into the running water of the sink and turned to face whatever it was that was casting the shadow. But as I turned, nothing was there. No shadow, no person, NOTHING. I nervously turned back to the sink and quickly finished brushing my teeth, with several furtive peeks in the mirror, and high-tailed it right out of the bathroom without a backwards glance.

Once I got into my room I took a calming breath and crawled into bed, snuggling myself into an extra comfy position. I reached for the familiar chain as I turned the lights out and started singing my favorite bedtime song softly to myself. That is the last thing I remember until I was jarred awake by my bed jolting violently. I was so startled that I sat bolt upright in confusion...and there he was staring right back at me. Again, I was frozen in fear as my heart began its now-familiar crescendo in my chest. My will to move melting away like the echoes of twilight suspended in dusk. I couldn't speak.

All I could do was feel the terror inside me grow like an unleashed animal, filling me with dread. We stared at each other in the silent darkness for what seemed like an eternity before he began moving towards me - again! His left hand reached the foot of my bed, his fingers seeming to caress the bedding, and his shadowy body started leaning forward eagerly as if he were going to climb into the bed with me. I squeezed my eyes shut. I didn't want to see it anymore. I couldn't!

Once my eyes were closed I began to hear a whisper deep in the back of my mind, fighting through the fog of fear. "It's ok," it said to me. "Turn on the light." But I couldn't move, couldn't budge - not an inch. I sat there transfixed, eyes clenched shut. The bed was now beginning to undulate beneath me. Closer to me...closer. The fear of him and his presence renewed the whisper in my mind. Now spoke again, louder. "Turn on the light," It beckoned. A pause and then sternly: "*NOW.*" Shaken free of the shackles of fear, I wrenched my eyes open as I flung my body towards my nightstand to pull the chain of my lamp.

The light seemed to blaze forth in a wave of relief and with agonizing slowness and trepidation, I looked over my shoulder. He was gone! Trembling with apprehension, I got out of bed and slowly, methodically, looked around my room. In the closet, under the bed, the dark places...anywhere I could think of, I looked. He was truly gone. Not a trace of him remained. With a relaxed sigh, I climbed back into bed and grabbed my little diary. I started writing everything down so that I would never forget. Trying not to leave out any detail, I wrote:

Tall man
Dark short hair
Dark eyes
Brown Jacket, kind of ripped and old
Wrinkles on his face, but not too many
Small thin lips, no smile at all
Looked lost and empty

As I wrote these things down, my mind was racing. Who was he? What did he want? Was he bad? As I asked these questions, I heard answers bubbling up to the surface of the chaos swirling in my mind. He was stuck here because he wasn't a good man and that fear that I felt in my core, he brought to others in life. I didn't understand the thoughts I was having; I was so unsure of myself and all of the things that I believed. Just like my dad, I believed things like this only happened in scary movies. And I didn't frighten easily, as my dad and I loved watching scary movies and suspenseful shows together in that early 80's melting pot of cinema.

It was never real...but this was different. This was *real* and it was happening in *my* house. The only thing that I was absolutely certain of at that very moment, as I sat looking over my diary with the first faint hint of a smile beginning to form was that this...thing, this shadow person: it didn't like the light and I controlled that. He didn't! I could send him away with one flick of my wrist. I was the light in the dark.

After that night, my bedtime routine was noticeably different. I had gotten the coolest new nightlight and it stayed on, *every night*. I still had the occasional odd experience in my house. Things would move around, noises that weren't easily explainable; but I never saw that shadow man again. With everything that had taken place over those few short days, I learned a lot about myself and about what was really out there.

I learned that I had strength; I learned that I could overcome fear and I learned that the light always takes away the dark. I never forgot this experience; even as I sit here and write these words, over three decades later as a married mother of four; it has shaped the woman I would become.

Always remember that you are in control of the light.

About the Author

Jessica Kawecki-Adams has been writing since childhood. Her poetry and short stories were a favorite with many of her teachers, winning awards throughout her academic years. Poetry and music were ways that Jessica connected with herself and her life. Bringing her much needed comfort while she put the ink on paper, or strumming the strings of a guitar and singing away. Growing up in a home where creativity was never stifled, and greatly encouraged; Jessica was gifted a vintage typewriter, much like the one that a favorite author of hers plied his craft upon. She spent many nights typing away on those long keys. That typewriter is still an item that she truly treasures.

She draws particular inspiration from her Polish Grandfather who lived through the horrors of World War Two solely by the virtue of his gift as a painter while a prisoner of war. Upon noticing the softness of his hands, he was conscripted to paint portraits of the officers and generals; showing her Grandfather that embodying your passions and creativity truly equals life.

Writing has always been a main passion for Jessica. Her other passions in life are her family, her spirituality, music and her business. She spends her days raising her children and being a wife and mother, and while her family slumbers, she works on her passions. Whether it is prepping her businesses next day of activity, writing whatever her mind has conjured up, or just singing while puttzing around her home and finally before bed, a little chanting and meditation to end the evening on a balanced note.

Jessica currently resides in Southern California

Email: JKA.Author@Gmail.com

Phone: 949-295-5176

Facebook Author Page: Jessica Kawecki-Adams Author

Facebook Business Group: Kissy Proof Lippies

Jade Delaney
Queen of Being

I'm sharing a little of my heart felt story with you. I actually have volumes of stories, lol!!! But the place to start is at the beginning.

I awakened almost five years ago, and yah, it was crazy wonderful, and scary all at the same time. Hands down the best roller coaster I've ever been on!

In this amazing adventure to see me, accept me, and loving me the way God the universe does. I found that I wasn't here just to exists, but to live, love, and laugh. As well as cry, and let go.

I've had everything, and lost everything. This includes home, children, and high paying job…. You think "this sounds crazy"!!! Not to mention the thought of jumping off a cliff lol!!! Which I did, but not to hurt myself, I did it to face my fears. I sat on the cliff looking down for about a half an hour. Thinking to myself "This is nuts "!!!

I remember my ex telling me that I was having a "midlife crisis" Still makes me laugh. Then I immediately thought "So does this mean I'm going to buy a corvette, and date an 18-year-old"?

On the contrary it wasn't, it was the open invitation from God. An invitation to live. Something that I'd never done really.

Also to trust, and grow, with the opportunity to share with everyone I could, this amazing love that I found. Through all of my trials, and tribulations. I've discovered that Faith taken in even one drop, can lead you to your dreams! To live passionately, without fear.

I am the Queen of Being
Being Love
Being True
Being the Light

About the Author

Aloha, my name is Joelynne "Jade" Delaney, I'm the mother of four beautiful children.

Join on me Facebook @ Queen of Being
Aloha to all of you on your Journey to Being 💗

Norma De La Mora
Ask and You Shall Receive

We all know life can change in a Split Second; it may give us many warnings and sometimes not at all.

My story starts on a Saturday afternoon. Started my day, like every other weekend; did the regular house chores, spent time with the kids and went about my day.

So, after a busy mid-morning I sat down next to my husband on the couch and talked about the details of my upcoming birthday. We had decided that I was going to have a night out with 14 of my closest girlfriends, we were going to rent a limousine, and go out for a night of dinner & dancing. I don't go out very much with the girls, but when I do I'm going to make it worthwhile!

During our conversation, we also decided we were going to take the kids down to the pumpkin patch.

It was October! Time to pick up a few pumpkins, so we can carve them up and put them outside our front porch. We agreed that everyone should go and start getting ready, it was getting late and it would be dark soon.

For some reason, I got the urge and great idea that I should make some yummy traditional snacks, (Churros) so when they come down after getting ready, they would enjoy some yummy snacks right before we left. In my household, they seem to be a favorite snack., so why not?

So, I started getting everything ready to deep fry them. I took a big pot out, nice long pair of barbecue tongs & poured lots of oil into the big pot. It has to be nice and full, get scorching hot so they can open up nicely. I stood there for a while, and made quite a few. I told myself okay you're done let's go get ready.

But then.... I second-guessed myself. I said no... I can make a few more by the time they eat them, they're going to want more; so, I decided to keep on making them. Which was a big huge mistake!

Lesson learned, always follow your Intuition or that gut feeling!

To be honest with you, I don't know exactly how and what happened. Everything happened so fast! I must have gotten careless, or just a plain freak accident not sure. All I remember is, that the tongs that I was holding opened up completely, and acting as a cupping hand splashing a great big puddle of scorching hot oil on me! Did I mention, I was only wearing a plain thin tank top! So NOT much protection. The hot oil landed all over my left arm, down to my wrist, on my chest and face. I could feel burning right below my eyes as well.

I was literally in shock! What did just happen? I didn't want to scream or scare the kids or my husband. I quietly and in disbelieve walked into the downstairs bathroom, I was trying to collect my thoughts. Trying to think; what just happened?! Did I really burn myself? What's going on!

At that point all my skin was Becoming red. and it was stinging everywhere. Pain was the word!

I didn't know what I should do, did not want alarm my kids or husband. But I also wanted to get proper care if needed. So, I quietly walked out and told my husband I burned myself...

With shocked looks on their faces, they all rushed towards me and chaos begun.

I was still trying to minimize the situation and I kept telling him that I was okay, that I was going to go take a shower with cold water to make it better. To my regret this made things worse. We ended up taking a trip to the local ER. I was in so much pain! It felt like everything was on fire!!
While my husband was driving, I was calling upon my healing Angels, Archangel Raphael please Surround me in a Cocoon of your emerald green healing light. Angels please help me!

Thankfully, when we got to the ER it wasn't busy. They were able to take me back to start care on me right away. At that point, I see my best friend walking in. She's a CNA at the hospital and so the crying game began! Watching her worried look and Tears going down her face, worried me even more! The nurse in charge said morphine! Let's give her a shot of morphine! Make her comfortable.

Luckily for me I was in great hands, in the hands of the divine & Great nurses and doctors! They right away cleaned and sterilized all my burns, surround me with cold packs special ointment. I was released the same day, after a few hours. I was told I had second and third-degree Burns, but I would heal, I would be in pain... but I will be okay.

After I go home I looked at my Burns and I couldn't help it but be filled with gratitude! Yes! I was in pain and I had burns on my upper body, but I had a gratitude! I knew it could had been worst! I know that my Angels and God were with me. Protecting my eyes!

I was looking at my face and I had two Burns right under my eyes; imagine if those drops of oil would have gone into my eyes! But yet they didn't. The healing process was very painful! Blisters were no fun! My clothing couldn't touch my skin without me jumping off my seat! I Couldn't tolerate warm water & cold water was so uncomfortable.

Every second and every hour I would call upon my healing Angels, thanking them for being here with me and taking care of me, as I notice it every day would be better. I was healing and I was healing fast!

As I was getting ready in the morning, I looked in the mirror and I notice I had a big blister right on my chin, I was beginning to scab and felt tight and looked horrible...I paused and I prayed.

Dear Archangel Raphael please help my burns heal, please surround my whole body with the emerald green healing light so I don't end up with horrible scars. (especially in my face)

I kid you not!! When I looked up after I was done praying, I looked in the mirror and where seconds ago I had seen my horrible painful looking scab there it was! I could see the shape of a Praying Angel!

I could see the wings with detail and the praying little hands. I quickly ran downstairs to show my husband, I said look, look they're sending me a sign that they're hearing my prayers and they're going to help me heal!!

I smiled and thanked them; this sure warmed up my heart. When God and the angels send, me signs I don't question them or try to figure out how they got there. I accept it with an open heart and gratitude.

I followed through the doctor's instructions, took my antibiotic and applied my ointments and kept on calling on my healing Angels. As every day went by I kept on healing and every day was a new surprise!

I would say I was pretty close to being a 100% better in less than 10 days! I was able to go on my birthday outing with my good friends, all I had to do was modify my dress; made it longer sleeves and added a little bit more fabric around my neck.

As I look back at those pictures I cannot tell that I had had 2nd to 3rd degree burns, less than 10 days before. When I think of the many times my Angels have been there for me. I cannot help but feel this immense gratitude. I Know there is nothing too big or too small for them to help me with.

ASK AND YOU SHALL RECEIVE!

Before I share my story with you, I'll start by saying I'm a very spiritual person; I believe that I am divinely protected, I believe in Angels, God and the higher Realm. That being said, I'm also human and sometimes I let ego & its doubt's take over.

My husband and I have been together for 18 years, and married for 14. We've had our ups and downs like every other couple, disagreements, struggles and so forth.

For some unknown reason; to be honest with you, I don't remember now, so it must have not been that important, we couldn't see eye-to-eye on a certain situation.

It became a big disagreement Between Two Egos and not our true selves. We were giving each other the silent treatment and every time we exchanged words it was to bring up another argument, things were becoming very unpleasant.

My ego was surrounding my mind with fear based thoughts, doubts, craziness! Did I really know this person; did I really love him? Does he love me?

My ego was trying to tell me that married couples shouldn't be having this kinds issues; this was not normal, maybe we had made a mistake.

After a few days like that; the weekend came around.
I decided that I would take out the kids for a drive.
I needed fresh air! I needed to get out of the house. So, I got my two kids ready my 12-year-old son and my three-year-old daughter. Put a few snacks together, got my purse the Keys and left without saying a word.

I put my daughter in her car seat I buckled her up & got into the driver's seat, waited patiently for my son to buckle his seatbelt. As I was getting ready to start the car I looked up at the rearview mirror and I saw my two children.

In my head, I thought... what are you doing? where are we going! I couldn't help it, I felt this overwhelming feeling of hopelessness! As I shrugged my shoulders; I lifted my hands up and said; I give up! I give up! I can't do this anymore!! As I said that; I caught myself.

I paused for a second & prayed, God, Angels! please help me, guide me, please send me a sign!! I Took a deep breath, collected myself and turned the key in the ignition. Has the car started so did the radio and the first words that I heard out if the radio loud & clear were:

"I won't give up, if you don't give up calling upon all Angels!! Singer(Train) calling upon all Angels

As I sat there listening to the song & lyrics; I knew my Angels were sending me a sign! Seconds ago, I was sitting there saying that I give up. Now, this song is telling me; they won't give up, if I don't give up!

Mind you, this is a song that I don't hear very often.

I've heard it a few times in my lifetime, but I had to look the title and singer up. Wow! I know that the Devine and Angels will not interfere with your free will. Once I asked, they sent me a sign that was so needed!

With tears in my eyes and a smile on my face, I thanked them for the message and with a tiny Giggle under my breath I said; you got me you guys got me good! I knew what I had to do. At that instant, I felt as the whole weight of the world had been lifted off my shoulders.

With those two phrases, they sent me; I realized that everything that is worth having, is worth working for, God & my Angels will always be by my side. Working as hard as I am, as long as I don't give up, THEY won't give up.

Sometimes we don't ask for help to family and friends because we don't want to Be a burden or the simple fact that we are a very private person.

Just know that you're never alone, that your team in heaven is always willing and ready to help you. Have faith and ask. We cannot forget that they love us unconditionally and they're eager and willing to help us in any way they can.

ASK AND YOU SHALL RECEIVE!

About the Author

I'm happily married to the love of my life Julio; we have two beautiful children Julian & Julyssa they are our daily Inspirations & a gifts from God. Business owner and entrepreneur. At an early age, I always gravitated to angel statues or books about angels, and I didn't know why. until I learned about the great Doreen Virtue and Sylvia Browne that's when my whole life changed!

I read every book by them that I could find & get my hands on. it was food for my soul! filling me with knowledge and great understanding, a powerful reminder of who I truly was! I knew I wanted to be of service, I wanted to be of help, even if it meant not to be like everyone else. I was on the search of the true knowing of my life purpose as a lightworker. Certified by the amazing Robert Reeves on peaceful protection, flower therapy healer, attracting abundance, connecting with your angels, finding and following your life purpose, The 15 Divine, nutrition for intuition. Connect with your angels with Kyle Gray.

Sharon Roebuck
* * * <u>Saved by GOD " The Voice of an Angel"</u> * * *

Hello and many blessing to you all on this beautiful day!!! My name is Sharon Roebuck and this is a story that changed my life to living it and not regretting life itself. I was born in upper state New York in 1965, in a family of 7 brothers and 1 sister. My parents moved a few times until we got to Simi Valley. When settled in with neighbors and with the area, our life changed.

In Simi Valley, my parents were out for the day. My dad was hanging around his friends and my mom was going to school at the time. No one was watching us when the police came over and told us "we had to pick up some trash in our neighbor's yard". One of my brothers said "run" and we all did. We all ran down into the embankment but me, I had skates on. I slipped and slide down the embankment and bent my arm in two different directions. It ended up being broken and they sent me to the hospital. When I was in the hospital they took everyone else into foster homes.

I was 8 years old at the time when I was put into a foster home. After my second foster home, they took me to Lancaster in southern California into yet another foster home. My mom's place wasn't far from my new foster home and I had lots of foster sisters and such a nice family. When they took me to start in a new school they said they had to send me to a different school. So, I went to special Ed and not long after that they took me to special Olympic classes. There I got to learn how to swim, bowl, skate and run track.

After a year, I got to go back home with a few brothers, but my father left and moved to Los Angeles. It was still the same old thing. No one was watching us. My mom was going to school and we had barely anything in the house, food or furniture. My bedroom became where I hid some of the time. My mom and me didn't see eye to eye and I thought we just hated each other. I tried talking to her but we always ended up yelling at each other. Either I just couldn't understand or she didn't have time to explain things to me.

Maybe with so many children to care for, going to school and trying to regain the love of her daughter, my sister Colleen to come back home. I feel possibly it was all too much for her. I didn't blame Colleen for not coming home, I didn't tell my mom the truth how I felt because she wouldn't listen anyways.

I know we had a dysfunctional family with some violence and yes I was angry sometimes. When you're in this type of situation some things are out of control and you think, the parent would change things, but my mom she was just watching the situation from the side lines. So, she wouldn't get hurt. She was a manipulator, a game player of the mind, trying to gain everyone's love, one at a time. I think that's why I always went to my friend's house. It was where I felt safe and learned what a healthy family was.

In 1982 my sister Colleen died at the age of 16 years of age. Many things happened at that time. I wish I could have fixed it all, but the way she went home is between Creator and her. When I was going to high school I decided to change the way I acted to the way I dressed. I got tired of people calling me stupid and retarded. But I think everyone changes themselves when going to high school. We all just want to fit in.

My mom changed the way she talked to me. She noticed me, maybe because I was the only daughter left. Either way the situation changed a little.

In 1983 I graduated from high school and a year later my life changed. I went over to my friend's house that's where I stayed most of the time, just to get away. When one of her friends came over and asked for a ride to her boyfriend's house, I said I could take her. Of course, I used my mom's car. So, I drove her to her boyfriend's house and on the way, back she asked to drive. I let her for some stupid reason?

When looking out the window a voice out of nowhere said, an angels voice told me, "take your watch off and put your arm through the car door handle." So, I did! The next thing I saw were the light of another car and then the lights went out! The whole car accident felt like a dream. I remember seeing the day turn to night and then night turn to day. Then it was like time moving fast, the day went past with clouds then rain, then night fell again. I then saw that there was a thin line of light ahead of me, no up no down, just the light was coming towards me and it was everywhere in front of me. I really didn't want to come back from this place I was in but Jesus told me through my heart that things were going to get better for me. Change is to come. I was so calm and so peaceful. I was aware that I was out of my body, back slightly behind my body, viewing my own self.

When a lady that came to help and when she began talking, after a bit, I knew I was back in my body. I then crawled out of the window and stumbled around. I looked at all the people who were watching and then I looked up to the sky. They took me to the hospital where they pulled the broken glass fragments out of my head and made sure I was ok. I was sent home with a few glass fragments in my head, with my mom yelling at me all the way home about the car. Sadly, she was more concerned about the car than me.

I was in shock for a few days wondering what I just experienced??? At the time, I didn't believe that much in God but my mom wanted us to go to church for some reason. My brother Shawn believed in God back then. I know now we all have dreams but at the time I thought I was going crazy when I started experiencing lucid and such vivid dreams, I was hearing guiding voices and having guiding thoughts. I began having thoughts of God. This played a part in my life experience which I now call voices!!!

In 1984 I met Victor in college in an art class and soon after that, in 1985, we got married. In 1986 I decided to try to become a hairstylist, so I went to school. This was a struggle with limited knowledge and I knew this but I wanted to learn and not give up. So, when going to school I had a spiritual experience, I call spirit. That day I was cold and not feeling well, but I had to go to beauty school. Just before I was going to leave I felt the cushions sink in and felt someone sit right beside me. I told Victor, "quick gab the camera I feel someone right next to me. Take a picture." I swear I looked so hard beside me wondering what or who was beside me! I didn't feel afraid but was in amazement. I knew there was someone there with their hands in front of them on their lap.

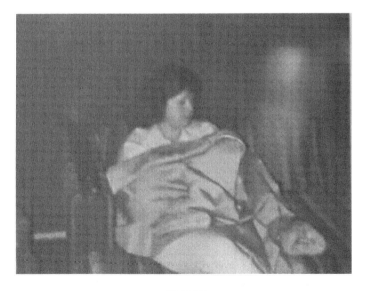

.... SPIRIT....

With the help of my husband I had to take the test twice to pass the State Board test. I was so happy to complete the school and the test that when I received my license in the mail, I looked for a job right away. Yay, I was at my first job as a hairstylist. After I worked as a hairstylist for years we decided to move to Sacramento so I could get to know my dad before his death. I had a few strange experiences that left me wondering just how these thoughts are popping into my thoughts and dreams? And how I was drawn to people I don't even know.

In 1996 we moved to Sacramento and stayed with relatives for a bit before we got to our apartment in Citrus Heights area of California. I had to take the bus to my job in Roseville, California, when on my way back home I walked from the bus stop to home, when I heard the voice of God ask, "Will you be open to me?" Of course, my mind said yes! When walking home my mind shook, "God"?!

Slowly the awareness of everything around me I started to notice. When we moved into another apartment in Fair Oaks, a friend took me to a class called Pathfinders, held at a metaphysical shop called Blossoming Path. There I started to understand about the things I was seeing, hearing and dreaming. It brought more into the light.

I started the literacy program at the library and still worked as a hairstylist. I know there was someone by my side guiding me, pushing me, encouraging me to be great in All of who I am. I know this sounds crazy but when driving to class, I saw Jesus driving an older small car. With my mind, I asked Jesus, would you stop by my place? I know and felt "Yes I can." I was so excited I shared this at class. I thought so much more of God to where it drove me crazy with so many questions and a constant wondering. When searching for God, God showed me the beauty in ALL of me.

I love the way God says hello, it feels like ALL love, to where it makes you smile, with this knowing of such love from God. I call it Gods Kiss!!! I know I had a guide with me most of the time. I also know Jesus was with me. Once, when I was told to go to a church, I did. When getting there, I saw God shine on the church. I felt a little scared, but was asked with such love and peace, "Why?" Only calm, peace, love, all are here to guide you. When I went into church I looked around and took pictures when I noticed my guide on the outside window watching me. I was wondering why she wouldn't come in? She said this is man's church which was for all in human form.

.... Guide....

The Christ consciousness became my awareness. After a while I knew I was being taught by Jesus and ALL that guides us by God. ALL is connected by God and God knows us like we know ourselves in ALL. Spirit explained all I experienced in simple ways I could understand. My guides voice said by God and ALL that you are supposed to experience it plays in favor of you hearing an angel clearly. The place I was in some call heaven. Again, the voice of Jesus let me know in my heart, that my life will change for the good. My guides voice . . . "There is no reason for us to lie, truth is like, I would say 2+2=4, do you argue with this?" I think no! My guides voice "why?" I said "I know it's right." My guides voice said "that truth and knowing it through your mind of being." I so love it when they say things because everything is done with all love through God. You can feel this through your entire being of body.

Heaven to some was explained to me. My guides voice shared, "What you call my thousands of people, is only a few to us." The perception is vastly different. When feeling the connection to heaven I see heaven brighter with such a clear blue sky but no sun. My guides voice shares, "because it just is". When in heaven, when entering all our humanness sheds, you feel this overwhelming peace, love and a connection to ALL. It's a vibration of love through your entire being.

When I'm connected and in heaven I look around I see the green rolling small mounds and a few small hills. Lots of beautiful individual blades of green grass and the flowers are so much brighter in color. There were a few roman stone buildings there but 1 in particular caught my eye. This roman building was away from all the others in a remote area. The building was the Hall of Angels with giant angel statues. When looking at it you can see all the Angel statues around the building so clear. The building and the stone statues were so very beautiful, I noticed no shadows anywhere, ALL is light!

I now also know some angels guide me in some things I do. Be it in heaven and/or heaven on Earth. I then see a stream of water with the grass hanging over it on both sides, you can clearly see the water moving "UP" stream, "UP" towards the valley hills. In the greeting, my past relatives appeared in spirit and I knew we were all connected. I knew I didn't know them in body here on earth. This experience is explained by the voice, "we choose before we come". An example was my dog came to me and cried to let me know soon she was to be with me. A cry before she was born as dog.

All I experienced was led by . . . the love of ALL that guides us ALL by God. Through ALL in connection they helped me to feel proud of me and who I am as an individual person. They showed me my life from the past, to help overcome all the hate I felt. Forgiveness is easy, it's the remembering the pain of the past that hurts us. What?! The Voice, "We all know and feel you, like yourself. Yes, God also". I ask, "In other words everything affects ALL through what guides us by God? The Voice, "YES, we feel what you feel." But we, as individuals share the joy of ALL that is here for we all came here with great strength, courage and ALL through what guides us by God supporting us living life here in our world.

The voice says, "I am that I am is a connection to all as an individual, like you have one body connected to all within yourself. It's all connected to everything you do, you say, you might even move, or throw out or shove in". The voice laughs and shares, "Imagine the universe is inside of you."

Gosh I am so thankful for all that guides me and all of us here that experience life day by day. I feel that all I experienced played a role in who I am as a person today. I am being great in all of me as simply as I can, one day at a time. As the years pass, it is now 2011. We moved to our first home. After we painted it and fixed it up a bit we were putting things in the place when my dad popped in my mind, "Dad!" I told my husband Victor, "Hey my dad, he's come to visit us." He was so happy for us at our first home. So, I said, "Hey I want a picture of you Dad!"

This is my Dad, Joe's spirit in orb form. This helped me to know, "all is good between us and there's nothing but LOVE!"

.... Joe's Spirit in orb form....

I am not an author or a writer I just want to share my story in hopes this will help others in their life. Life is worth living. This is our glory to experience it as we make it. I never thought I would be writing a chapter of my story of faith in God or faith within ourselves. God want us to be proud in the ALL we are. Maybe facing my fears in spelling will help get through what holds me back. By the grace of God and all through what I am supposed to experience, may it show me my glory and bless me through it all.

Before we come here we choose to live in what we want to experience and by ALL through guides us by God, guides and changes with us to lead us from our path. Victor and I now take care of my mom, in which I thought I would never do, but we take care of here in hope that I can grow a healthy respectful mother and daughter relationship. Forgiveness of all allows us to grow closer in friendship. I know with God Jesus showed me the way and all love and connection to ALL Lead me to the Christ Consciousness. I don't see much difference in God and Jesus, but know God is also all love and light and he feels more comfortable that way.

I believe differently in the power of prayer. Churches emit a lot of energy because of the power of prayer and faith in God through love. The energy of gathering in the name of God is high. If we all show kindness to one another like Jesus, this spreads like bread to all. Blessings to you all on this beautiful day of your and thank you for being here sharing your life with all we encounter along the way.

This is the end of my story, but the beginning of a new day. I will leave you with this one quote ... "If a tree falls in a forest and no one is around to hear it, does it make a sound? by George Berkely.

If a tree does fall or is in pain "There are some people who will feel this and hear the trees good-bye"

Hugs and LOVE, Sharon Roebuck

About the Author

I'm an Artist, & Read My Story You have in "Warrior Women with Angel Wings " That's All True & My Beginning...!!! 🖤
Roebucksharon@gmail.com

Conny Himenes
Angels; All My Life!

I work with Angels all the time, but I wanted to share my very first experience with one when I was about 7 or 8 in Germany.

I was getting off the bus as usual coming from school. Not a school bus, but a public bus. My mother has taught me from very young how to cross the street, no crossing guard or waiting to walk over to a traffic light.

She always said "wait until the bus leaves, look and then cross. Always wait until the bus leaves so you can see both ways"

Well that day I did something out of the ordinary, I jumped of the bus, and raced in front of the still parked bus across the street. For no reason as I recall. Full speed!

Next I felt a gust of cold air pass me by, I felt someone bring me to a dead stop, and heard the screeching of very loud brakes. I was stunned for a second, turned. No one was there, I ran back and around the back of the bus and ran across the street. I looked back.

A huge semi-truck had stopped a little way in front of the bus, the driver was running around looking under the truck, people were looking.

I looked down on my shoes, I only had one pair of shoes for school, brown velvet shoes. **They had tire tracks on them!**

Now I knew what they were looking for. They thought I was hit by that huge Semi-truck. I ran off and wiped the tire tracks off my velvet shoes because if my mother would find out, I would get a massive butt- whooping.

Yes, my Angel stopped me in full speed and saved my life.

This was the first time he intervened, and he did many times thereafter.

And he still by my side.

His name is Jedidiah. One time I asked him, "let me see what you look like", most of the time I just feel his presence to my left. That day I wanted to actually see him. He answered," what would you like me to look like"? Oh, I could choose! I smiled and in my head, was thinking of a specific animal, and poof, in front of me I saw, " a Magic Dragon ". Yes, just like Wished for.

I have had Angels around me my whole life, but there were times the shadows of this world clouded my vision. I could not see or feel them. Sometimes I needed others to remind me.

When my granddaughter Alyssa was about 4 years old she started seeing them. One day we were both sitting in my living room by ourselves. I was on the computer; she was sitting next to me with an old keyboard pretending to type. She was facing the hallway behind us. Out of the blue she said" grandma can you tell the lady down the hall to stop looking at me. She is pretty and looks like my mother but she needs to stop looking at me now". I carefully turned around and I could not see anything. That was the beginning of her seeing her Angel from time to time. When my other granddaughter Katelyn was visiting me from Nebraska, she said one day " grandma why do you have so many people living in your walls, are they Angels?"

Of course, I told her smiling.

When my grandson Christopher was two he started talking to "someone " he called Anja.

Many times, he would be in long conversations with her. When he was six he told me " Anja is still with me but I can't see her right now because I am getting older".

Many people have come in my life to remind me that Angels are with us always; I feel it's my gift to be able to see their Angels.

In 2005, my Reiki Master Lynette came into my life when I was at a very low point in my life. I was mourning my mother's death and I had just lost my job of 23 years. She introduced me to Reiki, which changed my life forever. It opened my eye to see what others sometimes fail to see. I was very hesitant when she first invited me to her house to "show" me Reiki. She did mention we would have a bite to eat and some wine afterwards. Well, that made the trip to her house worth it I figured. I was stalling, but finally I agreed. She put her hands on my head and I felt the energy! I was hooked! She gave me the Reiki 1 attunement that day. I saw numerous Angels; my guides and totems surround us as she performed the ritual. Several months later I did receive the Reiki Master Attunement. She never charged me a dime for her teaching and I made a promise to continue that gift she gave me.

Another person that helped me believe in myself was Denise Fall. I met her at a church, she was sitting on the other side. I couldn't stop looking at her, her light was so amazing, even though she tried to hide it. I had to get to know her. Well, I changed my seat and sat next to her. Eventually, we became friends and one day I had her do Reiki treatment on me. I felt like I had never felt before, like being transported straight up into Heaven. I felt like being comforted by hundreds of Angels. I had Reiki before and also do Reiki myself.

But no, I never had that kind of experience before. We decided to start a free Reiki share here in our town, and then I saw him. When she turns on Reiki, behind her, stand an enormous, amazing, majestic Angel. His glow almost blinds me. His energy is overwhelming at times. Denise and I did many free Reiki sessions for people. Many times, we would have a "Reiki Tupperware part" as we called it at a friend's house. She would invite people that never experienced Reiki before. Each time the whole room was filled with hundreds of Angels.

We continued our weekly free Reiki share together for 2 years and sadly for me, she moved. Even being thousands of miles away, when I need a healing, I call her and she sends her Angel to deliver the healing. It's quite overwhelming still when she sends him my way. My whole living room glows with golden and lavender light when he arrives.

I have continued our free Reiki share that we started together with the help of my fellow light workers Debbi and Miquel. Every Thursday she still sends her, as we call him " her big ass Angel" to our weekly Reiki share. The room still lights up. Now he stands behind Debbi so I can still see him each week.

Yes, Angels are everywhere and they have surround me, my family and friends all my life and I'm ever so grateful.

About the Author

I'm an Empath, Reiki master/teacher, Angel card Reader, Chrystal reiki master, kundalini Reiki master, Angel Realm Reader, intuitive I offer free Reiki treatments at a local Reiki Share once a week for over 4 years now. I also over free Reiki attunements for people with limited income.

Email: Himenesconny@gmail.com.

Carrie Bush
My Angel Mum

I was extremely sensitive as a child. The smallest things would upset me, and I would feel things very deeply. It took me years to understand that I was spiritual—an empath. I had a very happy childhood and wonderful, loving parents. I was always very close to my mum. She was my best friend, confidant, and supporter. She knew me inside and out. She could feel my emotions, my upsets, or pain without me needing to express myself to her. We were deeply connected to one another. As I grew up, she offered me endless support. She had become my rock.

I met the man I was to marry at eighteen years old; it was love at first sight. My parents welcomed him into our family, and we enjoyed many wonderful times together. At twenty-one, I fell pregnant with my first child. A beautiful boy who grew to be very much like myself—a caring, sensitive soul. As our family grew, so did the memories and time spent together. My mum would be with us often, still supporting and encouraging. She had a wonderful bond with my son, and I couldn't have felt more blessed.

Two years later, I fell pregnant with my daughter—a beautiful heaven-sent angel. My children made me feel a happiness inside that I didn't even know was possible. As my daughter grew, she and my son had a strong bond. Nothing gave me more pleasure than to just sit and watch them together. After some time, I became concerned that my daughter wasn't reaching all her milestones. She was thirteen months old. After a referral from the doctor, we sat in the hospital waiting room with her. Detailed checks were made, and it was revealed that our precious angel had cerebral palsy. Right then, my world fell apart.

I didn't understand about the condition, and through tears stinging my eyes, I asked the consultant, "Will she die?" He gave my arm a gentle rub and told us it would not affect her life span, and then continued to explain the condition to us. We sat in silence. Our baby girl, smiling happily, was oblivious to the information we had just been given. We were told our baby might not reach all her milestones and would find it difficult to crawl and walk. I was devastated. I felt as if our world had come crashing down around us.

Each appointment we attended would be spent with tears burning my eyes. I felt that familiar feeling of tightness in my throat from holding back my emotions. It was so painful. I had never felt anything like it before. At each appointment, we watched them pull our baby girl's legs while measuring her muscle movement. We wiped our little girl's tears whilst holding back our own. We sat in silence and dread each time she went into surgery to cut the muscles on her legs to allow better movement.

We had so many hospital visits, operations, casting of her legs, even Botox injected into her muscles. We hoped it would become less painful with each visit, but it never did. My heart was breaking.

Throughout all this time, my little girl was making progress slowly. She was happy, and nothing stopped her from joining in with her brother; she just found another way to do things! It was heartwarming to see that her spirit was so strong. She learnt to crawl. She pulled across the floor at first, but with a little determined look on her face showing her delight, she would shuffle herself behind her brother, laughing with joy. My mum never left our side.

She was there for advice, for cuddles, and words of encouragement. A couple of years later, I had bottled so many of my emotions inside that things became too much. Even though my daughter was happy and embracing life each day, I was still living with a deep inner pain and worry for her future. Would she ever walk? Would she be able to go to school?

Soon afterwards, I started to feel unwell and went on to contract viral meningitis. This totally knocked me out. I was trying to look after my two young children while finding it almost impossible to hold my head up from the pain. Of course, my wonderful husband and family rallied around to help. The doctor was coming daily to look after me and give me medication. One day, I suddenly woke with a huge rush of panic. I didn't know where it came from or why, but it was intense. I thought it was my time to die. It was a very scary feeling. I lay in bed at night crying at the thought of leaving my babies with no mother.

My mum was around to help each day, as always being the great tower of support. After a few weeks of feeling anxious and unwell, she sat and held my hand. She told me she knew I wasn't going to die and that I had to be positive about my daughter's life path. She said she felt she had come to us for a reason and that she felt deep in her heart she would be okay as she grew older. Something inside me just clicked. Yes, she was right; I couldn't let a doctor decide my daughter's future! I would let her guide us herself.

Things became better. My anxiety started to fade, and I felt positive about our future. As time went by, my daughter successfully learned to walk, a little wobbly at first, and using a dolly's pushchair for support. She was extremely proud of herself, and it was amazing to watch her progress. Over this time, I had started to see bright colors when I closed my eyes. It seemed very strange at first.

The colors were vivid; they would start as purple, blending into pink, and then green. I started to worry there was something wrong with my eyes! My dreaded anxiety started to creep back.; after being reassured by the optician that my eyes were fine, I felt a bit calmer. I continued to see the colors each time I closed my eyes.

It wasn't until a few years later that I came to realize they were angel colors and they were making a connection with me. I fell pregnant with my third child, another son. I can remember my mum saying, "He is a chosen baby. He's come to heal your family." As always, she was right.

He was a huge blessing to our family. The older two children adored him from the moment I brought him home. He was an angel. He would feed and sleep, and smile. Happiness radiated from his angelic face. Our family was complete. My daughter continued to make good progress, still doing some things a bit differently, but with that fabulously determined spirit.

She amazed people wherever she went. If she had a wobble and fell to the ground, she would refuse a hand to help her up, deciding instead to get up by herself with a big, proud smile on her face. She was a real inspiration. She certainly inspired me every day, and I knew she had a bright future ahead.

Time passed very quickly, and the children grew fast, as they do! Sadly, my mum became unwell and had a stroke. It was a devastating time, but, as always, I was in awe of that strong lady. She never complained or showed her fear, just said, "This has happened, so I must just deal with it." She was amazing, still worrying about us, reading my mind as accurately as ever! Even though she was going through her own inner pain, she started to make some progress, and I felt a sigh of relief. I knew Mum would be feeling better soon.

Over time, she became a little breathless. Tests at the hospital gave us devastating news that she had cancer. My world crumbled around me, but as always, that amazing lady stayed strong and just dealt with the news. She didn't tell my sister and I for some time that her cancer was terminal. I remember her voice on the phone being very calm. As before, she simply said, "When it's my time to go, I will be with my dad again. It's my life path."

I felt devastated inside, but I didn't cry. I wanted to stay as strong as she was. The children and I spent as much time with her as possible. When she was admitted into hospital I would go with her and sit by her side. Her spirit was always upbeat. We would sit and laugh. I felt so proud to have a strong mum. Time went fast, and our emotions were like riding a roller coaster. I told my children that Nanny was poorly. They were ten, eight, and three years old.

My beloved Mum passed away peacefully on the 29th November 2008. She had one tear fall from her eyes as she took her last breath. It gave me great comfort to think of her now being reunited with her dad. It was a warm feeling, but utterly devastating. Telling my children Nanny had died was the hardest thing I have ever had to do. The two older ones looked in shock. They cried and asked me lots of questions.

I sat calmly and answered each one as I wiped their tears away and held back my own. I wanted to get this right; I knew how incredibly close they were to her. I explained in great detail that she was now an angel. She would always look after them and guide them through their lives. My youngest didn't really understand what had happened. But what was truly incredible was that I would hear him talking in his sleep mumbling, "Nanny," and saying the word, "Eeyore," which was a teddy he had given her as a gift for her birthday just before her passing. He woke several mornings saying, "I saw Nanny." I sat stunned, asking him questions, and he would say, "Nanny cuddled." It was truly amazing. Although she had passed and my son was young, he still had this huge connection to her.

The older children struggled. My daughter cried often and seemed very concerned about me. My eldest son was very quiet. I worried about him, as I knew how sensitive he was. He developed anxiety; he felt worried he had cancer because he had kissed Nanny. It broke my heart. The only time I felt I could grieve was when my husband took my children out. I was drawn to being in my bedroom. I felt emotionally drained inside.

I spent a lot time dealing with my children's emotions so that they didn't grow up with any issues over her death. I was making huge progress with this; they were dealing with it better and seemed very comforted to know she was with them as their special angel. They would look at the stars and say, "That's Nanny's star," and we would see white feathers on the floor and they would shout, "That's from Nanny!"

I was pleased it hadn't had a bad effect on them. But inside, I was falling apart. I felt lost and that a part of me was missing. I would lay on my bed and message her using her mobile number. As I deleted the messages, I felt sure she had read them. By then, the colors I saw every time I closed my eyes were very strong, and I saw feathers everywhere I went. I could smell her perfume at random moments. I even felt a stroke of my hair! One evening as I was going to bed, I cried myself to sleep and said aloud, "I wish I could cuddle you, Mum."

I fell into a deep sleep, feeling drained from the day. I woke at 3:00 a.m., which had been happening a lot recently (I went on to find out this is the spiritual hour where you can connect with spirits). I was in tears when I woke. I had had a very real dream that my mum was with me. She said nothing, just lay with me, and we cuddled and cried. It was very real, and I could feel the love strongly. As I got up, I could still feel the warmth on my stomach where her head had been. I cried many tears, but they were tears of happiness. I felt completely blessed and very grateful that she had visited me.

After this, the connection with my mum and my angels grew very strong. I felt drawn to spiritual books. I had so many psychic readings, I lost count! It was giving me a great deal of comfort. It was helping me to grieve and deal with my loss.

More importantly, it allowed me to understand my connection to the angels. I am thankful for this learning time, as it changed my life. I started to dream most nights, always waking up in the spiritual hour between 3:00 and 4:00 a.m. The dreams were real, and I realized they were messages. Sometimes, they would be telling me what to do or would answer a problem. It was amazing!

After some time and much reading, I started to enjoy my life again. Anytime I felt upset, I would just talk to my mum and my angels. Every time afterwards, a feather would appear or her favorite song would play on the radio. By that time, my daughter had had a big operation, and she was just starting secondary school. It really took it out of her. She had to be in a wheelchair for six weeks to recover. She was not allowed to bear weight at all; it was horrible for her. She didn't have a great time at school either.

Two years after her operation, she had recovered well, but was feeling very negative and down about herself. I felt the strong guidance from my angels to homeschool her. She was nearly fourteen years old, and her determined spirit was fading fast. I knew I had to have her at home learning so I could spend time getting my girl back.

I would constantly ask my mum and my angels to help her. My daughter and I would talk endlessly every day about her asking her angels and Nanny to help her, about what we think is what we get back, and how a positive mind can change everything. This was very important to me. My daughter had been through so much, but always remained happy and strong. I wasn't going to let that go. I knew that my mum would help, and each time we asked, I could feel her presence. Soon, the changes in my daughter and her self-esteem were very noticeable.

My husband and my sons were seeing the difference. It had a positive effect on everyone. They started to manifest and use the law of attraction. The changes were magical. I couldn't have been happier. I started to call the children my three spiritual warriors!

They now feel the connection and guidance from their nanny just as strongly as I do. My three children are amazing. I could not be prouder of all that they have achieved and how far they have come. They are the kindest people, and they have a positive attitude about life. I am excited to know that they are going to bring big changes to this world. They are light workers. And they are blessed to be guided by the most special lady anyone could ask for!

Currently, I am still homeschooling my daughter. Every day she glows a little more; I can literally see her sparkle! Her self-worth is back, and our determined young lady is with us once more. While homeschooling her, I felt strongly guided by my angels to write fifteen books for children, a story to follow each Archangel. I call them my Angel babies. My angels have guided me to share this information with children.

Connecting with and talking about the angels has helped my daughter so much that I am proud to say she is now on a journey of self-healing with fantastic results already! She has recently been discharged from hospital care, and there are no more operations planned. She also was released from her physiotherapist's care who was amazed at my daughters results after a session. I have really enjoyed writing my books, and I hope they can help many children as they have helped my daughter.

I found each story easy to write; I felt the presence of my mum and my angels beside me with each word. They are most definitely divinely guided! After I finished the books, my angels gave me the ideas for many more. I have written every idea in a special notebook. I have already completed many more books, and I am excited about the release of these in 2018.

My angels also guided me to work with angel cards. I found I have a gift of being able to read them and also receive messages directly from spirits. This has since led me to providing angel card readings for clients with amazing feedback! I feel completely blessed and thankful to my angels for gifting me with this ability.

Each day I wake up, I am full of gratitude and positivity. The connection to my mum and my angels fills my heart with joy. Life is blissful and full of sparkle. My children are flourishing, and I am so proud that I feel I could burst! The day I was born, the angels placed me in the arms of a very special lady. A lady, who forever walks by my side: Mum, my angel.

About the Author

Carrie Bush is a devoted mother of three and a published author from the United Kingdom. Carrie has a qualification in childcare, and before becoming a mother herself, worked in nurseries and as a private nanny. She is very passionate about children's emotional wellbeing and believes strongly that mindfulness for children— helping them to focus, manage stress, and regulate their emotions—has a vital role to play.

Carrie has recently published a collection of fifteen Archangel books for children. She calls these her "angel babies!" Jodie, her daughter who has cerebral palsy, is her inspiration for the books. Carrie's angels guided her to share this information with others. Her three children have benefitted greatly too.

Her ethos is to inspire children at a young age to cope with issues before they become exaggerated in teenage years and into adulthood. Introducing children to Archangels—pure beings of light that show their individuality through their own color and specialty—help children to find their joy and sparkle. Carrie's books cover a range of topics that are important in everyday life, including healing, manifesting, friendship issues, loss of a pet, anxiety, and more.

Carrie's story is an inspiration to readers. After becoming concerned that her then young daughter wasn't reaching all her milestones, detailed checks revealed that her precious angel had cerebral palsy. Through years of upset and worry, Carrie discovered that with love, strength, hope, and faith, miracles do happen!

On dealing with the loss of her beloved mum, she found herself on a deep spiritual journey, which led her to find great comfort connecting to the Angels. Carrie's awakening changed her life and enabled her to see things differently. Carrie learned that a bond between a mother and child will always remain.

Book Link: https://www.amazon.co.uk/Carrie-M-Bush/e/B06XS2ZZYD/ref=dp_byline_cont_book_1

Facebook: @CarrieMBush

Twitter: @carriembush77

Instagram: /carriemariebush

Margaret Taylor
New Crone

Hello. My name is Margaret Taylor and I am proud to define myself as a New Crone. Proud, because the word "crone" historically was always associated with the wisdom, knowledge and experience of older women and commanded the respect and deference of younger men and women alike. I believe acknowledging and respecting the wisdom and life experiences of all those older than us – whatever our age – is an important part in creating more light and love, respect and consideration in this physical world of ours.

I am also an energy healer, artist, author and musician and so many other things. Just a short five years ago how I defined myself was very different! My journey to this place I'm at today has been so different from many others. I haven't had the accidents, illnesses or major traumas so many had that "activated" their gifts. Originally I was envious. They seemed to have such easy access to their guides and their guardian angels. I made it harder than it needed to be and through that process received the blessings of so much healing from Divine Source.

I finally realized my story is important because it is different than many others. Everyone can "activate" their connection to Divine Source and their guardian angels! Everyone has their own path to follow and it can be fun, fulfilling, empowering and scary to ask for and receive the releasing of fear and the return of parts of yourself. What a blessing this path has been for me!

I had a very normal upbringing in Iowa Midwest. We were blessed to be able to travel a lot - 7 of us in a 3-seater station wagon pulling a travel trailer. We got to see much of the United States and parts of Canada. Those were wonderful experiences. I received so many other blessings from my parents that I'm only now learning to appreciate fully.

My guardian angels have been around me my whole life. I just couldn't see, hear or feel them. Whenever my "guidance" got through the walls my head put up I would do the opposite – especially when I knew that what my gut was telling me would bring good things to me!

I never really realized until very recently how much my angels have done to protect me. They kept me safe when I was being stupid driving. They kept me safe when I fell asleep driving. I'm so grateful that they not only protected me but anybody else who might have been hurt by me.

I really became aware of them when I received a hug from my angel when I got the news that one of my sisters had passed. It was amazing and so powerful and so healing and I'm so grateful to this day for that kindness.

It wasn't until I walked away from my first marriage that I started opening up to learning about the amazing variety "Woo Woo" that is easily accessible today. A friend of mine to invited me to a Tarot class. And that opened up the floodgates into all of amazing rooms of "Woo Woo." I am so grateful for that invitation and for all of the help and guidance that my beautiful friend has given me over the years before and since! She is one of the many Earth Angels I have been blessed to know in this life.

My husband, a friend and I went to the Des Moines Metaphysical Fair a few years ago and we all signed up to have a reading with the same medium. In my session Archangel Gabriel came through and delivered a mind-blowing message. He told me about my spirit guides and guardian angels – things I knew next to nothing about at the time. He (yes – Archangel Gabriel appears male to me) gave me important information to help me move forward on my life path. I was so resistant! Because I was afraid – of everything!

Since then, I've learned that the heart wants what the heart wants and the heart KNOWS what will make me happy deep inside. And so, I've been actively seeking to let go of fear! I never imagined that my uneventful life in this lifetime would create so much fear and other unhealthy stuff to be let go of!

Add on to that the "stuff" from past lifetimes and it's been a journey of new experiences. And I'm so grateful for it!

My guides and guardian angels gifted me with learning about the history of Shamanism and all of the powerful and wonderful healing techniques that the Shamanic cultures had developed. I've also learned about so many other energy healing techniques and ways to receive information and guidance for and about yourself and others.

I've met so many wonderful people have learned so very much and I've been so blessed with all of the beautiful Angels and Archangels and Spirit guides who have been around me showing me all kinds of amazing things and pouring so much of their healing and their wisdom and their guidance into me into those who have come to me for help. I can't imagine living without open guidance and open access to their wisdom their humor they're fun into the joy and the peacefulness it comes with following their guidance and living the bliss.

I've learned so much that I never would have expected. And through it I've been blessed to be able to help others in so many wonderful and unique ways. Ways that our current medical system are not able to you. So many things that our modern medicine isn't able to understand and currently not willing to accept. And it's such a wonderful experience so healing and joyful to be able to help others and these unique and wonderful ways.

So, thank you angels for guiding me to hear and thank you for your patience and your understanding for never giving up on me. And thank you for all of the wonderful adventures that I know we're going to have in the future.

About the Author

Margaret (Maggie) Taylor can be reached at:

My website is WillowHorseRun.org My Facebook page is Willow horse run LLC Email is Margaret. Whr@ gmail.com Phone number is 515 210 - 3513

Pamela Lynch
You're Worth It!
The Shift From Feeling Unworthy To Wealthy

Have you ever lingered in those first luxurious first moments upon awakening and smiled with gratitude on your lips?

Thank you! Thank you! Thank you!

As consciousness greets me each morning, my blessings unfold. I experienced, if only for Nano seconds, a peaceful, blissful energy in the alpha state. I like to believe we return to the "other" side when we sleep, and when we awake, we are most connected to our spiritual being. I am appreciative when the moment lingers because I know my angels embrace and surround me.

There is a thin veil between the two worlds as we awaken into consciousness to greet a new adventure. We are born anew each day. We get to choose how we want to express our Self, yet it comes with a responsibility, an awareness, a desire to be present. How fortunate to have the freedom to linger in bed and feel gratitude. I am grateful for a good sleep, a comfortable bed, and pillow. There is a knowingness that today will be an amazing day, a day where I once again declare my mantra: *I love my life!*

It starts with asking questions of my angels: What is in my highest good to create today? Who do I want to *be*? What do I want to *do*? What do I want to *have*? It has been an incredible journey to get to this point. First, I must want to *be* the person to *do* what it takes to *have* what I want. We've had it backwards. We focus on the wanting, not the being. What does is feel like now to be the person who will have what I want?

So often, we get to teach what has been our deepest learning, and I am no different. I believe my beginnings are more like the majority than not. We are conceived as two sparks ignite and are born a brilliant light with pure potential. Why, then, is our brilliance extinguished at such a tender and innocent young age, leaving us to search through the rubble to find it again decades later? I'm certain my own light dimmed before I emerged from my mother's womb. Our experience influences our beliefs and shapes our personality, our preferences, our uniqueness. Everything is energy, even in the womb, and we merge their stories into our energetic, emotional bodies.

Forced to marry, my mom despised her husband even more than the bitterness and isolation she felt. They were in the Air Force and got stationed in France. Her devastation was compounded by her loss of her second daughter who died of SIDS at two months old. Her doctor advised her to have another baby. Trillions of souls asked, and I received the call, the gift, to gain entrance to be her third-born daughter. I came in to rescue my mom from her sorrow and shower her with light. Divine contracts are forgotten the instant we burst forth to begin our earthly adventure. It makes sense that we arrive here knowing everything, yet remember nothing. Rather, we must rely on the energy and beliefs of our parents, our caregivers, as handed down through our ancestors.

I felt my mother's despair and loneliness, and energetically took on her pain. Bitterly unhappy and lonely, she met my future stepdad and they instantly fell in love. He became her rescuer, and she no longer needed me to rescue her. The Air Force sent our biological family back to Canada, while my future dad had to stay in France for another year. My feelings of abandonment from two fathers blended with my mother's shame and grief. Intuitively, I felt her sense of loss, her sadness, and her feelings of not enough-ness. We mirror the emotions of our parents and our caregivers. When they are loving, trusting, and encouraging, we thrive. When they are sad, detached, hopeless, or angry, we feel not enough. Not knowing how to handle these confusing feelings, I shut down and kept silent until the age of three. I climbed up on my new aunt's lap and gazed happily up at her and said, "My old daddy didn't love me, but my new daddy does."

My mother and new father were so in love, my siblings and I felt like we were on the outside looking in. It was as if we were all waving our arms frantically about and saying, "Look at me. I want to be loved, too." Were we not good enough?

If only I could be lovable enough. If only I could be clever enough. If only . . .

To makes matters worse, I soon learned about the brutal strap of a military man, and fear griped me. I left my body and became the one who needed to be rescued. This was, of course, decades before I knew anything about our chakra system. It made sense that the belt across the buttocks and lower back damaged those energy centres. Since the root chakra and the crown chakra are connected, it is clear why I didn't feel safe, loved, or supported. It also explains why my connection to my spirit was blocked.

Fifty years later, it was time to heal. I visited an energy practitioner, and after only one minute, he said, "Pamela, the only thing I see is you have a broken heart."

This truth was locked so tightly in my heart, I didn't even see it there, and when I did, it rocked me to my core. There were so many broken hearts. I was tens of thousands of dollars in debt with soaring, high interest credit cards. I spiraled downwards financially, and over three years, several advisors suggested bankruptcy. It appeared my spirit guides were growing tired of me not "getting it." They decided I needed an intervention, and finally my faulty belief system started to unravel.

One of my Earth Angels received a message on my behalf that I no longer needed to be rescued. I was shocked. I'd never thought of myself as a rescuer or needing to be rescued. The lightbulb not only went on, it brought with it a symphony of lights. I saw the influence my parents had had on my finances, and how I relied on them to rescue me and my family. We got locked in the energetic game that confused the giving of money and material gifts with love. I so desperately wanted to be loved, I sabotaged the ability to earn money in order for them to rescue me.

I'd spent my youth looking outward for love, appreciation, approval, and validation. I found it in my second husband. Our financial relationship was the opposite side of the same coin. I was the breadwinner and become the rescuer for my husband. I later understood I had a financial karmic debt to him, and this was the lifetime to clear it. There was such relief when I knew our spiritual contract was complete! With a new awareness, I thought if *everything is energy, then that also includes money.* I needed to look closely at the root problem.

I'd spent my lifetime looking outwards for fulfillment when it is an inner game, and I am the creator. Underlying my feelings of abandonment and being unlovable was an unworthiness around money, which led to my inability to manifest financial abundance. It made me wonder, *how many others feel unworthy?*

The evidence showed up. I saw that the feeling of "not enough-ness" was rampant in our society. It was buried deep in our core beliefs. Yet on the surface, how often do we say, "I didn't get enough sleep, work, exercise, good nutrition. I don't have enough time. I didn't earn enough money. I haven't saved enough for retirement."

So many people seek a fulfilled and abundant life, yet so few feel worthy enough to explore the opportunity to achieve wealth. How do we begin to shift from feeling unworthy to feeling wealthy? First, through our awareness. We create more of what our attention is focused on and the vibration we resonate at. I was focused on debt, and guess what? I created more debt. My thoughts of lack vibrated out into the world and returned more lack. The job of the subconscious is to fulfill the command of the conscious mind *and* make true anything we *believe*. The more energy we give a thought, the faster it looks for evidence in our environment to support it.

Through neuroscience, we have learned that we can create a new neural pathway in the brain. It allows us to change our thoughts, behaviour, habits, and results. Every time we repeat a thought, the pathway becomes more ingrained. Let's use the belief that I must be rescued to receive money. Any time I trigger this belief, consciously or subconsciously, the neurotransmitters light up. My subconscious creates a situation to stop the flow of money. If I stay in that emotion, it deepens the false belief. The subconscious continues to find ways for me to repel money in order for me to be rescued. Since all our money comes from other people and resources, this is a problem.

When I looked for ways to see my value and to believe in myself, a shift happened. I saw money as energy, and it flowed in appreciation from me to others. I blessed the person receiving my money when I paid for my purchases. I saw money as a tool that circulated through our society in exchange for what we valued. It created a new pathway that became more ingrained and over-rode the old belief. I dug into coaching processes and meditations to heal and raise my vibration to love *all that is*. I chose to reclaim my brilliance. One process is to act *as if* what you want is already there, and feel as if you are that person. Remember the order: Be, do, have. I began to feel abundant by asking questions: Who do I need to *be* to be financially abundant? What would it feel like if I let go of the fear? Can I love and appreciate my last $300 in the bank? What would it feel like if I let go of the resistance to claim bankruptcy?

I focused on how I wanted to feel to live in appreciation. I celebrated every bill that arrived because I trusted I would have more than enough to pay it. Isn't it funny how the exact amount of money showed up? When I was down to that last $300, I decided to declare bankruptcy. I found myself in a pickle, but said no to being rescued. I trusted the process. My doubt and fear had kept me from remembering that was how it worked. The stories about unworthiness were the illusions. Our feelings are what is real. They are our guidance system.

Within two weeks of choosing to let go of any resistance, a miracle happened. I received the exact amount of money needed to pay off my high interest credit cards. Plus, I had enough left over to feel abundant with a positive balance in my bank account. The relief was immediate. The cheque arrived the day before I was due to meet with the company to declare bankruptcy. I had switched gears and disrupted my thought patterns to create a new neuro pathway.

A critical piece of my healing was learning to practice forgiveness. It was a huge impact to shift into feeling worthy, and it led me to reconnect with my spiritual aspect. Forgiveness is the most loving way to ignite our abundance. When we learn to forgive ourselves and others, we are able to reach out to heal our wounded children-within and our deep hurts. I finally acknowledged the pain, and instead of pushing it deep down inside into the darkness, I felt it. I nurtured it. I loved it.

Through my ability to forgive my fathers, I realized they loved me. They never meant to hurt me or make me feel abandoned as a toddler. I believed that story for five decades! It wasn't the true story. I knew both of my fathers loved me, and I was worthy of love. I embraced my new story.

A popular tool for forgiveness is the ancient Hawaiian practice of reconciliation and forgiveness, the Ho'oponopono prayer:

> *I am sorry.*
> *Please forgive me.*
> *I love you.*
> *Thank you.*

As you forgive the people who trigger you, see if there is another perspective to your story. Re-write it so it serves you as your present, loving self. Since learning to meditate, I tune into my divinity and connect the light from my root and crown chakras. I also focus on strengthening my throat chakra to speak my truth and focus on gratitude. Gratitude activates our whole brain into a high vibration. What are you grateful for?

A beautiful example of deep gratitude comes from a young man who shared his practice with his angels. He begins every morning with his mantra, "Thank You! Thank You! Thank You!" He doesn't ask his angels for help. He acknowledges they are there to bless him and thanks them with gratitude throughout the day. As he spoke, I heard the love and appreciation in his voice; my vibration shifted into peace and gratitude. As I felt this idea, I, too, gave much thanks to my own angels. He ignited a spark in me and inspired the opening to my story. It is as if the veil that darkened my heart lifted, and I arrived home after being absent for a lifetime.

I believe we choose to be here. Every person who stands in front of us is meant to share their message, a message we ache to hear. It is a soul contract we agreed to before we entered into our experience here on Earth. It is not only the obvious relationships. It is the passing of a stranger. It's the people with whom we travel through many lifetimes. It's the ones who touch our lives here ever so briefly, but have the most profound impacts on us. It's the baby girl who left my mother and opened the pathway for me to be here.

As I enter my sixtieth year of life, I hear the call to be the voice to let others know it is not too late to heal, forgive, or change whatever you want to *be*, *do*, or *have*. I intend to unravel this epidemic in our society where people feel not enough—not good enough, not lovable enough, not worthy enough. I invite you to join me to lead the shift from feeling unworthy to feeling wealthy. To step from the darkness and shine the light on your worthiness, your wealth, your well-being. Together we can believe and achieve anything. Each of us are worthy of love, abundance, forgiveness, freedom, compassion, appreciation, gratitude, and wealth.

I was deeply in debt one day and freed from its chains the next. I lived with a broken heart for five decades. Once my truths were revealed and I let go of my resistance, my heart healed, and the money flowed. It is never too late to change and embark on life's longest journey, the one from your head to your heart. It is not about shifting from your head to your heart; it is about bringing and accepting *all* aspects of yourself. It allows you to be aware of who you truly are, who *you* want to become, and how you want to *show up* in the world. The world wants you to show up as you. You were the one to get here. You see it's not about getting "there." It's about being here in this physical form. We are here for the experience, the adventure, the expansion, and the connection to others. We live in an infinite universe that is always expanding. We are a part of the expansion.

There is a field around us that allows us to tap into an infinite wisdom. We are being called to reconnect to it and heal ourselves to help heal the planet. The answer is though our reconnection to Source Energy. When we are stuck and our ego is running the show, we shut off the energy valve to the floodgates of our wisdom. We *are* Source Energy. It is time for us to see ourselves as we truly are: abundant, spiritual beings living in a friendly, safe, expanding Universe. Each of us deserves this. Striving for wealth allows us to positively impact and influence the vibration of the planet. It's not too late to create a legacy. Wealth is the epitome of well-being. It is not unattainable. When we live in the now, which is the only moment that exists, opportunities are abundant.

Are you ready for the transformation you desire, to awaken to a life you'd love? You are good enough right where you are. You have always been enough. It is time to choose the light, and *you* are the light you've been searching for your entire life. Are you open to shift from wounded child to warrior and bring your piece of the puzzle—your gift—to the world? It is *my* gift to see your potential, to help you go deep so you can dispel the feelings of unworthiness and ignite true wealth in your life. Because you are worth it!

About the Author

Pamela Lynch's mission is to help people raise their vibrations to shift from feeling unworthy to wealthy. As a Wealth Igniter and Spiritual Life Coach, Pamela coaches individuals to get to the root that is masking their abundance. She guides them go deep to dispel the feelings of unworthiness and to see the blocks to their abundance. Her gift is to help clients rediscover their purpose and see their potential to ignite true wealth. She sees the potential in others, their gifts, ideas, programs and business, and helps to promote them to the world. Pamela is also an inspiring speaker, author, and workshop leader. Her vision is to offer collaborative retreat opportunities in exotic paradises that are captivating and transforming. Pamela's ferocious determination, dedication to life learning, and her deep spiritual connection to herself and others were honed through her Shotokan Karate practice. She achieved the rank of first degree black belt when she was in her late 20s.

In addition, Pamela enjoyed 31 years in book publishing, developing skills, talents, and experiences from production to the boardroom. Her career culminated as a Web Producer, and she spent her last 13 years with Wiley Canada, creating websites and managing web content. In 2002, she relocated her family from Toronto to enjoy the benefits of working remotely in Kelowna for nine years. After a "right-sizing" in 2011, Pamela was certified as a Law of Attraction Coach through Christy Whitman's Quantum Success Coaching Academy. Clients are guided to uncover their limitations through the energy of the words they think, speak, and write. This helps them to get clear energetically, to realize limiting beliefs, and create a successful mindset to achieve their daily intentions. This marries well with her certification as a Dream Coach® with Marcia Wieder's proven 10-Step Process: you are guided with specific exercises in your Dream Coaching workbook to rediscover your purpose, align your dreams with your purpose, and create a project around your dream to take inspired action to create a dream-come-true life.

Pamela's dream is to speak to as many people as possible to help raise their awareness and vibrations to reconnect with their purpose and attract a purposeful and prosperous life. She believes we are spiritual beings who choose life on Earth for the experience, adventure, and expansion. Through healing ourselves, we help to heal the planet. Her own life experiences and challenges demonstrate that it is never too late to create a legacy, and she inspires others to embrace the knowledge that anything is possible and everyone is worth it! Pamela has proudly interviewed over 25 thought leaders about Conscious Business Conversations and spiritual awareness. The interviews are available through her website and SoundCloud. She is a consummate connector to people and ideas, and has interviewed many thought leaders, published *Journey into Joy* and is a contributing author in *Warrior Women with Angel Wings*. Pamela believes anything is possible, and her heartfelt message from the stage reveals everyone is born Worthy and Wealthy!

Her contact information:

Web site: *pamelalynch.com/*

Email: pamelaleelynch@gmail.com

As heard on SoundCloud: *https://soundcloud.com/pamela-lynch-1*

Facebook: *http://facebook.com/pamelaleelynch* and *https://www.facebook.com/groups/igniteyourwealth*

Twitter: *twitter.com/jazzedupnow*

Instagram: *instagram.com/WealthIgniter/*

Monique Hemingway
Alone

I entered this reality on a grey winter's day February 14, 1966, emerging from the warm comfort of my mother's womb on Valentine's Day. I took my first breath on the starchy, white sheets at Powell Memorial Hospital in rural Wyoming. Powell was a small town tucked away, and as such, there was no actual delivery room. My mother loved to tell me how she delivered me in a hospital bed right next to a man the doctors were desperately trying to resuscitate. In the confined space of the only operating room, one life was birthed while another was saved from the tight grip of death. What an appropriate metaphor for my life.

My young parents were high-school lovers who met at a dance complete with corsages, fruit punch, and awkward stolen kisses. Mother was a beautiful, uneducated seventeen-year-old from the wrong side of the tracks who dreamed of bigger things in faraway places and bought torrid romance books at the local Five & Dime. My twenty-year-old father came from a well-respected, affluent family whose ancestors were amongst the first homesteaders. Marriage was something they were expected to do, not something they wanted. It was the natural choice in 1966 when Mother suddenly found herself pregnant. My father wanted me aborted. My mother, being a good Catholic girl, refused. She saved my life as I would later save hers.

After my birth, my paternal grandmother's first words to her son were, "Well, she looks like you. There is no denying it now." I was a cute little burden, bundled up tightly and already being judged, blamed, and scrutinized. Her words slid right off of her son. When I was older, my father told me that he was captivated and mesmerized the moment he held me. He said if ever there was a princess born, it was me.

Usually, firstborns are given honorable names passed down through generations. At the time, the chosen names for girls included Mary, Julie, and Kathy. My mom defied both tradition and conventionalism and crowned me Monique. I was named after a stripper in a racy French novel my mother devoured. Perhaps she thought by giving me an exotic name, her life would seem more filled with *Joie de Vivre* and she'd live like the carefree characters in her books who led exciting lives. *Oui!*

All was bliss until my father got drafted, called away to fight a war he didn't understand in a land he did not know. Deep into the muggy jungles of Vietcong, my father proudly went. Uncle Sam armed him with a shiny new machine gun to shoot the enemy and unknowingly, also sprayed him with Agent Orange.

I got left behind with my disconnected seventeen-year-old mother. She was forced to grow up fast, trying to feed a baby in between fighting her own demons and wrestling her inner pain. At less than a month old, I already had my first taste of both physical and emotional abandonment.

We lived, or rather existed, in a tiny house with white trim and tall pine trees that swayed in the wind. There were wicker rocking chairs on the front porch and a big welcome mat for muddy feet. We shared this home with my stoic, alcoholic grandfather and my cheery grandmother who kept busy trying to keep up appearances.

When Mother and Grandma went off to work, I was left alone with Grandfather. He was the local Ford mechanic, trusted and loved. A tough cowboy, what you would call a man's man. Bones knotted by arthritis, his mind marinated in alcohol, and his soul was tormented in a private agony I would soon meet.

In those brief moments when he was sober, I knew, as a little girl, that he truly adored me. But those moments didn't last long. When the alcohol came out, so did his darkest self. He tried to keep the monster at bay, but it always escaped. The monster had hot, heavy breath that smelled of Certs, cheap beer, and Camel cigarettes. His callused, oil-stained hands fondled and poked me under my bleached cloth diaper. Afterwards, he spoiled me with sugar cookies and a warm bottle. The sugar eased my confusion and became a sweet reward for my silence. In my silence, I was alone.

Growing up, I always knew something was amiss between my grandfather and me. I didn't consciously know why I didn't trust him, but I knew I couldn't. When I entered adulthood the flashbacks and memories started pouring in. All the pieces came together under the care of a professional therapist. I was regressed back to infancy. Each time, the horrible memories surfaced in detail. I was able to uncover the truth that had been gnawing away inside of me. It was ready to be set free. When I told my mother about my repressed memories, she confirmed my suspicions.

For two years, my daddy was a brown-paper parcel wrapped with tattered string delivered every few weeks to our door. The box always had an odd, musty odor; a foreign smell from a foreign land. Within the box were Polaroids of a face I vaguely remembered. In every picture, my father had a cigarette dangling out of his mouth. Nicotine was his only solace to cover the pain and fear of being separated from his family. Later, Mother told me there had been drugs too. There was always some token of love packed in the parcel just for me. Usually, he sent exotic pajamas from Asia. Mommy took lots of pictures to send back to him, praying the envelope did not get returned MIA or KIA.

In 1968, my father returned home. He eagerly hugged and kissed Mother and me, but he was different. He was nervous, on edge. Loud noises made him jump.
He was present, but his mind was elsewhere. He returned in one piece, but his heart and mind were not at peace. Unsettled, he locked everything up in his mind. He brought the void home with him and sunk into it alone.

In 1969, we packed up and headed west to California, the land of sunshine, white sand, and glossy dreams! Father seemed to snap out of his mood. Coming back to life, he was excited for a fresh start. We set out on a grand, new adventure with hope in our hearts. At last, I could sleep in my crib, undisturbed from my grandfather's prying hands and poking fingers.

The road ahead led us to Santa Ana, California. We were living the American dream in a three-bedroom house with a big yard and asphalt driveway. My father became an aerospace machinist who made parts for rocket ships headed to the moon. I was so proud of him. My heart overflowed with love. The year 1970 arrived, and with it, my new baby sister. Unlike me, she was planned. I was disappointed because I asked God for a brother, but in time, she became my best friend. I felt the seclusion that had been my life alone start to fall away.

Around this time, the true cracks appeared. Cracks in the marriage, and literally cracks on my father's hands. He might've survived Vietnam, but not the effects of Agent Orange. He was in physical pain as his skin blistered, bled, and peeled off. Agent Orange attacked his nervous system and caused acute burning sensations from the inside. The mental pain was the hardest to endure. His mind replayed the looping scenes of horror over and over in graphic detail, and they never blurred or eased up. My mother didn't understand because he refused to talk about it. They refused to talk to me about it, but I knew, I always knew. Mother was now twenty-one with two children under five. Worn out, she became numb and alone. In this American dream, we were all suffocating under a blanket of denial.

With each passing year, the yelling and screaming between Mother and Father got louder and more difficult to ignore. Father, now intensely paranoid, was keeping tabs on my distraught mother. His jealousy came out in fits of rage with slaps across Mother's emotionless face. I held my sister close to me in the hopes of muffling her ears from the cruel, acid insults that my father, caught in the turmoil of PTSD and Agent Orange, spewed at her. The words "whore" and "slut" flew out of his mouth, along with droplets of spittle. Watching him, I realized that father was a monster too. He was angry and Mother was numb and my sister and I were alone.

About this time, I experienced a huge gift. Angels entered my life and changed it forever. I know it sounds crazy, but it's true. It's all true. Bright, shimmery, multi-colored light beings swirled above my bed each night. Enveloped by their love, I instantly recognized them. They spoke with me telepathically. They showered me with joy in my time of deep darkness. I told my parents about the angelic visits. They shooed me away matter-of-factly, explaining that it was just my imagination.

They already had more than they could handle; they didn't need a weirdo daughter "messing it all up." I took their truth and made it my truth, figuring somehow that I must have made it all up. After that, when the angels appeared, I shut my eyes and ignored them. I closed off my mind to silence them and banished them back to live in my imagination. Slowly, they retreated, and once again, I was alone.

The cracks turned into chasms that cut deeper and wider. My grandpa committed suicide in 1976. The alcohol and guilt had finally taken their toll. He locked himself in a garage with the car running. The note he left simply said: *Have fun.* My grandmother went to her grave saying it was just an accident. He died alone.

My mother started to rebel. She wanted to be free no matter what the cost. She went to night school to earn her high-school diploma, which pissed off my father. One night, in the wee hours before dawn, I heard Father coming home. He was greeted by Mother demanding, "Who is Jackie?" Followed by, "Where is your wedding ring?" There were terrible words and blows, which came to a crescendo when my mother told him she was done. Father responded by swallowing pills and saying he wanted to die. Alone in my dark room, I called out to my banished angels. "Please," I begged, "don't let my daddy die!" They answered my prayers. He didn't die.

Instead, in a horrific fit of rage, he dragged Mother into the bathroom by her hair and placed his war-ravaged hands around her neck. The same hands that lovingly held me were now choking the life out of my mother. In my bed, I lay paralyzed with fear, hoping that my sister didn't hear any of the chaos. How was I going to protect her from something that was bigger than any of us? Mother was struggling, coughing, and fighting for her life. In that moment, somewhere deep within, a power overcame me. I bolted into the bathroom and pounded my tiny fists into Father's back.

"No, no, no!" I screamed. I will never forget the sound of my mother's skull hitting the bare tile floor as he let go, and then turned around and hugged me. Lovingly, I wiped the hot tears streaming down his angry, red face. At nine years, old, I had a flash of clarity and understood that I was a healer. Even in the midst of such horror, I saw the possibility of salvation. We were together at 3:00 a.m. in that tiny bathroom, all of us so alone.

Like something out of a surreal horror film, my mother crawled past my father and I holding each other and called the police. Later, I watched out of the living room window as my father was put into the back of the cop car and hauled off. He never came back to live with us. Their divorce was as bitter as their hatred for each other. Inwardly, I blamed myself. Had I not been conceived; they would have never married.

Mother had to get a job with long hours since Father didn't pay child support. She couldn't afford a babysitter. At ten years, old, I was left in charge of my five-year-old sister. We were latch-key kids left at home alone. Slowly, life somehow managed to move forward. My father stuck around for a few years, and we visited on weekends. He and my mother never again exchanged words. We were dropped off in silence and picked up in silence. He got remarried and had another child with his new wife, Kim. I finally got my brother, a beautiful boy named Michael John Lance. Sadly, my half-brother didn't live to see his first birthday. He died, alone in his crib, of SIDS. I attended the funeral where a small, blue coffin held his precious body. That vision still burns in my mind.

No child should ever have to see their sibling buried. Losing his son pushed my father over the edge. He took off, disappeared, abandoning my sister and me. No child support, no contact, no birthday gifts or Christmas cards. He went off alone to fight the battles in his mind. Abandoned by Father, my sister and I were left to live with a burgeoning alcoholic of a mother.

Everything happened quickly. My body developed breasts. I was the first one to wear a bra in the fifth grade. I started to notice the boys noticing me. I was clever and hustled them. For twenty-five cents, I would lift my shirt and flash them my Sears training bra. They liked it, and I liked the attention. It made me feel wanted and not so much alone. In junior high, boys paid even more attention. Lifting my blouse was not enough for these horny, hormone-fueled creatures. Nope, they wanted to tongue kiss and grope me too! It felt awkward, weird, and slobbery. Not wanting to be alone, I obliged.

In high school, my bottom became round to match my firm breasts and as my legs got longer, my skirts got shorter, and my high-heels higher. How could they not pay attention? Sadly, what I didn't understand was that they wanted attention back. Losing my virginity was not a happy memory. The whole event was what we now call date rape.

My so-called boyfriend of a few weeks didn't give a shit that I kept saying no. Against my wishes, he too turned into a monster that pounced on me and had sex with me until it hurt, tore me open, and made me bleed. When he was finished, he got up, walked out, and left my house. Not a word was spoken. No kisses, no hugs, not even a, "Thank you, I had a nice time!"
At fourteen years, old, sprawled on my twin bed surrounded by bloody sheets, I sobbed. In between tears, I remember thinking how his semen smelled faintly like hydrogen peroxide.

I wanted that scent, his vile scent, *off* of me. I stumbled into the bathroom and filled up the tub. I lay for hours in that tub scrubbing and soaking, trying desperately to cleanse myself, desperately trying to reclaim my dignity. The next day, as I walked to the bus stop, he drove right past me and nonchalantly waved.

I pulled myself together and made it through high school. I realized I could hide behind make-up, perfect hair, and pretty clothes. I got people to look at the outside, so they would never ask about the inside. Like so many girls in Hollywood, I was a great actress. I hid behind the façade surrounded by popular friends and even a new boyfriend, but inside I was completely empty. Somehow, I maintained a connection to Spirit. Mostly, I prayed that I wouldn't get fat, ugly, or pregnant. I didn't discuss the spirit world with anyone. I didn't want them to think I was weird.

My mom slowly drowned herself in endless Bacardi and Cokes that she'd start drinking at 6:00 a.m. from coffee cups, thinking she was fooling us. She also acquired a new husband who became her priority. My sister and I were five years apart and complete opposites. My once-best-friend and I were living in the same house, living separate miserable lives, trying to be brave. We were both so alone. I entered college and that's where the nervous breakdown happened. I dropped out of college two years in, right before finals. I was even on the honor roll; but I couldn't do it anymore. I couldn't keep up. I couldn't keep the pain inside. It wanted to boil over. I developed an insidious eating disorder.

Most days, I survived on three pepperonis, a Diet Coke, and a dollop of whipped cream for dessert. A few years later, it turned into Bulimia. My mind thought it was in control, but I was horribly out of control. I suffered from Exercise Bulimia, along with vomiting after binging on mass amounts of food. Ipecac syrup became my best friend, as it induced vomiting. I experienced the ultimate humiliation after a binge when I swallowed the syrup and didn't make it to the bathroom on time.

At twenty, instead of being on top of the world, I was on top of my bed covered in my own hot vomit. Never had I felt such despair; never had I felt so alone. I knew the vomiting had to stop, but I couldn't get control of the bingeing. Then the disorder swung into obesity. Over the next thirty years, I watched the numbers yo-yo up and down the scale. I could never maintain my weight. It was either going down or going up like a dizzy see-saw that never finds equilibrium.

I carried on. I pushed forward alone. That's what strong independent girls do, right? We become Wonder Women. We power through everything in our search for perfection. We don't ask for help. Nobody ever offered it to me anyhow. At that point, if somebody reached out to me, I didn't trust them. I got a job, I made money. I searched for a man to love me. Admittedly, I searched with a lot of men, forever hoping that somewhere there was a man who could love me enough to validate me and make me whole again.

The years faded into each other with a combination of failed relationships and wild sexual promiscuity. There were bouts of celibacy when I shut myself off from life, feeling too fat to participate. One bleak night, I found myself on a cliff, contemplating driving off of it. That was when my angels returned. They said nothing, but they filled my car with an immense energy that sparked my will to live. At last, I realized that the validation I needed was within me.
I needed to realize my worth. It was not going to come from an outside source. It was something I needed to do, and I needed to do it on my own. I dug deep, I meditated, I cried, I screamed and then I told my story. I did healings to release my sexual shame. I called back my angels from childhood, asking for their healing presence.

They never left I had simply pushed them away. Slowly but surely, I started to emerge. My beautiful light within began to burst forth. I promised myself and my angels never to dim myself again. My gifts opened to me, all this time awaiting my own self-discovery. In 2001, I tracked down my father.

Finally, I got to hear his side of the story and not just the one my mother told me for years. I saw that he was a beautiful man. A hurt man, yes but also an intelligent, loving, kind, and peaceful man. I looked into his eyes and realized I was my father's daughter. I forgave him. I saw the aloneness that was etched in his face. He had suffered enough. We both had.

Sadly, a few years later, at the age of sixty-two, he was diagnosed with lung cancer. My sister and I flew to Wyoming to say our goodbyes. We held him and loved him. Through his morphine haze, his eyes told me that he knew we were there and that he was not alone. I walked out of the hospital knowing it would be the last time I saw him. It was ironic how hard it was to leave someone who had left me so many years earlier. That is the beauty of forgiveness.

My mother met her fate at the age of sixty-two as well. She went into a coma when her colon stopped working and sepsis set in after years of alcohol abuse. My sister and I had to take her off of life support. Again, we had to say our goodbyes prematurely. I told her she was the best mother for me. I thanked her for her sacrifices as well as her mistakes. In a moment of clarity, she turned to me. Her eyes, so sadly said *thank you*. Ten minutes later, she was gone. With her, I took my first breath, and now I was with her as she took her last.

Today, I am without any parents or grandparents. I am divorced and completely on my own. I am truly alone and thriving! I've come to know that I've never been alone. I have been surrounded by angels always. At times, I shunned them, yet they never stopped believing in me. They knew when to show themselves and when to stand back so I could show myself the way. They infused me with the power and the determination to move forward and move beyond.

When I couldn't pull through, they dragged me through. I may have felt alone, but I always had the sense within me that I would survive. I had an inner knowing that I would somehow make a difference to this world. My inner flame may have flickered, but my angels fanned it to keep it from burning out. They gave me strength until I was brave enough to look at my darkest parts and bring them up to light. When I was finally able to integrate my mind, body, and soul, I became whole, and that is vastly different than being alone.

About the Author

Monique Hemingway is an Author, Psychic-Medium, Channel, and Healer. She is a mother, sister, and daughter whose goal is to help both men and women recognize and awaken the God/Goddess within. She lives in Southern California with her two young children who keep her both grounded and on her toes!

Monique is amongst one of the most sought-after and recognized Psychic-Mediums and maintains an international clientele roster. She is a media presence, having appeared on television, radio, and in printed publications. Monique discovered her intuitive gifts in her forties after suffering six miscarriages, losses which inspired her to embark on a spiritual path of healing herself and guiding others on how to do the same for themselves.

In addition to her work as a prolific Medium, she is also an accomplished writer and poet. Monique is working on a new book of poems and essays based on her many years of professional Medium work. Her writing focuses on erotic poetry as a means to help men and women integrate the sacred aspects of their sexuality as a means to heal their minds, bodies, and souls.

Monique can be reached at:
www.moniquehemingway.com
monique@moniquehemingway.com

Vivian Martinez
My Story

This is my story about finding peace and love, and how a camera and the help of angels guided me to it.

Like many others, I was brought up in a dysfunctional family. My parents, two brothers, and I grew up in Southern California. I am the middle child and the only girl. I always thought that being the only girl in our family gave me the right to be spoiled. It certainly was not. Although my parents loved us dearly, they just did not know how to show their love or compassion.

Mom and Dad grew up in very stressful households, which had been handed down from generation to generation. As a child, I often wondered why I had even been born into that family. I always felt different from everyone else; I never felt like I fit in anywhere. At one point in my young life, I even thought that maybe I had been adopted!

I wasn't aware of it at the time, but all of what I endured growing up was part of my journey to discover who I was and to recognize the importance of changing our family dynamics. My parents were my greatest teachers in my life, and I love them very much for that.

In my early twenties, I was given a 35-mm camera, which used film in those days. My older brother's friend had found the camera on the ground while driving back from a trip to the mountains. He had given the camera to my brother, but he had no use for it, so he gave it to me. I was very excited to receive it. It was the first camera I had ever owned.

I discovered photography in high school when I took the class as an elective. I was a very shy, quiet, and awkward kid in high school and never wanted to be center of attention. The camera was a big part of me. It gave me a way to express myself without using words. It helped me to discover a creative side that I never realized existed within me.

I always loved the outdoors and adventure. I really enjoyed taking drives by myself, just me and my camera. The more I would venture off into nature, the more connected I felt to Earth. The more I felt connected to Earth, the more I had a connection to myself. Amid nature and wildlife was where I felt most peaceful within, and the more at peace I became, the more open I was to love. The love for others, and most importantly, the love I had for myself.

As time went on, I had gone through many transformations in my life. Each time, I felt more connected with myself and my three beautiful children. I have always had a very strong connection to my precious grandchildren too. I made many discoveries throughout my journey, and one of those discoveries was my connection to the angels and the non-physical beings that exist among us.

It all started with my camera and taking pictures at night. Orbs started showing up in my pictures. Lots of them. I did some research on orbs to see what they were. Though there were a few opinions about orbs, I always felt very comfortable with them. I could not see them with my eyes in the beginning, only in my pictures.

I learned to say a special prayer whenever I intentionally set out to photograph them. After some time, they started appearing in my daytime photos too, but not as many. I even started videotaping the orbs in motion. I had gone to my very first retreat in Mount Shasta. I made a big transformation at that three-day retreat. I noticed that I started getting other beings in my photographs, like nature fairies. One of my most memorable adventures and when a photograph opportunity was gifted to me, was during a solo road trip to the state of Washington from California.

On my drive, back to California, I had stopped to rest in Oregon. I parked by a body of water that had many birds around. I brought out my camera and took some shots of the birds on the water. I noticed a swarm of flying things that I thought were bugs coming towards me. There were so many that I had to leave because I didn't know what they were. I was able to see them, but I could not make them out. They were about a half an inch in size. As I got into my car to leave, they followed me and were hovering above me. I rolled down my window and took two pictures of them.

When I finally got home, I started looking through my pictures. I discovered the most amazing picture of these creatures!

People have looked at the photograph, and some believe they are fairies and some say angels. I believe it is up to each individual and what they see through their own eyes.

This photo is beautiful, amazing, and real. I feel it was gifted to me, and I am extremely honored. After taking it, I realized that anything is possible when there is love in your heart, trust, and belief. I want to thank the angels for always being by my side throughout my existence on Earth. I love you, and I know you love me unconditionally. I now have the peace and the love that I've always searched for. Thank you for guiding me toward knowing that it was always inside of me.

Hope you find yours. Just believe.

About the Author

Vivian Martinez is a Radiology Assistant at a local hospital in Sacramento, California. She has three wonderful children and two precious grandchildren. Her passions are wildlife photography and being out in nature and wildlife. Vivian is a Certified Angel Card Reader, Fairyologist, and Angel Therapy Practitioner certified by Doreen Virtue. She was a guest speaker on the Angelic Realms Radio show, speaking about her experiences with Angels and Fairies. Vivian is a Precognitive Dreamer Intuitive and has experiences of Claircognizance and Clairsentience. She was on a mission to discover her truth. In her pursuit of truth, she discovered energy healing and became a Certified Reiki Master. Vivian has a passion for helping people and animals to find comfort, peace, and healing. To view Vivian's photographs, visit: *www.smugmug.com*

Joanne McLeod
Rainbow Skies and Feather Pathways

How do I begin to express my 47 years on this earth plane?

Here is my story:

Witchy Poo, Bible, Frogs and Fairies

I have always been spiritual and I've always been a little peculiar, I dance to the beat of my own inner drum.
I acknowledge my dark and light side and would label myself a Mystic Angel the two sides of me were apparent at an early age the obsession with bible and saying I wanted to be a nun when I grew up, I'm not from a catholic family. In contrast my long dark untamable wavy locks with the regular threat to turn family members into frogs earnt me the pet name Witchy Poo!

Age 7 all I wanted for Christmas was a plastic crystal ball that had a slot for playing cards to give readings.

I knew fairies existed partly due to McLeod legend of the fairy flag of protection. The tale goes that the son of the chief clan's man fell in love with a fairy and they had a child thus I am descendant of fairies that explains a lot! Also, my Granny would tell me of the Devonshire little fold n when Auntie had seen one but my favorite was how Rainbows were made by fairies hanging out their clothes to dry.

Wow that's me down there!

I married young and became a mum the month before I was 23. During Josephine's birth my Soul had detached from my body and there I was floating by the ceiling watching her make her way into the world.

Almost 4 years later number 1 son Alexander was born and again I watched his birth from outside my body. However, this time a door way opened in the delivery room wall and stood in the door way were my deceased Gran, Auntie, Grandpa and Great Grandad smiling and waving to me.

Let me clear I was not drugged up I had been given something the first day Wednesday and refused anything after that it was now Sunday evening. Jimi's birth 4 years later on Christmas day, I remained in my body it was a quicker birth.

Soul contracts and get what you can cope with.

Alex was diagnosed with ADHD and Autism and Jimi with Autism life was a struggle of coping with daily meltdowns, rushing to take them home from school from regular incidents, trying to teach my bright boys when they were permanently excluded from mainstream school until I won battle to find a suitable place for them.

Contrary to belief that autistic people don't have any empathy; I observe that my boys are hyper sensitive to the emotions of other and at times it's too overwhelming to be around people.

I was sleep deprived still waiting for Alex to sleep the night even though he is 20! Plus, trying to hold down a job. My escape time was reading all I could on Angels, Fairies, the paranormal etc.

Angels guide me

Angels guided me in my daily work life as a care worker. When I worked with the elderly I sensed where I was needed and even claricognitively heard patience call to me. I got to one lady during the night in time for me to hold her hand as she passed away and to stop a man from falling out of bed.

Angel Leigh

In 2005 my marriage began to crumble.

I treated myself to a birthday Past life regression n my awakening began.

In July, this year my family had the devastating news that my youngest brother had an inoperable Brain Tumor.

I sat home alone crying when I was overcome with a feeling of calm and peace I looked up to see the almost solid for of a beautiful lady she had black long wavy hair a frilly long red dress, colorful wooden beads she looked like she came from ancient Peru. I was not scared I sensed she is my guardian angel, she emanated love, warmth and comfort in my mind.

In my mind, I asked her name and heard Angel Leigh.

Rainbow skies and Angel whispers.

After my marriage broke up I was vulnerable and low at this time I met my youngest son Williams Dad.

He has severe mental health Issues is a Narcissist. The boys' behavior went off the scale at this time as we were living in fear I naively thought I was protecting my kids and taking all the abuse which he did to me on every level.

I don't want to dwell too much on that time we've survived are happy now it made us stronger united.

One night as I slept I heard my name I was told to wake up and get up which I did to find William's Dad in a compromising position leaning over sleeping Josephine with hand out stretched to touch her it doesn't bear thinking about what would have happened without Angel Leigh waking me.

Thru the stress of the time I sadly suffered a late miscarriage 13th November 2007 I named her Poppy, she was due 1st May 2008.

1st May 2008 my Stepdad passed away, the day after I had a visitation from him he showed me the rainbow bridge, I could see home the big white mansion and children playing near the stream on luscious grass. As I stood on the edge of the bridge Charlie let go of my hand told me I couldn't walk over the bridge with him and waved goodbye.

I fell pregnant again with William in 2008 and this year I qualified as a hypnotherapist /life coach which opened my intuition more and Did Reiki 1 during which I discovered I could see Auras.

Still the volatile relationship I asked the Angels to keep William safe to term I saw many Rainbows during his pregnancy.

It is only recently that I have made the connection to William being my Rainbow baby as he was due 12th November 2008 a year after lost Poppy.

The Angels were determined William would survive his birth was eventful. He was born by emergency caesarian 2nd November 2008 as he lay transversely.

The doctor began to shake when she opened me up and saw William. He was wrapped entirely in his umbilical cord; it was wrapped twice around his neck with his hands tied to his neck it coiled all around his tiny body and looped over his toes.

The top consultant walked in at this point wearing a white shirt, beige trousers. He said he had come straight from the golf course as he had feeling he was needed at work. He asked permission to climb aboard mummy which I gratefully gave him.

He untangled William, he was born a lovely shade of purple and not breathing. My blood pressure was low and I wasn't well but I was aware of medical team working hard to revive William that seemed like an eternity until the magical sound of William crying.

William also has Autism and ADHD he is very sweet natured and affectionate; I call him my Cherub child he is my gift from the Angels. He is now 8 and still tells me he looked down from the spirit world and chose me to be his lovely Muma!

Feather Pathways

In May 2009, my beloved Grandad passed away, I was devastated. The day we scattered his ashes I saw huge white feathers at me feet leading all the way to the passenger seat of my uncle's car.

The feather pathways continued for months afterwards. At times of sadness, stress I've since been sent a lot of feathers, I found 1 inside a folded up new pair of leggings that was in a sealed bag, 1 appeared stuck in my top mid conversation with my friend, even landing at my feet in a public toilet!

One Boxing Day when kids were with their Dad I lay crying in the bath a feather landing in my bath. I said wow thank you did that really happen and in answer a second one floated to me!

2013 April, I went to a workshop at the local spiritualist church where I had an emotional reunion with Poppy. I felt her clamber onto my lap, cup my face in her tiny hands and smother my face in kisses. I heard her say as I sobbed "Don't cry Muma its ok I'm here "

The next day I broke down as William did exactly the same!

November that year sat in the spiritualist church congregation I stared in awe that I could see ethereal outlines of spirits queuing up on stage awaiting their turn and

November 13 continued.

Among the queue I recognized my paternal grandparents! I felt the hairs on the back of neck rise as they stepped forward. They foretold my brother had 6 months to live and that I had to sort a family situation, no easy task!

Angel Lady who held open the door.

2014 I googled Angel workshops up come lady who changed my world and Doreen Virtue was coming to London as a single mum could I afford to go?!

February, I went to the Angel card workshop with the special lady. There was supposed to be 4 people taking part but only 2 of us turned up. The other lady had a panic attack chose to leave so I had a 1 to 1 lesson. Everything clicked it was a milestone moment which helped me decide to go to the Doreen virtue training September 2014.

May 2014 my brother's health rapidly deteriorated friends and family over took the hospital ward to be with him in his final hours. The family vicar stood by his bedside praying I was saying my own prayer to the Angels when the Vicar mentioned Angels! Dad turned to me and Said Jo believes in Angels at that point my legs gave way.

Leading up to his funeral I couldn't face writing my brother's farewell card to go on the funeral floral arrangement.
He appeared before me and in characteristically colourful language told me to get on with it!

September 2014 the first person I saw at the Doreen virtue training each of the 4 days was the Angel lady!

In spring 2015 I received an email from her asking if I would be interested in doing Readings for a company at a large mind body spirit festival. I had never done a reading for money let alone anything like this. I had a test reading with the lovely manager and may 2015 I worked at the show. I certainly got thru on a wing and a prayer, must have done ok as got asked to do the autumn fayre.

Whilst at the autumn fayre I plucked the courage to ask to try doing readings on their phone line. I did so on 1st October 2015 working my care job by day n phone readings night times.

I now work full time doing the phone readings at home. My quality of life has improved so much and I have more time with the kids I am so blessed.

My future is manifesting brightly with a new opportunity I can't say too much about yet!

If anyone was moved by my story or needs to talk as going thru similar, please get in touch.

Feb 2017

As I lay in bed I chatted to the Angels thanking them for guiding me in my life and for choosing me to work with them. I asked if I was being of service enough.

When I awoke next to my face on my pillow was an Angel shape made of cotton. Later that week I commented on Facebook of painting by a famous English Angel lady. The painting relates to my recent evolving opportunity prompting me to try again as I had last year and their reply didn't reach me. This time all's well.

About the Author

My name is Joanne McLeod I live in Greater London England, with my 3 sons, 3 cats and lively puppy. My daughter lives nearby.

I would certainly describe myself as a Warrior Woman and I have both faery and Angel Wings Tattooed on my back!

My Angel Lee, guide Peter and door keeper Silver Wing of Many Feathers and well as the Arch Angels I now work with have shown themselves to me, sent many signs, to protect, guide, support and comfort me whether I've asked them or not!

Serena Brinderson
My Soul Whispers

My heart is racing, my breath quick and rhythmic, the spirits hiding in the trees are dancing. They move and intertwine in the shadows, making them hard to follow, but nonetheless, they are jumping from one juniper's dark imprint to the next. My small feet and legs carry me home. I run to my room, kneel down, and look out the window, watching from a safe distance. After being mesmerized by the dance of the tree spirits, I soon crawl into bed and pass from one dream to the next. Morning comes, and I move in between worlds from the magic of nature, feeling, listening, and seeing the light of the All that surrounds me back to the constant reminders of everyday life. I am silent about what I see; it is my secret that no one would believe if I told them.

The secret that my mom continually offers is the sense of awe and wisdom that God is everywhere and everything, accompanied with the essence of undying gratitude for the present moment. She guides my brother and me along, singing hymns, dancing, and painting, always finding joy and

315

laughter amid the shades of internal distress within her own self-doubt. Holding onto her faith and its confined structure, which brings her the security and strength to handle her challenges with grace. Though the structure is narrow, riddled with guilt and judgement, which differs from the undying truth that I feel—that we are infinite. I recognize that in a flower, the ocean, the clouds, and most importantly, in the entirety of my being. I know the Divine resides within me, but I'm taught that God is outside of us and He is here to save us. And so, my self-doubt began early on, and the journey back to my soul begins.

My eyes are closed in prayer as I lie on the top of a hill amid the wild grass and flowers. I see a glimpse of myself in a forest teaching a group of people and leading what feels like a ritual. As I embody this vision in my teenage self, I sense the deep fulfillment and acceptance of what I hold dear. Seeing it clearly plants the seed that I want to nourish. Moving closer to independence, I start my college search looking for that vision; I travel to Alaska, Montana, and Vermont. Surrounded by the tall pine trees straddling the lake and the ocean, I feel the connection I am looking for in Juneau, Alaska. My body confirms this truth with the unexplainable peace I feel here. And I speak with passion about my desire to go to Alaska, yet I am discouraged based on the lack of worldly benefit. I choose to succumb.

The slow undercurrent of being in a place that isn't where I need or want to be begins to eat at me. My entire being feels displaced, but my mind rationalizes the practicality, which creates a nonverbal expression through my physical body. The clouds of depression fill my days and roll into a listless fog, creeping through my mood, getting thicker and thicker. I feel trapped and lost in the lack of visibility of myself, and I question who I am and what I am striving to become. My soul is stifled and calls out with a muffled melancholy-ridden voice. It's hard to hear and decipher the message, but I know I have to leave this place.

In a winding and twisting path, I find myself again in the concepts and ideas of art school. They are conveyed through materials and images, which make my spirit soar. They give me life, purpose. It is a platform for me to speak in a way that nourishes and enriches my being. I am connected creating sculptures, photographs, and installations with intention. Messages come to me through pictures and are expressed in each piece I conceive. Moving from one project to the next, I feel inspired; my heart is opening to myself and who I am. This coincides with a love of practicing Yoga, opening me up and expanding my awareness of self. I begin to connect deeply with my body and continually become awakened to why I have certain belief systems and veils of protection.

As the barriers slowly begin to fall away, shedding a skin or layer of the past, I step into the essence of my being. Each step brings me closer to my roots—teaching Yoga, marriage, and children. My physical body begins to speak with me more and more frequently through food allergies, environmental allergies, headaches, body/joint pain, and fatigue. I continue dwindling my diet, but working, being a mom, and getting my Master's degree part-time is taking its toll. Feeling alone and carrying a huge weight of supporting a family without a partner capable of sharing the load of it all, my body and spirit, day by day, are less and less cherished until there is very little left.

There is a glimpse and flickering recognition as I turn to leave the front door of our house, and I see clearly, without a doubt, that I have to leave my marriage, otherwise my children will believe this is what a partnership is and looks like. I cannot fathom seeing my daughter being where I am. I would never wish it upon her, and with a firm stand, I know I will not allow my son to believe that this how you treat a woman who you love. So, I come to a reckoning and step away from our marriage, if not for myself, then for our kids.

I search out and pursue a deeper connection to something as I let go of the relationship that challenged me, made me grow, gave me strength as a provider, and took so much from me. I find the practice that nourishes my spirit in a way that has never been done. I deeply feel a connection to my soul, and it sings through pranayama, mantra, kriyas, and meditation. I recognize myself, my situation, the circumstances, my past with more and more clarity at an accelerated rate. My intuition is stronger than ever; I see the divine all around me in a butterfly that crosses my path, in a sunset, in the beauty of my life and how it continues to unfold.

I have the chills, every hair on my body is standing tall, and I know what I am hearing rings truth, and this is my acknowledgement. The vision of my art and of books that I will create to bring healing to those by sharing my journey is crystal clear; I feel it—my purpose. And yet knowing this, I finish my Master's and get a job as a first-grade teacher. Every day that I go to work, my body speaks to me, at first subtly, then with greater fatigue, joint pain, and headaches. As the year moves forward, my symptoms worsen and begin to be unbearable. I can barely get through a day; my cognitive function is slowing, my diet consists of two or three vegetables, and my migraines are frequent. I come home from work and go straight to bed, all the while my two children are home playing. My meditations every day clearly state: *leave your job; this is not what you are here to do.*

In my bed, barely able to move with a horrible kidney pain and migraine, I see that I have to let go of my job or it will kill me. As I gain strength back, I return to my job in order to find a replacement. Now on disability and diagnosed with Chronic Fatigue, Fibromyalgia, Immune Deficiency, and/or Lyme Disease, I begin the slow recovery back to my soul's purpose of creating art, writing, and sharing my story, following my connection to the divine guidance that I receive. As I listen more and more closely to my spirit and essence, I build strength.

The soft voice inside that calls to me, that I feel in my body, that sings truth, is my soul. It often is quiet, like the soft footsteps in the night that we are told do not exist, or the gut feeling that just comes to you but is put off as a fluke, or the wish that lights you up but that you push out of your mind as a fantasy. It is not the logical, practical, or rational part of you, but nonetheless, it is *you*. It is the place we find fulfillment, trust, and faith. Inherently, we are born to trust and have faith in the world around us until we are taught otherwise. This can occur in any environment in a million different ways, but ultimately somewhere along the line, we learn we shouldn't trust ourselves, that it's inevitable.

Our challenges and growth bring us back to the whispers of truth to grow into the assurance of ourselves and our own guidance, finding our way by listening to the quiet whispers.

About the Author

My yogic path started very young and it evolved into my way of being. The beginning stages started in the physical realm as a vinyasa teacher, as life progressed and I faced deeply challenging aspects of life and myself. Divorce and chronic illness sent me searching for answers beyond the physical and into the spiritual. I came to connect with aspects of myself as a healer, intuitive and spiritual teacher through my own daily meditation and affirmation practice.

These tools have been the key to my continued education as I received a Master's in Art of Teaching at USC and also studied to become a Reiki Master, Shambala practitioner, Intuitive, Kundalini Teacher and Yoga Instructor. I am honored to share my journey and growth as way of supporting those searching for connection in the wake of isolation, for love and forgiveness despite fear and judgement, and letting go of resistance for freedom.

Maeve Grace
My Path

The towering wave of the tsunami loomed nearer and nearer.
I knew I could not escape it. My heart pounded with fear and
anticipation; I knew the tremendous wall of water would
crush me in an instant. I wondered if I would experience
pain; I wondered what it would be like to drown, to let the
water fill my lungs and release me from my physical sheath.
I felt disaster with far ranging effects was about to strike; yet,
the voice of peace within me spoke that this would not be the
end. I knew this to be true somehow; my faith was sure that
my eternal soul would not suffer or stop.

Yet, my heart ached for what I had not yet been able to
experience in this earth sojourn; my future grandchildren,
robust health, travel, creative exploration, peace of mind. As
the wave rushed over me I was stunned by the beautiful aqua
clarity of the water. I could see the sun's rays brilliantly
streaming down from the surface. It illuminated everything
around me, yet the sheer liquid pressure made it impossible

for me to rise to the top. I was swept along by the tremendous force; yet I was surprised that I wasn't being crushed at all. My father's voice rang in my ears "don't panic!"; one of the many, many times I had heard that lifesaving advice, just as it had been instilled during a near-drowning event in my childhood. I realized that I was still alive, yet I was keenly aware that I could not stay that way for long without oxygen.

I prayed that somehow, I would be lifted to the top of the water. I stroked upwards furiously, but it was not enough to propel me to the lifesaving surface. I swam and swam until I could no longer hold my breath; my lungs gasped for the air element my survival so desperately depended on. As I gulped water into my lungs I braced for pain and deliverance. But I did not die. After some moments, I realized that I was literally able to breathe under water. I was shocked and amazed! And as my logical mind informed me of the impossibility of this, I awoke.

This recurring tsunami dream came to me at least weekly for the better part of 2 years. After a lifetime of receiving information from nature for navigating the world around me, I knew that the dreams were a message. I understood that the clarity of the water reflected something about my ability to stay in a clear space regardless of the chaos swirling around me, the sun's rays bringing illumination in the form of guidance from my meditations and prayers. But given the circumstances I found myself in both personally and professionally, I didn't feel clear at all. As a government executive in charge of administration services for a large department, a billion-dollar budget and the support for several statewide programs, I found myself in a maelstrom of politics and transition at the beginning of the economic downturn.

The constant, overwhelming need to find ways to function with fewer resources; the burdensome responsibility of implementing the legacy visions of high-ranking politicians; tending to staff needs for reassurance because they were afraid of losing their jobs; and answering the demands for information and remedy from a frustrated legislature and their constituency, too often had me feeling like I was drowning at the end of a 12 to 16-hour day. Managing the care for my mother who was suffering the dreadful march of Alzheimer's, yet still deserving of the dignity of assisted independence, filled every moment of the time I was not at work and beyond; into my sleep and dreams. My young adult children and my husband were cast to the back-burner as I juggled to simply keep my head above water, and I missed them with every fiber of my being.

I missed the experiences we could have been sharing, the closeness we had cultivated all our lives together, the completeness I always felt in the embrace of my little family. Our daughters were recently graduated from college, building their adult lives, and I feared that I would lose the thread that had always kept us close as they embarked into adulthood with very little access to their mother. I missed my husband and my friends, who did what they could to comfort me, but who also found it very hard to understand the depth of my turmoil. I truly was drowning. I was wrung out, depleted, feeling completely lost.

Then came my mother's diagnosis of terminal cancer and her death 3 months later in June of 2008. Simultaneously, the top layer of the state department I worked for experienced a major transition with new, and in some cases, hostile political appointees coming in. I felt like every day was a call to battle and I never knew where the next "bullet" was going to come from. I became hyper-vigilant against the negativity in my environment, and was stunned by the level of toxicity directed at me and my staff. I felt I was losing my grip on the life raft of faith and hope that had somehow kept me afloat throughout my crazy life. I started to fall apart physically; chronic and dangerous symptoms began to manifest, landing me in the emergency room more than once, and it was at this point that the water in my tsunami dreams lost its clarity. All I could see as I would get tumbled around in the powerful waves was murky darkness.

Symbolism attributed to Carl Jung is that a tsunami represents some great spiritual change; the washing away of the old and the beginning of new growth. And in fact, as I shall share, that was exactly the message of my recurring dreams. Significant changes and spiritual growth were certainly in store for me. So yes, check. Tsunami dreams may occur when we are feeling overwhelmed, or when we are afraid we won't be able to cope or adjust with what we see or feel coming in our future. Absolutely, not being able to see what was ahead, I was terrified for my psychic and physical survival.

Another check. These dreams remind us that if we don't confront and deal with things that are out of balance in our life, they will confront us first. A great big check, as I was to find out. Murky water is a warning to address one's self-care. Check, check, check, as my body was so eloquently telling me. It was time for me to make some big changes, no mistake. But I had no idea where to turn first; a new assignment in the State? At my level, it was not likely I would be able to escape the volatile dynamic of the downturn and the politics around that.

Quit working? It just didn't fit into the retirement numbers I had run for my exit strategy. I needed to work to make sure the girls college costs were paid off and to provide security for the future. Could I fight back against the swirling political dysfunction I lived in daily? I was so beat up from endlessly working to simply continue doing the right things for the right reasons in an environment that was all about the sound bite and the people be damned, that I could only choose the battles where it felt like everything I stood for was at stake.

The battles to maintain my integrity and that of my area of responsibility, whittled away more at my fragile health. I prayed and meditated and prayed some more for guidance, but could not see clearly a way to shift my path. Finally, one evening when I was at the lowest of my lows, my husband mentioned that I might want to consider an early retirement. After my first response of "are you crazy?!" I started to wonder if he had thrown me a literal lifeline.

Funny what form our angels can take. This man; my practical, solid, non-emotional and not very sensitive husband, who for reasons of his own had not always been there for me in the past, had brought a glimmer of something I might be able to hold onto. Was it possible? Could I trust him to support me, not just financially but also emotionally, if I made this move? God knows I had supported him in the past! Would the reduced pension from early retirement be enough to take care of our needs in the future? If I did not do this, what would happen to my health? Would I be able to persevere for another 5 to 10 years without falling apart?

I looked at the numbers again and again. *If* we lived simply; *if* I found something I enjoyed doing and worked part time; *if* we weren't confronted by any major setbacks; a lot of *ifs*! I just didn't know how it could work! But the murky tsunami dreams continued. The toxicity at work only increased. I was tormented by a sense of impending doom if I stayed. My hubby had offered me a glimmer of hope. That glimmer was all I had to hang onto. I had to make a leap of faith.

I officially retired from my 30-year career in State service August 2010, at the age of 52. The months leading up to that decision were filled with constant budget and personnel reduction drills; impossible demands on my time while averaging 11 meetings a day; and several political end-runs by some of my peers and by my Cabinet level counterpart. I was reminded constantly why it would be a good time to devise my exit strategy. The day our Director announced his own retirement "for personal reasons" the writing was on the wall. When I learned that the man appointed as interim Director was one of the most contentious of my peer executives, I knew that it was time for me to leave.

I remembered all too clearly the day he pointed to his oversized glass sculpture of a scorpion and told me that he *was* the scorpion. He warned me that just as was the fate of the frog in the old fable, the frog who wanted to believe the promise of the scorpion that it would not be harmed for carrying him across the flood, it was the scorpion's nature to sting and he would not hesitate to do so. I submitted my paperwork and announced my retirement to him a few weeks after he was appointed as interim Director. He seemed to be angry to receive the news, which surprised me a bit given some of the challenges of our past relationship, but I was resolved. I needed to take this risk in the hopes of creating balance and healing freedom in my life. So, in a few short months I quietly left for good, without fanfare or celebration.

I wish I could say that leaving my career gave me a sense of relief. Unfortunately, at least for a time, the toxicity tried to pull me back in. As the days turned into weeks I learned of things that were happening in my old environment that made it impossible to find my joy. The leadership team I left in charge were decimated; the interim Director terminated their executive and managerial appointments, and those people he was not able to fire he buried in dead-end assignments within the organization. Word on the streets was that he was in a vengeful mood because I retired before he could fire me.

Rumors were spread about me that I found out about because they were questioned by those who knew me. The network server I had been left access to until my old responsibilities had all transitioned was hacked and many of my files destroyed (fortunately I had backups). The following investigation found that the breach was generated by the interim Director's office, but that information was quickly covered up. I was shocked; ashamed and horrified at these revelations. I had put my faith in the Universe that things would be better if I left all that behind, and this was the result? Was I such a bad actor in a prior life that I deserved the meanest kinds of character assassination?

Did I deserve such a dishonorable exit after a 30-year career as a devoted public servant? Was my prior team; that group of intelligent, loyal, and dedicated souls, implicated just by their association with me? I may have escaped the direct wrath, but it was lobbed instead onto the people who had worked for me, people I deeply cared about! Had we all been forsaken by faith and hope and love and God? Rather than feeling liberated by my newfound freedom, I felt completely crushed in ways that I had not experienced in the tsunamis of my dreams.

In my desperate attempts to feel better I reminded myself that if I looked around, there were others who had experienced far worse. So why didn't that provide any relief? Answers were not immediately available. I put into place the only plan I could come up with; to wake up each day and do my best to face life anew.

It's taken me seven years to find a solid footing back into faith and hope and a daily awareness of the Creator in my life. Not that I had lost it; I just couldn't *feel* it anymore. I remember when I retired, I intentionally dedicated my heart and soul to becoming the embodiment of healing love, then quickly realized that the spiritual path is not for the faint of heart. Apparently, I had to walk through the experience of being shattered at the level of my deepest values, everything I thought to be true about me and the world, and all I had learned about how to be a responsible, productive citizen, to have a place to rise from. Isn't that the way of it? It's usually through our crucifixion that we rise to learn the story of our own resurrection. And despite the pain there was never a more certain direction for me; I was born to live in connection with the Divine.

What I ultimately re-membered; what I learned at the core of my being, is that we are never alone. The Universe provided a host of helpers for me find my way back. And sometimes our blessing angels show up in interesting ways. Mine showed up in the form of my funny, crusty hubby; some dear, close friends; and a couple of learning opportunities that supported my heart and spirit. By following the threads of creativity and love that came to my awareness I began to walk in the light again. One friend steered me towards a board seat for a charitable foundation. It gifted me with a sense of purpose and a way to focus on giving back to the world. Another dear friend led me through the process of becoming certified to teach sacred mandala art.

I then could help others explore the gift of their inherent, inspired creativity while reconnecting with my own. I was introduced to Angelic Reiki through friends; I'm so glad I listened to my inner voice and became an Angelic Reiki Master. The connection to pure light and love has helped me to heal myself and to become a healing presence in the world. I joined with a dear friend to explore a deep level of dialogue skills and tools, through a powerfully transformative program where every person is recognized as having sacred worth and value. We spent two years with a cohort learning about mindfulness, how to invoke deep compassion – both internal and external, our creative freedom to make choices outside of our default defenses, and our complete interdependence with all of humanity. This practice has been truly life changing and has helped me to step into my authentic voice while continuously inviting others to do the same, regardless of where we might stand on an issue.

Through these opportunities and a daily exploration of where my true gifts lie, I have risen step-by-step from the ashes to a newfound strength and presence, and the "peace that surpasses all understanding"[1]. It's been a process for sure; I've had to uncover and release a trunk full of personal baggage. The deep internal excavation of real and perceived wounds has been excruciating at times. My faulty belief system about myself and my environment; that the world is a hostile place and that I constantly need to protect myself or risk becoming a martyr, had to be deconstructed so that I could re-member and reclaim what was True.

Throughout, I've been surprised at how interior the journey is; no external action on my part could have brought me through the 'eye of the needle'. I learned that the True Path can only be traveled from the inside out.

The magic that has revealed itself through my journey has buoyed my Soul and helped me to re-member daily miracles. As I've moved beyond trauma and grown more reflective, memories of how I've been protected all my life have come flooding back about events that defy logical explanation. Like the time, I felt a screaming internal alarm before the van I was riding in with six other people rolled several times down a snowy embankment; yet all of us walked away from the accident. I believe beyond a doubt that the precognitive warning allowed me to invoke prayers that helped support a positive outcome.

Or the time I was jogging full speed to an exercise class during my lunch hour, when I tripped and went completely airborne before falling harmlessly to the ground as though I had landed on feathers. Or the time I was driving mountain roads late at night and was not able to stop my car in time to avoid the tree that had fallen across the road; instead I drove right through it as though the tree was not there at all – without a single bump or scratch. I might question that one myself had my passenger not experienced the same thing I did!

I love how the enchantment of life continues to show up, even still. Early after my State retirement and as a charity board member, basking in the glow of the like-minded community at a planning retreat on the Monterey Bay, I was the first to spot a low flying meteor tumbling directly overhead.

It was not quite dusk and still very bright outside; so, at first we did not understand the bluish white blazing light that left a swirling, zig zagging streak that glowed for hours in the darkening sky. The next day we learned that a single Leonids meteor had been sighted nearby. I felt certain there was a symbolic message and my research uncovered the meaning that significant changes would be coming or unfolding; and while the changes could be unsettling, they would be in line with a greater good. That has very much been my experience ever since!

Working as a dialogue program intern and on contract with a couple of state departments later gave me the opportunity to re-member forgiveness, for myself and for my past detractors and wounding experiences. With a newfound ability to see through more neutral eyes, I was able to witness the humanity and vulnerability underneath the defensive actions that can occur between individuals and groups; especially during times of change and the high stress that comes along with it.

I understand now how my own previous lack of awareness and my programmed expectation of conflict and negative outcomes became the perfect fuel to feed the toxicity in the environment I closed my career with. For the first time in my life I could comfortably speak without fear and from a place of compassion, even when the sharing of information may have been uncomfortable for me or the receiver. Through this work my faith in humanity and my own ability to navigate relationships has been restored.

Using mandala art as a tool for self-awareness continues to strengthen the connection between my gut (intuition), heart (love), and mind (wisdom). It has allowed my inherent, God-given creativity to re-emerge from the deep well of my woundedness, through the portal to the subconscious this form of art-in-a-circle creates. I notice that I have an increasing clarity and more balanced thinking. Mandala has helped me to embrace my "hyper-sensitivity" and re-cognize it for the gift it is. Walking others through this creative process and being witness to the profound shifts that have occurred, has been a powerful reminder that I can never anticipate the impact of my presence or what I been given to share as I allow the divine to work through me. The energetic current and the messages brought forward from the guides and angels have had life changing effects for me and my students.

I've had students experience a spontaneous ability to channel information from divine sources; heart openings that have changed their relationships and their lives; the use of mandala as a tool to replace their habitual addictive substances. Mandala has helped me and those I've worked with to re-member infinite possibility.

This precious life, with its many ups and downs, has taught me what I have finally been able to reclaim, to re-member; a foundation and the tools to help me continue the journey to Spirit. My Mom's Alzheimer's and ultimately her death helped me to re-member the Sacred. She made her transition with an ease and grace that was remarkable given her personality and life experiences. It was my deep honor to stay present as her witness.

The dismal effects of the economic downturn on my husband's business, which had me working part-time to help keep it afloat far longer than I had anticipated, helped me to re-claim the gift of faith; I knew we would be okay (we were and we still are!). Watching and learning as every single one of my old management team landed firmly on their feet after such painful disruption; promoting and excelling in ways that were beyond my imagining, helped me to re-member trust.

Things happen for a reason, and everything ultimately works out for good when I stay open to growth and change.

I am able now to fully appreciate that what threatened so many times to destroy me simply brought me closer to my own divinity. Every painful experience was designed to help ensure that I did not try to fall backwards; that I continued toward the light. For me, it was through stepping into my commitment to the Path that the real magic began. The nature allies that have always come to me through dreams are just one aspect of the enchanted tools Creation can offer.

I honor their messages with deep gratitude, even as I realize that the reason they have been so present in my dreams is because I am willing to look to their symbolism. I now understand that our higher power; our great I AM presence uses language through our subconscious that we can understand if we are able to slow down enough to notice. Learning this has strengthened my ability to stay present. As time goes on, the messages I receive from these gifts have become more frequent and easier to interpret. I have been able to feel my Soul re-awakening to my conscious mind; the holistic integration movement toward my *becoming*. I have re-membered and experienced for the first time in my life, that life is a celebration. It's all a dance. I am blessed and delighted to be part of the troupe.

About the Author

Debbie Baker, Author, Dialogue Practitioner, Certified Mandala Art Facilitator

As Founder of Creative Consciousness Rising, Debbie is committed to programs that support reflective awareness, of ourselves, each other, and the world; one human connection at a time. She works with others in personal and business settings to facilitate understanding of the power of living compassionately, through creativity and awareness, and mindfully honoring how we are all truly interdependent. In sharing intentional dialogue, healing mandala art, and other creativity tools, Debbie is passionate about helping others to explore their ability to heal themselves and the world, from the inside out.

As a retired State government executive since 2010, Debbie has worked with a variety of audiences to help them experience their inherent gifts of inspired creativity, balance, and peace through creative mandala art. In 2011 she co-authored *Sacred Creations - The Healing Power of Mandalas*; an inspirational book of mandala art, testimonials, and empowering quotes.

Her interest in the practice of healthy and effective dialogue led her to a 2-year skills development program through the Bread of Life, Sacramento, California, which she graduated from in 2014. As a certified Dynamic Dialogue mentor, Debbie works with individuals, business, and governmental groups to help create safe learning cultures where every person is recognized as having sacred worth and value. Writing under the pseudonym Maeve Grace, Debbie has contributed to the anthology *Warrior Women with Angel Wings; Stories of Love, Hope, Faith, Courage and Angels*, released Summer 2017.

Maggie Dunaway
IF ONLY

It was 1965, our son was two, and I was five months pregnant with our second child. My husband was a drug store assistant manager, and I took our toddler to his store one day for a short visit. Then, before we headed home, I bought a bag of hard horehound drop candies, and when I bit into one, a broken piece scraped the roof of my mouth.

I awoke in the middle of that night with a painful swelling where the broken candy had cut me. I wondered briefly if I was developing an infection, and by noon the next day, I was sure something was wrong. A visit to my general practitioner (GP) confirmed I'd been hit with not one, but two bacterial infections: strep throat and trench mouth. The doctor prescribed an antibiotic for the strep throat, but mentioned no specific treatment for the trench mouth. When I returned for a follow-up visit the next week, The GP said the strep throat was much better, but the he again prescribed nothing to address the trench mouth, which remained extremely painful.

Unable to chew anything solid, but not knowing what else to do, I continued to dose myself with aspirin until I went to my next scheduled maternity exam. To my astounded relief, when my OB-GYN saw I'd lost all nine pounds I'd gained since getting pregnant, she had me admitted to the hospital. After being hooked up to an IV, an internist swabbed my mouth with gentian violet, a solution that left my gums a bright violet-purple. Although the treatment had historically been used to cure trench mouth, the recent advent of antibiotics had relegated it to pharmacy back shelves, apparently out of sight and mind of my GP. Thankfully, the solution worked almost immediately, and I was soon allowed to return home.

Three months later, my husband's company placed him on "vacation relief", which meant he would be on the road every weekday through the coming spring and summer. Since I was by then eight months pregnant, and we had only one car, we temporarily moved in with my parents. Our relocation meant finding a new OB-GYN, and the closest one to my parents' house turned out to be less than stellar, e.g., although she knew I'd been seriously ill three months before, she didn't do a single comprehensive exam during the final month of my pregnancy.

A week past my due date, I finally went into labor late one afternoon. When my contractions faded away several hours after I arrived at the hospital, my new doctor asked whether I wanted to return home or have her induce labor. Naïve about the process, I blithely opted for inducement. It turned out to be a terrible mistake. While my first labor had lasted eight hours, and had been painful, but bearable, this one immediately became excruciatingly hard, and lasted less than an hour. I had only a few moments with our new baby boy before I was inexplicably drugged into a deep sleep.

It was the next morning before my husband gently awakened me. He said the pediatrician had just told him our baby was not doing well; in fact, he had less than a fifty percent chance of surviving. We hurried to the nursery where we were shocked to see our baby struggling so hard, it seemed each inhalation was torturous. Devastated, we returned to my room to await the inevitable.

A week later, while my husband was home for the weekend, we were taking a drive when I realized I was hemorrhaging. We rushed back to the hospital I'd barely left, where I learned one of my episiotomy stitches had come loose. After the incision was repaired, I was, unbelievably, wheeled upstairs to the same maternity ward where our baby had died. When my suite-mate's newborn was brought to her for nursing, I fell apart, called my husband, and minutes later, checked myself out against medical advice.

My whole family was devastated by the loss of our baby, and did everything they could to ease our pain. After a few weeks, my mother asked if I'd like her to pack up the baby's things, which still sat in my childhood bedroom. I told her no, I wanted to do it myself, and cried throughout the most devastating activity I've ever performed.

For weeks, afterward, my mind and heart were haunted with the words "if only". If only our baby had lived, he and his brother could have enjoyed a precious lifetime connection. If only he had lived, our family would already have been complete. If only I hadn't gotten so sick at such an important stage in his development, maybe things would have been different. If only I'd received more competent medical care, maybe the labor wouldn't have been so stressful for him. The painful musings went on and on and on.

Then one day when I was taking a shower, I suddenly felt I was being touched by a warm hand. I instantly understood that all my backward-looking "if only" longings were pointless. Instead, I needed to begin looking forward, to plan how I would accept our loss and move on, hopefully to have another child. Since the medical circumstances that had occurred during this pregnancy were extremely unusual, I realized they were highly unlikely to recur. And we had no other inherent risks such as diabetes or RH Factor, so my next pregnancy would probably be as uneventful as my first.

Finally, at peace, I accepted, and have since believed, that an angel came to me that day, and imbued me with eye-opening spiritual wisdom. I've received several more signs of heavenly guardianship over the years, but none more life changing and precious than the first.

About the Author

Maggie Dunaway has always been an avid reader. She was an English major at the Davis and Berkeley campuses of the University of California before being hired in 1969 "off the street," i.e., not through any political connections, as a Correspondence Specialist and Manager in Governor Ronald Reagan's office.

Her position led to her being hired in 1972 as a Governmental Program Analyst at the California State Department of Social Services where she worked as a regulatory development specialist, and then as a consultant to county welfare departments for both Child and Adult Protective Services. In 1990, Maggie switched subject areas and became an analyst and consultant for the State Department of Developmental Services where she established and ran a statewide program for persons with developmental disabilities transitioning from state hospitals into local adult family homes.

Maggie retired from her professional career in 2001 and didn't start talking openly about her spiritual experiences until years later, often receiving the reaction of blank looks from folks who hadn't yet experienced any themselves. She hopes that in providing her work history, her readers will be reassured by her thirty-two years of serious, largely analytical work, that she's been as analytical in determining her spiritual beliefs as in analyzing a statute or developing regulations for a new statewide program, and appreciate that she's not a "flake" or one who invents spiritual experiences as an answer to some of life's greatest mysteries. But rather, she's one who, fairly early on in life, has seen and read enough to realize that human history has been replete with conclusions believed to be eternal that have later gone by the wayside after humans gained new and/or greater knowledge about the world and how it works.

Maggie's bottom line is this: Unless something drastically different eventually develops in the area of human awareness, she will continue to work on the premise that "anything is possible" since there's always the chance that humans simply haven't yet determined all the "how's" and "whys" of our world's infinite list of "what's." Following this credo, she became quite secure in her spiritual beliefs by the early 2000s.

Nevertheless, she wishes to share that the meeting with Sundi Sturgeon and her husband, Joe, opened the door to quantum leaps in her knowledge of worlds beyond her own. Originally connecting through business, they soon became close friends, and when the couple recounted their angelic experiences in Happy Valley—a secluded area close to Maggie's Northern California home—her skin quivered with goose bumps for forty-five minutes straight! There's no doubt in her mind that these folks are holy messengers, and she blesses the work they have done and continue to do for her and countless others.

Sarah Brown Nisse
Growing Up Physic

It all started with butterflies. I have absolutely no recollection of this, as I was only three years old at the time, but my mother recalls the memory vividly. It was about three o'clock in the morning and I was supposed to be sound asleep. Mom was a pretty light sleeper and awoke to the distant sounds of me talking. As she got up to investigate, she could hear my toddler-self sitting up in my bed, carrying on a full-blown conversation with someone, and giggling. She snuck into my dimly lit room, scattered with every stuffed animal known to man, and asked "Sarah, who are you playing with?"

Mom said it was my reaction that made the hair on the back of her neck stand up. I immediately sat up straight, eyes wide with that *I'm definitely in big trouble* look, and pretended like I wasn't doing anything. She prompted again "Sarah, it's okay, you can tell me. Who are you playing with?"

"She told me not to tell you" I replied.

"Who told you? You can tell me" She goaded.

"It's a secret. I'm not supposed to tell". I was a stubborn and persistent as any three-year-old.

Mom had to switch strategies. She lightened her tone, knelt beside my bed, and acted as though she really wanted to take part in my early morning, top secret adventure.

"What game are you playing? Can I play too?"

Let's just say that mom knew how to crack me like an egg. She said I immediately got excited and spilled the beans: "We're playing with the butterflies! Orange ones! Big ones! They're everywhere".

"Oh really! Who else is here?" Mom figured she'd give it one more try as she started pretending to see the butterflies everywhere.

"Grandma Joanie" I replied.

Cue all the blood sinking out of my mom's face. "Oh." was all that my Mom could sputter as her mind raced around the fact that I was talking to her dead Mother.

I had only met Grandma Joanie once. I was 9 months old at the time and my mom had made the long flight with an infant from California to Ohio. Grandma died just 19 months later. The last thing that she said to my mom before she died was that she wished she had met me more than once and was able to watch me grow.

Even more serendipitous to this timing was the fact that this butterfly playdate happened on January 14, 1989. Grandma Joanie's Birthday was on January 13th, and she died of Hodgkin's Lymphoma just on January 15, 1988. So here we were: Mom, me, and the ghost of Grandma Joanie, all in my bedroom playing with butterflies on that single-day, One Year Anniversary between Grandma's Birth and Death.

Mom was positive that I was carrying on a full conversation with someone before she entered my room, but she still wasn't convinced that I wasn't making it up. Who knows, I could've heard Grandma Joanie's name mentioned somewhere and created a butterfly filled adventure, right? Good thing my mom had a quick solution. She walked into her closet and pulled out a dusty shoe box with old photos in it. One of the photos was of Grandma Joanie and all of her sisters, cousins, aunts, friends, etc. We are a Catholic family so I don't have to relay to you the sheer number of people in the picture-- if you get my drift. Ultimately, it was one of those old sepias toned photos that has about 20 women, all dressed the same, with the same damn hair style in it.

She came back into my room with the photo. "Sarah, can you show me who you were playing with?"

I didn't even take time to study the picture. She said I just pointed straight to Grandma Joanie, standing and smiling between all the other women of her time.

"Her" I said, while tapping on her face. "Grandma Joanie".

Chills ran down moms' spine as she got very quiet and examined the room. She wasn't sure what she was waiting for. Maybe Grandma would just appear out of nowhere, maybe Grandma was standing right behind her, maybe a stuffed animal would move? Who knew.

"Is she still here Sarah?" She managed to stutter.

"No mommy, she left. The butterflies did too."

Mom tucked me back in and went back to sleep with the knowing that what just happened was quite miraculous, but worried because she had a sneaking suspicion that this type of occurrence with her young, but obviously gifted daughter was far from over.

I didn't hear about this story until I was a teenager. Parts of me wished she would have told me earlier, because it would've made the rest of my psychic experiences easier to deal with. The butterfly event was just one of many experiences I've had in my life. I don't remember that event, or Grandma Joanie coming to see me. My earliest memories have to do with the departed, and they are not fun nor heartfelt memories.

I can remember being five years old, laying in my bed at night, and feeling absolutely terrified. The lights were out, and the dim, cat shaped nightlight did not emit enough shine to illuminate away the people, beings, creatures, and unknowns that lurked through my room. It would always start with the sounds of footsteps. We had carpet in our suburban, 2100 sq. ft. standard neighborhood home. As with every night, about five minutes past lights out, I would start to hear the slow squish of one foot, then another, slowly making its way down the hallway and towards my bedroom. I would curl up into the tightest ball I could and bring the blankets up to my ears and around my eyes in an attempt to stomp out the noises and sights that haunted me.

Then the shadow men would appear. Their bodies made up of static like from a television and outlined in the general shape of a male. They would always look straight ahead and I would audibly *hear* their footsteps approach my bed. Then they would stop. I was always too scared to look, but there were a few times I did. I would hold my breath, clench my

344

body, and slowly pull the covers down from their safe place over my eyes. The men would just be standing next to my bed. Staring at the wall. I'd yelp with fear and contemplate going to sleep in mom's room, again, like every other night. But I would be frozen in terror. How the heck am I supposed to get up and run down the long, haunted hallway into a different room when there are static figures standing next to me?

Eventually the shadow men would disappear. I couldn't tell you how long they would stay, what they would do, or what made them go away. All I know is that the next phase of my evening would get very interesting.

As an adult, I have a healthy fear around mirrors. In fact, mirrors are absolutely NOT allowed in the bedroom. If my husband and I are looking for a place to live, and there's mirrors in the bedroom, it's not our house. This is because an entire wall of my childhood bedroom, which were my closet doors, were full mirrors. When I was a teenager, I heard somewhere that mirrors are the passageways to other dimensions. This made complete sense to me…

Initiate evening *Phase Two*. After the shadow men, would disappear, all hell would break loose. That whole "mirrors are passageways to other dimensions" thing – yeah, let's just say that would happen. I would be transported into a world of vibrant color. I could still see everything in my bedroom:

Bed? Check.

Desk? Check.

Stuffed Animal Stack? Check.

Night stand? Check.

Dresser? Check.

But each of these pieces would now be overshadowed by glorious plants, animals, and beings. I would watch my mirrored closet doors as glowing pink lights would begin to manifest within. These lights, now orbs, would pop out of the mirror and begin to gently float throughout the room, glowing and pulsing with hypnotizing rhythms and magnificent colors. Where they would land, plant-like organisms that I have never seen before and I doubt I ever will again would sprout up and out of my carpet. I would look onto the roof of my bedroom where I would see insect-like creatures, both foreign and unrecognizable, crawling around the ceiling then sputtering down the walls as they made these weird clicking noises. I'd hear huffing and breathing across the room and look over to see a strange horse-dog looking hybrid with lizard scales sniffing around.

All of this would be coming out of my mirrored closet doors. No joke. At that young of an age you could say that I was over imaginative or hallucinating...but I kept seeing these things, these creatures, every single night until I was around twelve years old.

If I slept in my mom's room, which ultimately happened most of the time until I was about 10, the same events would occur. Only there weren't mirrors in her room, so the creatures and beings would flow in from the part of the hallway where my room was. Yeah, they followed me. I can vividly remember one night an animal like creature was floating through the air, it looked like a mix between an eel and a goat, and the way that it moved looked like it was effortlessly swimming and dancing through water. This creature changed directions and started coming directly toward my face, not even aware that I was there. I reached my hands out to block it and as I touched it I felt this strange current run through my body, then I noticed that the creature just started dissolving until it completely disappeared.

I was around 11 at that time, and I learned something valuable that night. I had never touched the beings before. I discovered that if I did, they would dissolve. I HAD POWER. The next several weeks were spent bopping around my room tapping all of the orbs, strange plants, animals, humanoids, etc. It turned into a game for me. I still didn't have the bravery to touch the Shadow Men, but these dimensional beings: Hell, Yeah!

Both the shadow men and the dimensional activity stopped shortly after I discovered my new found "tapping" power. As an adult, I'd like to experience the beauty and magic of those other worlds again. At that youthful age, I was probably just excited to get some damn sleep for the first time in 8 years. However, my adventures with the other realms weren't over yet. A new phase simply began.

Looking back, I thought I had a normal childhood and young adult hood. But as I examine it more, I realize that I kept a lot of my everyday experiences a huge secret from everyone close to me. When I was young, I would walk down the street and know when someone was about to die, or when someone just did a really terrible thing. It seemed completely normal to know these things. I inherently knew not to talk about it, just like I knew not to tell my friends about the ghost people that were in their houses or the intricacies of their parent's relationships. I also didn't have many good friends growing up. Authenticity and a genuine personality, from a psychic's point of view, are easy to pick out, whether you're seven, seventeen, or twenty-seven.

Growing up psychic, I found that if you ignore the activity it only gets stronger. That's where phase three started. I was now deep into my teenage years. The shadow men and dimensional mirror creatures no longer haunted me, instead I was getting great sleep then waking up in the morning to some dead person standing in my room. As soon as we would lock eyes, they would realize that I could see them. They would get palpably excited, like you would feel the whole ominous-dead person-in my room energy disappear, and then they'd beeline for my bed!

A lot of screaming happened back then.

Most of the time it would be a single person, standing in my doorway, dressed in period-style clothing: a woman in a dress and bonnet with a white apron, a man dressed like an old lumberjack, a kid wearing saddle shoes and a cute little suit. They'd show up about once a week, and I can honestly tell you that you NEVER get used to dead people standing in your room. I didn't have the luxury back then of knowing they were dead. Meaning that they didn't have some pearly white glow around them or a big sign saying "I'm dead, I'm not real". Nope. These people looked as real and alive to me as anyone who you would pass on the street. If there was ever an intruder in my house, I would probably just think it was a dead person and roll over and fall back asleep. Seriously though, my husband is in law enforcement and I don't allow him to have the gun near me at night because I'd probably shoot a hole in the wall once a week.

As I got older, the activity intensified. During high school, I would sometimes be home alone in the morning. As a daily activity, I would be in the kitchen making tea and my lunch for the school day. One morning I forgot my tea mug in the kitchen. I had just been in there a split second before, and everything was normal. When I turned to walk back into the kitchen, every single cupboard door, the oven door, the refrigerator and freezer doors, were wide open. All within less than a second.

Things really got strange in September of 2001. It was early September and I was a Junior in High School at that time. I woke up to a regular morning (no dead people) and opened the blinds in my room, just as I do every morning. I lived in a small, coastal California town that was often foggy, moist and dewy. This meant that dew often developed on the single pane windows our freezing house was blessed with. As I looked out the window to take in the morning fog, I noticed a peculiar drawing in the dew. As I looked closer it looked as though there was a simple drawing of a plane and two tall rectangles. I thought it was weird, and maybe my Dad was playing a joke on me. He was a big smoker and would spend a lot of time outside savoring his cigarettes. Maybe he was messing with my window?

I walk out of my room and find him enjoying his morning coffee.

"Hey Dad! Did you go near my window this morning?" I queried.

"No. I walked around the block, why?" His curiosity was piqued.

I suspiciously countered "well, there's a weird drawing on my window. Did you see anything out there?"

"No, nothing. What's the drawing?"

"It looks like a kid did it. Probably just a joke from a classmate" I replied.

Two days later was 9/11/2001, when terrorists flew a plane into the Twin Towers in New York City. The drawing stayed on my window for about a year. I just figured the dew formed around it and kept it there. When we moved out of that house, I tried to Windex the drawing out of the window and realized it was etched into the glass…from the inside. Right above my sleeping head.

Growing up psychic was, for lack of a better word, interesting. I navigated the strange path as easily as I knew how. When I entered college, I had huge aspirations to become a Virologist for the CDC. I studied Microbiology and expected "normal" 9-5 job upon graduation. As you can probably guess, that didn't happen. Spirit had other plans for me and quickly ushered me into the field of Intuition, Whole Body Health, and Deep Cellular Healing. I now trust the process and have found ways to work with Spirit. My favorite types of clients are the psychic children and their often-exasperated parents. I was there once, and understand how scary it can be. As tough as my initiation into this field was, I am so very thankful that I am here and can now assist others on this path.

About the Author

Sarah's greatest joy seeds from illuminating the light which lives within you. She is a spiritual powerhouse when it comes to aiding others in clearing away any perceived blocks and limitations. As an Intuitive and Healer, she works with your guidance to develop a custom framework which assists you in seeing the world through new and spectacular eyes: through the eyes of Spirit. Her life's work ignites the intuition in others, attuning and aligning their energy at the Soul Level.

Sarah lives in beautiful Monterey California where she works as a Psychic Medium. The transformational process she uses with her clients includes a mixture of Energy Healing, Shamanic Healing, Channeling, Remote Viewing, DNA Activation, and Animal Communication. Sarah facilitates healings, teaches workshops, and leads retreats throughout the world. You can find more about her at www.TheIllumanaProject.com

Robin Markowitz
Flames

It's hard to write a story when your still at the beginning, but I will try my best. My life was sort of like a maze or labyrinth of sorts. I started my mission long before I met my twin flame, though most of my mission I had to complete alone. I've learned that people are just mirrors. Sometimes we like the things that reflect back to us, and sometimes we don't. Well, my mirror cracked when I was very young. I manifested cancer at a young age and faced my first of many visits with death.

My mother also died, crumbling any sense of stability I had. Before she left, she passed her karma in the form of addictions to me. My vibration dropped lower and lower, and I manifested a sort of hell-on-earth existence. I chose to have many difficult experiences in the next ten-year period.

The first was a near-fatal car accident in which I broke over thirty bones, shattering my pelvis. That was the beginning of my training as a healer. I have always been very spiritual, but back then, that looked more like having religious sense. After my car accident, I spent some time in Israel, learning many things about many religions. I went back to school and studied psychology and theology. I then moved on to my soul-mate relationship.

It was a very deep connection with an evolved member of my soul family who came to teach me hard lessons in love. My problem was that I was still very much asleep, and I hung on to long. This caused much suffering. The relationship was amazing at first, but I didn't understand at the time that I already belonged to someone else. The breakup sent me into depression and anxiety. It was there that I found myself. I had to complete myself as a person. When we become complete, we get a complete person reflected back. A lot of this matrix is an optical illusion of sorts, leading you back to yourself.

 For a long time, I tried fixing the reflection in the mirror instead of fixing myself. I had to learn to love myself completely, flaws and all. When we don't love every aspect of who we are or the experiences that made us, we can create soul splits. This process I went through this loss and it is what opened my heart chakra. We all have to experience grief in some form. It's this loss that opens us up to unconditional love.

I met my twin flame in a synchronistic way. We had a mutual friend and ended up in the same place at the same time. My twin flame was very much awake, but I wasn't. The encounter was the first time I sensed energy. I could tell he was shielding me in some way when I was around him. The energy that one experiences with their twin flame is powerful. Twins encounter each other to reunite after completing themselves and to undertake a mission. Things happened rapidly from there. I began to wake up immediately.

I began downloading information from being around my twin flame, including the word twin flame! I began to shed the layers of my old life, and that included anything not serving me.

We both remembered we were healers and became Reiki Masters/Teachers. I replaced the pharmaceuticals I was on with CBD and energy healing. Much as the caterpillar turns into the butterfly, I began to learn and evolve. I'd heard that each twin-flame couple is here to heal fifty-million people. That resonated true with me. We started a healing business and began our mission of healing the world. We are currently running a large spiritual community on Facebook and strengthening the grid.

Our purpose is to help shift this planet into higher levels of consciousness with Divine love. We are here to teach unconditional love, a different paradigm from the current one, which is very conditional. We are still healing ourselves and learning as we go, but this gives us hope for humanity. We work with higher vibrational entities, some known as angels and extraterrestrials. We are teaching and seeding this planet with love and compassion. We transmute negative energies, having learned how to perfect alchemy. When we merged our two polarities together, we literally merged heaven and earth together. We are learning how to easily manifest the things we need or want. In any spiritual union, peace, love, and harmony are the key. We are learning how to assess higher dimensions, as well as dispensing Akashic knowledge.

I had a kundalini awakening along with my spiritual awakening. This opened all of my chakras, and I reached enlightenment. My third eye continues to expand, and as it does, I see through things more and more. I'm finding that the rabbit hole is infinite, and the more you learn, the more you realize that you know nothing. The veil, as in my ego, vanished. I had a profound experience where I merged with and became my higher self. I began the ascension process and began repairing and activating my DNA. I realized all of the knowledge of the cosmos is stored in my DNA, and my mission became to access it.

My twin flame and I are working on getting back to a pure state. The purer the channel, the stronger you will be. The more we've use our gifts to help others, the stronger they've become. We don't have a current plan for things; we literally just go with the flow. With every day, it's something different. I do know that a big part of our mission entails our contract to have two children. They, along with other crystal children, will save this planet.

About the Author

Robin Markowitz currently lives in Pittsburgh with her husband. They are twin-flame healers and own Sparks of Divine Light Healing. Robin is an angelic channel, Reiki Master/Teacher, Chi Energy Healer, astrologer, and psychic. She uses live feeds to teach ascension on Facebook.

She helps people navigate through their spiritual awakenings and is working on many collaborations aimed at helping shift the planet into higher levels of consciousness. Robin integrates many aspects into her holistic health modules, merging spirituality and health to cure serious illnesses.

Victoria Zillo
Ocean Breeze-Surfing the Big Waves

As immigrants, we move around the globe with invisible luggage, full of hopes and dreams, seeking new experiences and a better future, facing different challenges and obstacles that bring lots of self-discovering valuable moments. Being 4,412 miles away from my family wasn't always easy at an emotional level. I grew up in a very loving and caring family of five where sitting all together for supper was a daily ritual, and no excuses were allowed to miss that moment. Now, I recognize the great value of the connection and unity that those moments brought to us; daily, they gave us the right tools to have integrity as human beings. My parents' sayings and highlighted words, such as honesty, empathy, love, and care, among others, will stick with me for life.

We grow up and make our own decisions, though I had never imagined moving this far from my family. I think, at an unconscious level, I was honoring my father and his love and admiration for this country. They would travel often, and I would do the same, but we weren't able to spend holidays together due to job schedules. Those times were, and still are, the hardest. Just by remembering what an Italian-Spanish celebration we would have! From getting dressed to setting up a big table full of amazing dishes, to having friends and other family members join us. My life was easy, happy, and full of blessings. Back then, my worries were only a bad hair day, the guy I liked who didn't like me, someone bullying me, or me being mean to somebody else.

After many years on American soil, meeting people from all over the world, making new friends, and creating a family with others who have chosen my same path, it's gotten easier to be this far away. We help lift each other with daily situations, but most important is they are a phone call away when unexpected life events happen.

While coping with my aunt's uncertain death, not knowing when or how that happened, my father—her only direct living family member—took the emotional blame and responsibility. He never said it, but I knew it when he told me the news. I was really worried for him; I felt a lot of pain in his voice. My mom, my sisters, and myself would try to protect him and shower him with daily love. We couldn't predict the internal process he was going through. A few weeks after my aunt's passing, I got a phone call with my sisters telling me that our father was taken to the hospital after having a heart attack in my mother's arms. He was brought back to life and had been placed in ICU in an induced comma to be stabilized.

I don't remember if I said anything to them; I probably did. When I hung up, I couldn't breathe, didn't know what to do, and I couldn't stop crying. Not being able to control the situation or shorten the distance drove me insane. I only wanted to be there with my family.

A friend of mine booked me a flight for the following morning, which was my mom's sixtieth birthday. A week before, we spoke to my dad about how to celebrate her, and he said he would do something she would never forget! Crazy or not, none of us will forget that birthday.

Another friend made up my suitcase, and my boyfriend at that time was nowhere to be found. We weren't going through a good time either. I flew nine hours, but it felt as if I would never land. When I arrived in my country, one of my sisters picked me up, and we went straight to the hospital where my mom and my other sister were waiting for me. It was winter time, cold, grey, a rainy evening. We bonded in a group hug and cried together for some time.

I still had the need to celebrate my mom. I had to wish her a happy birthday, and I also asked her to allow my father his will by letting him go if he wanted to. Still today, I don't know why I said it. I walked into my father's room to see him on a bed connected to every possible machine that you can imagine assisting him to breathe, urinate, and be fed. The different beeps, the monitors, and the lights turning on and off were scary.

Days went by, and we adjusted to a different routine with visitation hours, prayers, healing stones, caressing, massaging his legs, talking and singing his favorites songs, attaching family pictures to the wall for the moment he would come back. After some days, the doctors decided to stop the sedation. When he woke, he was in a good spirit. He wanted to go to work and mentioned all the things he had to do.

All the facts were true; my mom and sisters were talking and laughing with him, and I was an observer from the outside. It made me really sad. I wanted so badly to hug him and to look into his eyes and let him know how much I loved him. We chose not to tell him that I was there to prevent him from worrying about how severe the situation was. He had been having health issues before, and I never had the urge to travel. I knew this time was different, and I was even more assured when he told my mom he was with his mother and she came to take him (my grandma had passed away over forty-five years earlier). My mom didn't get it; I was already grieving.

He was also asking for his tennis shoes and saying he wanted to be at the beach in Miami, the place he always mentioned for where he wanted his ashes to be spread when he died. One of my sisters asked him if she could go too, and he said he would go now and she would go later. Some nights, I didn't even want to go to the hospital. I was emotionally drained and would be sitting outside, peeping through the door, not able to talk or have contact with him. At one point, the cardiologist said he would allow me in the following day. That day never came. Back under sedation he went because his breathing wasn't normal. We went back to the start, back into sedation. It been eleven days already. I wanted a miracle so badly.

One evening, I was the last one to visit him. I kissed him goodnight, caressing his head, holding his hand to my chest, and I gave him as many kisses as I could.
I could feel my silent tears rolling down my face. Then I walked away because the nurse came in to let me know visitation hours were over. My hand was glued to his, and I didn't want to leave. I really wanted to stay that night.

In the morning, I woke with someone caressing my back, like a breeze. I really felt it. Our dog was sleeping next to me, and at that same moment, he woke up and looked around and cried. A few minutes after, the phone rang. It was the hospital saying my father was unstable and we had to rush in. I knew right then that he was gone. I saw my mom and my sister getting ready, but how could I be the one to give them the news?

When we arrived at ICU, no one would acknowledge our presence. I held my mom's hand and told her it was not good. She refused to hear, but no one was brave enough to walk into my father's room until the nurse came by and gave us her condolences. My mom asked her, "What do you mean?" By the end of her question, she went in his room, and I followed her.

While she was talking to the doctor, I got close to my father, gave him a kiss, and whispered, "I will always love you." My mom, in her need to protect me, pulled me away from him. I was already a grow woman, but mothers will always protect their kids from anything.

My sisters were crying outside, unable to get closer to the room. One of them was interrogating another doctor while immersed in her pain, and they chose not to see my father at all. We stayed at the hospital until he was cleared to be transferred to the funeral home, otherwise my mom would've felt that she was abandoning him after forty-three years together.

Honestly, we didn't know how to start a new day. We were all grieving in different ways. I wasn't able to cry in front of my mom because, as the eldest child, I felt I had to be strong for her, so I did it in silence. My father was that person I looked up to, the one I wanted to make proud in every step I took. He was so intelligent and a hard-working man. Heaven knows how proud I was to have him as my father. He told me once when I shared something I was going through, "I trust your judgment and your instinct, and I know that what you decide will be the right path." Those words would give rebirth to my spiritual path that, for social reasons, I wasn't able to live freely.

I decided to stay in my country longer than what I had originally planned. While my faith in the states was being managed and my strength tested by others, a week after my dad passed, my boyfriend broke up with me over the phone. By then, we had been living together for two and a half years. A few days later, my manager at work, knowing what I was going through and after telling me to take all the time I needed, decided to fire me. The pain and emptiness I was feeling didn't leave space for any other emotions than my father being gone. After three months, it was time to take back charge of my life. I came back to the states, to the home I shared with my now ex-boyfriend, only to see that all my stuff was hidden. He had sold some of my things, and another female had been there. I wasn't affected, but I couldn't believe someone could act like that with the pain I was going through.

My grieving process came with panic attacks, social anxiety, and insomnia. The doctor diagnosed me with depression and prescribed one of those emotion-numbing pills that I refused to depend on. I told her I was not a symptom; I was going through something that is a part of life, and I was going to heal on my own terms.

I got my job back and found a new home right by the ocean where I would start over and reconnect with myself. It took a lot of tears, prayers, strange symptoms, self-talk, books, and journaling. It turned out to be my safe place, my shelter. I was still broken inside, but those walls made me feel safe and content. I also joined a meditation group where I was able to release and decompress.

Strength, acceptance, and faith would be tested for some time to come. The family dog had to be put to sleep after fourteen years with us, and shortly after, my grandmother passed away. I could only wonder about the lessons to be learned, knowing we would always be connected at a different level, like when they visited me in dreams where we would get to talk, laugh, and hug each other.

Time keeps moving, and losing a dear one isn't something we are emotionally prepared for. It is a hard process. While I was putting my shattered pieces together, I accepted that everything that happened was meant to happen that way, and at the moment it took place, all that would bring self-growth helped me to overcome fears, to take chances, and to fall in love with life again.

My approach to life and to people changed. I didn't need to be right or to have the control in everything. I understood that making mistakes are only lessons that redirect us to focus on our purposes in life, that we have a destiny, and there are things, people, and situations we will go through no matter how hard we try to avoid them. We also have free will, and is up to us to make the best of the worst situation. Acceptance, patience, and *love* are the most powerful feelings, regardless of your race or religion. We are all connected. Those feelings are beautiful medicine for a broken heart.

Isn't that the meaning of life—to learn how to surf the big waves without losing your balance and getting back up if you ever fall?

About the Author

Victoria Zillo have a bachelor degree in communication and studied psychology but for personal reasons she didn't graduate. Passionate for every form of self-expression she took acting classes, drawing and writing were some of the ways to be in tune with her true self and find balance between routine and what she feels is her soul calling.

From host to manager working in the hospitality industry living in survival mode, she met people from all over the world and all walks of life, what made her realize that we are all at service and wonder herself if we are truly serving our purpose in life.

She grew up knowing that there is a lot more to life than living in automatic mode; reading and studying about the universal laws and how everything is energy, how we use it from thoughts to taking action or no action and the ripple effect that has on us and others.

In different stages of her life she allowed fear to take over, fear of rejection, of not being good enough, of failing, today she knows that you only fail if you don't try; when something don't go as we expected it helps you to push harder if you are willing to leave fear, pride and ego behind.

As an empath, she wants to help, inspired and encourage others, specially teenagers and young adults to learn how to live a life to their higher potential.

VictoriaZilloMaktub@gmail.com

Paulette Kouffman Sherman
How My Dark Night of the Soul Led Me to My Legacy

It was the day before my 41st birthday, and I sat in a hospital office with a breast surgeon and my husband.

"It turns out that the lump was bigger than we expected, and it is the Triple Negative kind, which is more aggressive. So, you will need chemotherapy and radiation and your hair will probably all fall out, even your eyebrows," the doctor said (or some semblance of that).

"Will I be able to work and play with my kids?" I asked, thinking that a year is a long time.

"Everyone is different. You will need to wait and see how you feel."

My head spun. Life would definitely be sidetracked in the short run, and I also wondered if I would live through this experience and whether life would return to normal.

The next day, I went for a walk on the beach near our house and asked Spirit whether I was going to die. I was scared to leave behind my then one-year-old daughter and three-year-old son. I heard internally, "No, you will have a rough year, but you will get through this."

I asked, "Have I done everything that I was sent here to do?"

I heard, "Yes, you did the five major things you set out to do—marrying your soulmate, having a boy and girl, buying an apartment on the beach, being a therapist, and publishing a book, but you still have a legacy of at least twenty-two books left to write."

I was still trying to figure out how to be there for my clients and kids during my treatment, how to commute ninety minutes each way to the hospital by train, and how to sit in the hospital all day for my treatments. But it was a clear message; my soul's purpose was to create a legacy of books to leave my messages behind, and there was no arguing with that.

My mother and husband weren't happy. "Twenty-two books right *now*? Shouldn't you focus on getting better?" they asked.

It isn't for me to judge, I thought. So, stubbornly, I declared that I'd figure it all out as I went, and that I would just self-publish to start because that timeframe would be faster. I asked my then three-year-old son what I should call my publishing house, and he said, "Parachute Jump Publishing," after the iconic Brooklyn Eiffel-Tower-looking structure that we often visited near our house.

It became a symbol of hope and love for us, and Coney Island had always been a place of dreams for me. When I first moved there, I was single at thirty-three years old, and I'd walk to the Parachute Jump and daydream about meeting my future husband and starting a family. This was also during a period when I wrote and published my first dating book, and my dream to become a published author with Simon & Schuster came true.

Then I dated my husband, a fellow therapist. We courted in the area, and he proposed right next to the Parachute Jump! At thirty-six, I again walked there, hoping to get pregnant naturally, which happened on our first try with our son. I did the same thing for our daughter and got pregnant with her at the age of thirty-nine, naturally. So, maybe I superstitiously imparted my Parachute Jump pilgrimage with secret powers for co-creating my dreams. Magical thinking, I know, but we all need some harmless magic from time to time. And I definitely needed all the help I could get.

So, I began writing my books in notebooks at the hospital, transcribing them into my laptop when I had time. Help came out of the woodwork. I found my cover designer, Sara Blum, from Beyond Words/Atria Books (the publisher of my first book) on LinkedIn, and she designed many of my self-published books at a discounted price so that I could put them on Amazon one after another. I created some short children's books and a number of longer ones. Some of the longer books were edited by Julie Clayton who also gave me a great rate. I then made hope chests for my husband and two kids and began to put in my books special letters and memorabilia.

My sister visited me from California and told me she didn't want me to go through this year of treatment just working and being stoic. She suggested that if I didn't go to a support group, I should call an angel intuitive she knew from California and speak to him by phone. I thought phone sessions were convenient since I was an hour commute to the city and was feeling exhausted. I also thought that it would be interesting to hear what he said about the spiritual meaning of my illness and whether I'd be okay. So, I called Christopher Dilts of *www.Askanangel.com* with that intention.

Not only did we discuss the spiritual meaning of my illness, Chris agreed that I had a legacy of books to write, and he began to describe to me the one I was currently writing— *When Mars Women Date*—and explained why it was important for our society. He also said I would write several books about my breast cancer experience that would help other women going through it. I was impressed, and I started speaking to him by phone weekly on Wednesdays. Now, it's been five years of Wednesday sessions! Often, we would do meditations to help me to connect to my soul's mission and Spirit. I learned how to connect to the unconditional love of Spirit and my angels in order to overcome pain and fear and how to move into a state of peace and centeredness so that I could be led. I opened to guidance, which helped me surrender more to Spirit than to be directed by my mind and ego.

Books poured through me, and the latest one (book #21 five years later) was published by Llewellyn. It was about how I used bath rituals to connect with Spirit and how others could too. It seemed to bring my spiritual practice full circle so that I could share it in a new way. I am now working on the last book in my legacy (book #22), and I feel that there are at least fifteen more books that I'd also love to write. Now, I surrender to the flow, life energy, and excitement of these messages of love that will hopefully help others and that have helped me. I no longer listen to the thoughts that say I don't have time to write these books because I have faith that we are here to do our soul's purpose, and we will get unexpected help and guidance along the way.

I learned a few things from my cancer experience as well. I learned that Spirit is stronger than my body, and it can carry me through darkness into more light and love when I keep the faith and remember to connect there. Sometimes we need a wakeup call from Spirit to shift things and to pay attention to our soul's purpose, even if it's inconvenient or sounds crazy. Connecting with our soul's purpose raises our vibration, brings us joy and life energy, and gives us meaning. It allows us to help others by sharing our gifts. And leaving a legacy is a way to continue to share our love even after we aren't physically here.

Hopefully, people won't have to go through the harrowing physical experience that I did to have these realizations. This is one reason that I wrote *The Book of Sacred Baths,* so that others could create a habit and take twenty minutes out of their busy days to connect with Spirit, to get guidance, to connect with their angels and their soul missions. Then they could take that new wisdom and consciousness out into the world.

I am grateful that I have thrived and survived for the past five years since my diagnosis, and that although the cancer is gone, I am changed. During this time, I've made wonderful memories with my family and some positive changes in my lifestyle. After having been a therapist for eighteen years, I'm so glad that I met my earth angel, Chris, at a time I wanted support. I had a chance to experience being the client, and that will probably help me in my work as a counselor and coach. I have had the opportunity to do therapy with a few cancer survivors as well. It makes me see that there is a bigger picture and all is connected even at those dark times when nothing seems to make sense. These challenging periods or "dark nights of the soul" are often our biggest opportunities for growth because they are when we are most willing to listen and surrender to a larger plan. I had help in being empowered through change, and my hope is that my work and books will inspire others to do so as well.

About the Author

Dr. Paulette Kouffman Sherman is a psychologist, life coach, Relationship expert & the author of, *The Book of Sacred Baths: 52 Bathing Rituals to Revitalize Your Spirit*, published by Llewellyn and *Dating from the Inside Out: How to Use the Law of Attraction in Matters of the Heart*, published by Atria Books. She has written 21 books, translated into 6 languages.

She has a private practice in Manhattan, does international phone coaching on relationships and runs, *My Dating and Relationship School* in NYC which offers groups, events and classes to help individuals and couples unblock obstacles to love. Paulette was a Relationship expert on Fox 5, Channel 11, the CBS Early Show & the AM Northwest Early Show and a radio guest on the Curtis Sliwa show, NPR's Cityscape, Unity Radio's 'The Soul-Directed Life, Pathways and others. She was quoted in MSN.com, USA Weekend, the NY Post, Newsweek, Lifetime.com, More, Match.com, Foxnews.com, Fox Business, Crains, Better Homes & Gardens, Reader's Digest, Redbook, Glamour, Forbes, Woman's Day, Metro newspapers, Men's Health, Men's Fitness, Marie Claire, Seventeen, Men's Fitness, Bustle, New York Magazine, Woman's Day, Web MD, Everyday Health, Elle, Psychology Today, Complete Woman magazine, the Huffington Post, Guideposts and the NY Times.

She was just featured in a Relationship advice video series for Guidepost Magazine as well as a Relationship Expert Q&A article in their Feb/March 2017 issue.

Her websites are www.DrPauletteSherman.com and www.MyDatingandRelationshipSchool.com . You can also join her at Twitter: @kpaulet; FB: https://www.facebook.com/pauletteshermangroup/ ; Instagram: https://www.instagram.com/paulette_sherman/ ; Pinterest: https://www.pinterest.com/kpaulet/

Maude Schellhous
My Journey

It was one of the first sunny days in Northern Oregon that year. The kind of day that wakes up cold and soggy and then transforms to crisp, with blue sky peeling back the clouds of winter. I had yet to experience my new town without the rain and gloom, having just moved there in December, and I wanted to explore everything: every old theater, art museum, funky boutique, restaurant and bar. My level of excitement grew as I navigated through the city streets, anticipating my exploration like an antsy little child running onto the playground for the first time.

As I pulled onto what looked like a promising street I was just able to squeeze my little car into a parallel space and got out. As I stepped out of the familiar cocoon of my car, the gravel crunched under my carefully chosen for the occasion boots & I excitedly scrambled up the curb and headed towards the first promising boutique.

As I moved towards the store something unexpected happened. As if I had walked into a giant rubber band I was repelled away from the store. Confused as to what might've happened, I began moving towards the door once again. The same resistant feeling came over me, this time combined with a barrage of thoughts pounding into my brain:" you can't go in there. You're not cool enough to go in there. You don't look cool. Nobody else is in there and so all eyes will be upon you. You can't go in there. "bewildered and discouraged, I turned away and walked down the street. A few doors down stood a small gallery, filled with eclectic art pieces that called to me. I stood in front of the gallery with the same thoughts racing through my mind. "You can't go in there. You are not cool enough to be in there. You suck." A dizzying, nauseating feeling washed over me, and I walked back to my car, dejected and alone.

I wish I could say that I recognized that abhorrent combination of thoughts and feelings for what it was that day: Social Anxiety. I didn't. I slunk back home, feeling like something was terribly wrong with me, but not knowing what. I spoke to no one about my experience, or the other many other alarming anxious experiences I would have over the next few months and years. As time went on, I began to anticipate anxiety coming on, and I would cancel plans and avoid outings to "escape" the clutches of anxiety. It wasn't until much later that I would learn what I was experiencing, and ultimately overcome it with a combination of nurturing myself, positive self-talk and hypnotherapy.

The next two and a half years of my life would prove to be the most challenging years of my life. I had moved away from my home state of sunny Northern California to Northern

Oregon, land of lush green foliage and sullen gray skies. I had moved for what I considered to be the best reason of all: romantic love. I had left home at a time when everything seemed to be going my way: I had many wonderful, true friends, and my hypnotherapy business that I loved was finally thriving. Things were really in the flow. Until I decided I should ditch it all for romantic love. An ex-boyfriend of mine had moved several times since we had last been together, and had been working hard to convince me that we should move in together and begin again. And although my intuition and my friends told me repeatedly that this would not be one of my better ideas my heart seemed to provide direct opposition. The more often my intuition tried to quietly tell me in its' soft, consistent voice to stay put the more I pushed it out of the way. It seemed that each time a friend provided wise counsel regarding thinking over my decision my resolve to leave stubbornly strengthened.

I packed up my things and moved in early December, and arrived in the middle of an ice storm. My new home looked beautiful and romantic. There was snow on the roof and upon the trees surrounding it. I immediately pictured a plume of smoke wafting out of the chimney and imagined the cozy goodness of sipping hot chocolate in the living room by the fireplace with my beau. As I alluded to earlier, my new life was not to become cozy or romantic. Within the first few days of my arrival my boyfriend began behaving in a possessive and controlling manner. It was the same possessive and controlling manner that I had grown to recognize from our past relationship, but had conveniently forgotten about in my desire to romanticize the possibility of our future together. And of course, things began to quickly disintegrate from there. I found myself feeling afraid to reach out to make connections in my new city, as each time I did those connections were angrily discouraged by my boyfriend. As time went by I became isolated and lonely, and my self-esteem began to plummet.

If you have ever been in a relationship with someone who is abusive you probably recognize the traits that I just described as classic traits of an abuser. I did not recognize them as such, but I did realize that I had been ignoring my own intuition; my own inner wisdom. And rather than do something about that, I dug in my heels and became more determined to make my new life "work' anyway. Before long, I became pregnant. This pregnancy brought me great joy, and I could think and talk of nothing else. No longer would I feel lonely and isolated. No longer would I long to be a mother. One of my greatest wishes was coming true! Over the next few months I planned every step of the pregnancy and delivery process that I could. My partner took a backseat in the planning, but I didn't mind at all. I chose a team of two wonderful midwives, and considered having a water birth in a beautiful birthing facility. By this time, I was pretty sure that my boyfriend would not make an ideal father for our baby, but I chose to believe that I could make up for it, and that everything would turn out well in the end.

The next few months shook those beliefs to the core. By the time the morning of my first scheduled sonogram came I was more than ready for it. What an exciting day, after all. Not only would we be able to have the babies' health and heartbeat checked—we would also find out if we were having a boy or a girl. However, when the sonogram technician told us that the baby was a little boy I could tell something was amiss by the way she hesitated. I thought for sure something in the equipment or camera was not working as it should when she told us that she would return with a doctor to go over some information with us. Within five minutes a doctor was in the room, and I was unable to absorb much of the information he shared about the baby. He seemed to be saying that a birth defect had been detected, and that even though the baby was perfectly healthy within my womb that the child could not live once he breathed in oxygen. Time stood still as I sat nodding numbly in the hospital room. How could this be happening? I had felt so positive about being pregnant, and so excited to welcome this baby into the world. I understood what people mean when they say their world was shattered. I was sobbing uncontrollably by the time we stepped into the parking lot, and the next few weeks were excruciating as we struggled to make a decision that we never thought we would have to make. In the end, I made the decision to end the pregnancy and tumbled into a sea of grief.

I have heard it said that when we are vulnerable we make decisions that we would not make if we are feeling strong. I made the decision to marry my boyfriend soon after the loss of the baby. We were married three days when he became physically abusive, holding me down and slapping my face again and again until I was bruised and bleeding. Amazingly, this is the time that I was able to look inside myself and see the light within. I remembered that there had been a time when I had felt good about myself. There had been a time that I could go out in public without experiencing shortness of breath and heart palpitations. A time that I had been healthy. A time that I had been strong. I asked my new husband to leave the house three days later, and begun the process of healing.

I moved back home to California, and was once again surrounded by loved ones. Then I began to evaluate what I thought I needed to do next. I knew what I didn't want, but I had no idea what I wanted, so I simply told myself that I wanted to know what I wanted. This desire to simply know what it was that I wanted was the crack in the door that I had shut around myself, and around my heart. The light began to shine through that crack, and as the light got brighter that crack in the door began to get wider. Finally, the door broke open completely, and my light was able to fully shine. Today I am grateful for every single one of the experiences I have shared. My light shines brightly because of them. My light shines brilliantly because of who I am and because of the culmination of my life experiences. Your light shines brilliantly because of who you are and what you have experienced. Let us all be the light that we carry within us.

About the Author

Maude Schellhous is a Certified Clinical Hypnotherapist & Behavioral Therapist living & working in Sacramento, CA. She helped thousands of people reach their goals and often achieve what they did not think was possible. It is Maude's belief that discovering inner wisdom holds a path to many different areas of our subconscious where we can unlock blockages that can hold us back mentally, emotionally, spiritually, and physically. You can contact Maude at: Maude@sacramentohypnotherapy.com, or by phone: (916)549-5109.

Thomas Valentine Holick
The Spiritual Journey of Women in the Nation

 I would like to say that it is an honor to be in this beautiful
book with so many wonderful and amazing spiritual women.
Women have a roll in this life that is ever so demanding with
work, family, home, children and a lot of you are
entrepreneurs and business owners and spiritual leaders
that help within your Communities. Women were born to be
leaders and are masters at multi-tasking. I must give credit
where credit is due. There are some amazing spiritual
women in history that have been called to lead and have
mastered the gift of spiritual love, guidance, mentoring,
teaching and self-sacrifice for the benefit of others.

It brings one woman in particular to mind when I reflect on
this subject, Mother Teresa. Mother Teresa's devotional work
among the poor and dying of India, won a noble prize for
peace in 1979. Known in the Catholic Church as Saint Mother
Teresa of Calcutta, she was born Agnes Gonxha Bojaxhiu in
Skopje, Macedonia, on August 27th, 1910. She was an
Albanian-Indian Roman Catholic Nun and Missionary. She

dedicated her life to the work of Christ, light work and continued to until September 5th, 1997 when she passed away. She faced many trials and tribulations during her time as a nun and missionary but she never lost faith in her path forward in Christianity.

I have seen so much of her in a lot of the spiritual women of today and I am pleased with the Spiritual Sisterhood movement, moving forward at great speed. I had a vision about the women of the world and they were gathering and praying, and preparing their household, schools, churches, neighborhoods and friends for the times ahead and I have seen the angels touching their heart and souls to fill them with the love for themselves and other women to succeed in their spiritual journey as they worked toward their very own spiritual anointment and purpose to come to pass with a heart full of faith, hope and love.

This vision showed me what it would be like with communal love and acceptance of one another. Women are known for being warriors and leaders in this life and that is what makes for stronger family ties that bind. Men are warriors as well and when their spouses stand behind them with prayer to strengthen them as they battle the ways of this world, they become champions. Christ says in the bible to pray for your husbands. (Father, help my husband to trust in You with all his heart, not depending on his own understanding, but acknowledging You in all his ways, so he knows what direction our family should take. (Proverbs 3:5-6).

(Pray diligently for him, for Christ shall make a way for his soul to be lead, by your faith.)

I can honestly say that I have met some amazing women on my spiritual journey in my lifetime. I met a woman who was a Reverend and African Shaman who was a guardian of the 80-acre parcel of mountain land in Northern California alongside a man known as a yogi, (A **yogi** (sometimes spelled jogi) is a practitioner of **yoga**.) She was a guide into the Mountains of Northern California in a town called Middleton, for those who were seeking spiritual enlightenment or for their life purpose. She was an amazingly strong woman who shared her wisdom and spiritual insight to anyone who truly was seeking the spiritual light in this life and she done that kind of work for 25 dedicated years if not more. She was able to speak in the language of the Holy Spirit and pray for your healing.

Times have changed so much over the past 40 years with women now in ministry and becoming head of households and raising children on their own, that the way of light is not so cut and dry as we were once taught it was. God says, (Where two or more are gathered in my name, so shall I be.) Matthew 18:20. Women of faith are gathering from all over the world these days and lending support in ways one would never believe was possible. Just as my vision showed me it was coming to pass and I am thankful to still be here to see it come to full fruition. Mothers, daughters, sisters, grandmothers are the keepers of the light and stories yet untold. Fathers, sons, brothers, grandfathers are the protectors of the light and to the keepers of the light, behold.

There is a great deal to learn about the feminine spirit for it is resilient in so many ways and yet tender with the message of Christ, but yet fierce in prayer. I have been fortunate enough to see how the divine feminine spirit has its place in the walk of this life and how much good it has bestowed upon the hearts, souls and minds of those in this world.

Today I want to say to you, continue to share your light and love unto your Sisters for they are in need of your light and support. Speak to their hearts about Christ and let them know he loves them and that he has a plan for them for you are the light barer for all to see when you walk in the light of Christ. Let your light forever shine for that piece of light you share unto her, will be the same light she gives to her mother, sister, daughter, son, brother, father or friend, grandparent or maybe even an abandoned child living on the streets that in which that light you placed in someone else, saved his life, that very same night through the one you touched that day.

The circle of life & light is never ending, just like unto the words (Alpha & Omega) the beginning, and the ending, it all comes back to the beginning, forever eternal, like unto the emblem of infinity. I praise the Sisters Unite movement and look forward to seeing how far your journeys take you as you reach for the stars and pull down a piece of heaven for all those to see that Christ's love is so very real and forgiveness is only a knee away.

The world is your stage and the angels are watching you and beside you every day and night. I pray your lives be filled with happiness and fulfillment and that peace follows you all the days of your life, as today I celebrate the women of ministry and collaboration, good-will and love for children, the elderly and one another as a whole, for without your courage and never ending devotion to home, family, community and spiritual faith and sisterly love, where would we, as a nation be? I wish every one of you the very best life has to offer and you have all my respect as a brilliant light unto the world. I am wishing you rainbows of love and many golden roses from heaven above.

About the Author

Thomas Valentine Holick, born Spiritual Healer and an Inductee of the Baseball Hall of Fame was born in Linden, New Jersey. 'Valentine' 'Tommy', '18KKid','Young Sizzling' Hurler', 'T- Bird', 'The Strike Out Artist' are the many names he is called, after he pitched (18) strike outs in a row, as a baseball pitcher at 11 years old, in 1968. He was placed in the Athletic Hall of Fame in his home town of Linden, New Jersey. In 2013, he was inducted into the "Baseball Hall of Fame," in Cooperstown, New York. Valentine has been placed in the Hall of Fame within the "Library of Honorary Mention." There has been no one ever that I am aware of, in history that has accomplished what Thomas Valentine Holick achieved at such a young age.

The story of his young life, playing baseball at 5 years old and the discovery of his rare talent in the sport, and healing intuition that led to this inspirational story, which continues to unfold today. His message for baseball today, gives many hope for the pureness of the game and its ability to bring people together, not only for the competition, and the glamour of winning, but to encourage people to be the best they can be; a message many can relate to.

To Quote: "Twists and turns, strategies, and tricks, to defeat the opposing team, only encourage new, young players to ignore some of their natural ability, while forcing a role, an approach to teaching the game that may present poorly in the outcome of age," He has said. These insights Valentine has for the sport, have been born through experience. The special gift of 'sight' and healing of life and people is interwoven into his many talents. Valentine has lived in Hawaii now for 27 years and continues his avid following of the game and his spiritual practice of healing and bringing forth spiritual messages he is anointed to bring to us all.

52365521R00215

Made in the USA
San Bernardino, CA
19 August 2017